COMMUNITY COLLEGE LEADERSHIP
AND ADMINISTRATION

"Carlos Nevarez and J. Luke Wood have taken the important first steps in bringing the education of community college administrators into the 21st century. From its survey analysis beginnings to its case study presentations, this book goes beyond war stories to a higher level of theorizing the role of administrators in this rapidly growing segment of the nation's education system."

—Gene V. Glass, Regents' Professor, Mary Lou Fulton Institute & Graduate School of Education, Arizona State University

"Leadership of America's community colleges continues to be one of higher education's greatest challenges. Carlos Nevarez and J. Luke Wood have focused on exactly the right combination of talents and skills the next generation of presidents and administrators will need to successfully lead our community colleges in the future."

—Brice W. Harris, Chancellor, Los Rios Community Colleges

"The breadth and depth of this book is unequaled. As a leadership practitioner, I find the applications useful and compelling. The chapter on the community college's role in the achievement gap is 'must-reading' for the next generation of community college executives."

—Ned Doffoney, Chancellor, North Orange County Community College

"As a community college leader, a practitioner, and an adjunct faculty member at a major university, I am impressed with this volume for many reasons. It is a contemporary look at leadership today—a very realistic analysis of the changes facing higher education today, especially community colleges. It presents authentic, practical ways to develop leadership skills to confront those challenges. The case study approach is one we are using in our own Talent Management Initiative with the purpose of 'growing our own' talented leaders. This methodology will result in developing the kind of visionary, skilled leaders who will be able to solve the multifaceted, complex issues higher education leaders routinely face. The time is ripe for the kinds of fresh thinking and new approaches to leading community colleges that are exemplified in this book. It will be an invaluable resource for practitioners, students, and faculty alike."

—Rufus Glasper, Chancellor, Maricopa Community Colleges

COMMUNITY COLLEGE
LEADERSHIP AND
ADMINISTRATION

M. Christopher Brown II
GENERAL EDITOR

Vol. 3

PETER LANG
New York • Washington, D.C./Baltimore • Bern
Frankfurt • Berlin • Brussels • Vienna • Oxford

Carlos Nevarez and J. Luke Wood

COMMUNITY COLLEGE LEADERSHIP AND ADMINISTRATION

THEORY, PRACTICE, AND CHANGE

PETER LANG
New York • Washington, D.C./Baltimore • Bern
Frankfurt • Berlin • Brussels • Vienna • Oxford

Library of Congress Cataloging-in-Publication Data

Nevarez, Carlos.
Community college leadership and administration:
theory, practice, and change / Carlos Nevarez, J. Luke Wood.
p. cm. — (Education management: contexts, constituents,
and communities; v. 3)
Includes bibliographical references.
1. Community colleges—Administration. 2. Community college presidents.
3. Educational change. I. Wood, J. Luke. II. Title.
LB2341.N43   378.1'01–dc22   2010012744
ISBN 978-1-4331-0796-2 (hardcover)
ISBN 978-1-4331-0795-5 (paperback)
ISSN 1947-6256

Bibliographic information published by **Die Deutsche Nationalbibliothek**.
Die Deutsche Nationalbibliothek lists this publication in the "Deutsche
Nationalbibliografie"; detailed bibliographic data is available
on the Internet at http://dnb.d-nb.de/.

TABLE OF CONTENTS

PREFACE

A large numbers of community college leaders and administrators are retiring and will continue to leave administrative positions now and in the years to come. Thus, there is a great need to prepare the next cadre of community college leaders focused on advancing the vision and mission of community colleges: (a) open access to education; (b) comprehensive educational programming; (c) serving the community; (d) teaching and learning; (e) lifelong learning; and (f) student success. In order to do so, leaders are needed who possess: (1) the ability to engage in critical thinking, analysis and reflection; (2) the ability to transfer academic knowledge (e.g., theory, models, research) into practice to address issues which arise in professional and social settings; (3) knowledge, appreciation, and inclusiveness with regards to diversity; (4) the ability to confront issues and resolve conflicts; (5) a well developed moral compass; and (6) the political savvy, social networks, and disposition to drive change in the community college.

The need to prepare a new kind of community college leader is of the utmost importance, as the roles and duties of community college leaders have changed greatly from previous generations. Leaders today need to realize the fundamental organizational changes required to better meet the needs of affiliated constituents and the necessity for growth and transformation of individuals and institutions. This will better enable them to guide their institutions in increasing educational outcomes and prepare them for a world market. For leaders to be effective in meeting accountability demands and responsibilities; ongoing traditional professional development opportunities need to be created and supported. Additionally, new trainings need to be aligned with contemporary leadership challenges. This allows leaders of colleges to guide their institutions in the midst of ambiguity, change, and pressures (e.g., financial, political) never before faced by community colleges. Community colleges will continue to face challenging times. Thus, there is a need to develop visionary leaders who can turn challenges into opportunities.

This textbook serves as a tool in training the 21ˢᵗ-century community college leader and administrator. An in-depth review of community college literature quickly reveals a dearth of literature focused on community college leadership and administration. Further, the minimal literature which exists on this topic is out of date, with the majority of sources being published two to three decades ago. We began with a survey administered to community college leaders to gain insights about contemporary issues influencing community colleges. Based on the leaders' responses, we undertook a thorough review of existing books, articles, reports, and other scholarly works on the topic. This was done in an effort to develop a core textbook that best addressed the needs of prospective and current community college leaders. Additionally, a case study follows each chapter. These case studies are written by community college chancellors, presidents, former presidents, and vice presidents, representing various national regions. Cases present issues which are anything but simplistic. Rather, they are dynamic, complex, and multifaceted in nature. The case studies serve to challenge readers to consider the intricacies of issues involved in community college leadership by promoting problem-solving skills and analytical thinking.

A review of the literature and leaders' responses supports and makes a request to educational administration and leadership programs to further prepare leaders who will work successfully in diverse, complex, and dynamic community colleges. The profession of educational administration and leadership must prepare leaders who have a strong commitment to improving community colleges. Leadership and change are invariably connected: leaders influence colleges' culture and climate, including the moral domains which ultimately affect student academic performance. This textbook will emphasize leadership, change, politics, community college mission, leadership theories/models, and research and practice as common strands which run throughout. A particular emphasis is placed on deconstructing and constructing new approaches to how community college leadership is viewed, practiced, and envisioned. In doing so, the authors have made great efforts to not simply restate common practices, but develop new models (e.g., leadership, change, case study framework) focused on facilitating leadership innovativeness. The option to continue to perpetuate sameness was not an option in writing this text. Rather, the authors challenged themselves, and subsequently readers, to think and create new approaches to leading community colleges. This sentiment was driven by the fact that a great majority of leadership practices are simply not effective. In all, the status of community colleges and the future trajectory of these institutions, serve as a guiding framework for this text. The intention was to challenge prospective and current leaders to think differently in addressing the multitude of issues impacting community colleges while being solution oriented in how challenges are addressed and resolved.

This textbook will provide a variety of content chapters specific to community college leadership and change. Additionally, each chapter concludes with the presentation of a case study which requires leaders to use the information presented in each chapter to resolve a dilemma. These chapters include:

- Chapter 1: The Community College Vision and Mission
  This chapter focuses on clarifying, articulating, explaining and examining the vision and mission of the community college, as well as its influence on the functions and operations of the institution. Focus is given to critically examining the role and changing nature of these concepts in leading today's community college. We also discuss the importance of leaders' integrating the values of the community college vision and mission within their everyday leadership practices.

- Chapter 2: Historical Legacy of Community Colleges
  This chapter provides an overview of the history of the junior-community college with primary focus given to its origins. In doing so, this chapter will include the following: (1) an examination of social and philosophical forces which led to the development of the junior college; (2) an overview of the individuals who promoted its creation, specifically William Rainey Harper; and (3) a historical snapshot of the development of the junior-community college through seven periods.

- Chapter 3: Leadership and Leadership Theory
  This chapter will focus on leadership and leadership theory in relation to the community college. The following areas will be addressed: (a) differences, and commonalities between leadership and administration; (b) an examination of leadership styles (e.g., authoritarian, transactional, transformational); (c) an overview of primary leadership theories (e.g., trait-theory, behavioral theory, contingency-situational theory); and (d) a presentation of leadership approaches (e.g., bureaucratic leadership, democratic leadership, political leadership.

- Chapter 4: Achievement Gap and the Role of Community Colleges
  This chapter examines the community college achievement gap. In doing so, we present: (a) the p-12 influence on the community college achievement gap; (b) the personal and social benefits of postsecondary education; (c) persistence research and models; (d) the community college achievement

gap model, which identifies factors directly influencing two-year-college achievement disparities; (e) minority male initiatives; and (f) the guiding steps for community college leaders to address the achievement gap through the presentation of the Achievement Gap Action Model.

- Chapter 5: Ethical Leadership and Decision Making
  This chapter presents the concept of ethics as it relates to leadership in the community college. Focus is given to: (a) the importance of knowing the codes of ethics which govern the profession of community college leadership; (b) using multiple ethical paradigms (e.g., ethic of justice, ethic of critique, ethic of care, ethic of profession); and (c) employing ethical decision-making models.

- Chapter 6: Faculty in the Community College
  This chapter focuses on faculty in the community college. Specific attention is given to three areas: (1) faculty demographics (e.g., full-time vs. part-time faculty, tenure status, teaching load, degree status, rank, salary and job satisfaction); (2) faculty preparation and development programs; and (3) the current status of faculty diversity and the benefits of diversification.

- Chapter 7: Demographic Trends
  This chapter introduces select demographic information on community colleges that focuses on: (a) institutional characteristics; (b) students' characteristics; (c) faculty characteristics; and (d) administrators' characteristics. Demographic trends are contextualized as an opportunity to further meet the changing needs of an increasingly diverse student population.

- Chapter 8: Leadership in Student Affairs
  This chapter focuses on student affairs leadership in the community college. Specific attention will be given to four areas: (1) the disconnect between academic affairs and student affairs and its implications to student learning and personal development; (2) foundational and guiding student affairs documents (e.g., the Student Learning Initiative, Principles of Good Practice, Student Personnel Point of View); (3) the core functions of student affairs in relation to effective leadership practices; and (4) student development theory, with a primary focus on psycho-social theories.

- Chapter 9: Community College Finance
  This chapter examines finance in the community college and includes: (a) an overview of revenue streams for public two-year colleges; (b) an

examination of community college expenditures; and c) funding of college for students. Particular attention is placed on assessing whether the overall picture of community college finance is in line with the mission of these institutions.

- Chapter 10: Community College Governance
  This chapter will focus on governance in the community college. Information presented will be framed in accordance with a Conceptual Model of Community College Governance which depicts governance in these institutions. The focus of this chapter is twofold: (1) to provide an overview of the general governance processes at the state, local, and campus levels; and (2) to present four influences (i.e., national, statewide and local needs; ideological differences; internal influences; and external influences), which serve to "truly" guide governance in these institutions.

- Chapter 11: Leadership Development in the Community College
  This chapter focuses on the role of leadership development in preparing community college leaders. Therefore, we will: (a) examine challenges and opportunities facing community college leaders; (b) address the skills needed to successfully confront these challenges; (c) identify various leadership development programs designed for community college leaders; and (d) discuss the need for assessing the success of these programs.

- Chapter 12: Emerging Trends
  This chapter will summarize the mission of the community college in light of emerging trends facing these institutions. Particular attention is paid to: (a) challenges to "open-access"; (b) bachelor's degrees; (c) the presidential initiative on community colleges; (d) increasing numbers of part-time faculty; (e) new and returning students; and (f) minority-student initiatives.

A case study follows each chapter, based upon chapter content. These case studies are written by community college chancellors, presidents, former presidents, and vice presidents, representative of various national locales. These executive educational leaders provide scenarios relevant to the everyday realities of community colleges. While challenging leaders to consider the intricacies of issues involved in community college leadership, cases present issues which are anything but simplistic. Rather, they are dynamic, complex, and multifaceted in nature. These dynamic issues call for dynamic leaders who can lead community colleges to better actualize their mission. Case studies are designed to encourage leaders to use chapter content to resolve a leadership dilemma. The authors have designed a case study framework to guide leaders in analyzing various cases and ultimately determining what resolution(s) should be enacted, if any.

Case study analysis is a good way to develop reflective leaders capable of solving and analyzing challenges facing organizations. This is done through the use of real case scenarios which originate from the everyday leadership practices of executive leaders. Through the presentation and analysis of factual scenarios, aspiring and current leaders will be able to develop analytical and problem-solving skills required to resolve the cases. These skills are paramount to the success of community college leaders.

Case Study Framework

We encourage leaders to use the following steps in analyzing cases. These steps will guide you in finding a resolution to the scenario; be mindful that these steps are not linear. Depending upon the content of the case, the steps may be co-dependent, multi-dimensional and fluid. Approaching case study analysis in this manner, will allow leaders to form a broader outlook on the intricacies specific to core elements of the case.

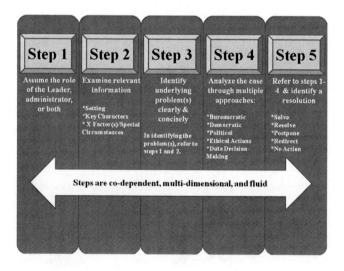

Figure 1 Graphical Depiction of the Nevarez-Wood Leadership Case Study Framework

Step 1: Assume the role of leader, administrator, or both.

Step 2: Examine Relevant Information. List integral information that provides context and clarity to key elements of the case. These include, but are not limited to:

- *Setting*—Describe the overall characteristics of the setting. For example, ask yourself: Is the organization located in an urban, rural or suburban area? What is the demographic makeup of the institution's stakeholders? Is the setting public or private?
- *Key Characters/Groups*—Identify the primary individuals or groups involved in the case. Note their relationship to each other and to the organization.
- *Special Circumstances/X factor(s)*—Note special circumstances which give light to important elements in the case. For example, ask yourself: What is the historical interplay between key characters/groups in the case? What are the formal and informal power relationships that exist within the case? What are the institutional culture and/or values of the organization? What are the allowed behaviors and climate in the setting?

Step 3: Identify Underlying Problem(s) clearly and concisely. In identifying the problem(s), refer to information collected in steps 1 and 2.

Step 4: Analyze the case through multiple approaches.

Leadership Approaches

- Bureaucratic Approach—Conflict is presumed to be resolvable through the use of existing rules and regulations. If this does not suffice, then it is the responsibility of management to resolve the issue.
- Democratic Approach—Assumes a human relations approach in which central characters involved with the case are sought out and included in resolving the case. This approach follows a "shared authority model."
- Political Approach—The political approach does not adhere to specific decision-making structures; rather, it utilizes any structure (e.g., bureaucratic, democratic) to gain influence over others. This approach in not necessarily concerned with how actions will impact the entire organization, rather how actions will play out in the subunit in which the leader resides.

Ethical Courses of Action

- In resolving the case, consider the ethical implications of potential decisions. For instance, are they compassionate, equitable, professional, and lawful?

Data Decision Making

- Data can be used as a tool to identify problems and to develop solutions in resolving the case study. What current data within the case study needs to be considered? What additional data could be gained that can influence the resolution of the case?

Step 5: Refer to the steps above in identifying an overall resolution to the case study. Select one (or more if needed) of the following options and explain your answer: *Solve; Resolve; Postpone; Redirect, No Action.*

Individuals seeking supplementary resources (e.g., additional case studies, power points outlines of each chapter, leadership inventories, newsfeeds) should see the following site: www.communitycollegeleadership.net.

Case Study Matrix

Case Study	Mission	History	Leadership Theory	Achievement Gap	Ethics	Faculty	Demographic Trends	Student Affairs	Finance	Governance	Leadership Development	Emerging Trends
The Problem Student by President Mark G. Edelstein					P	S		S				
Pressures of Fund Raising by President Gayle Hytrek									P			S
Leadership in Transition by President Edwin Massey	S		P								S	
A House Divided by President Karen Nicodemus	S	S	S			S	S		S	S	P	
Facilitating Student Behavior by former President Jim Riggs	S					S		P			S	
Accommodating Displaced Workers by President Edna Baehre & VP of Public Relations Patrick Early	P	S					S			S		S
Student Friendly Campus Services by		P						S				S
President Edna Baehre, VP of Student Affairs Winnie Black & VP Stuart Savin												
Converging Issues as an Opportunity for Change by President Cathryn Addy	S								S			P
Funding Remediation Efforts by President Eduardo Marti	S			P		S			S			
When Language & College Policies Collide by President and Superintendent Francisco Rodriguez	S					P	S	S				S
An Athletic Scandal? By Chancellor Ned Doffoney		S						S		P		
College Influences by President Cynthia Azari	S		S	S				P				S

Key: P= Primary chapter content focus; S= Secondary chapter content focus

ACKNOWLEDGMENTS

The majority of this text was written in the basement of the library, "the dungeon," at California State University, Sacramento. This inescapable setting allowed the authors time and space to examine, analyze and critique existing sources on community college leadership and administration. This provided for critical exchange, which translated into the creation of various conceptual models, styles, and approaches. In doing so, we hope this work serves as a guide to give opportunities and increase the educational success of those *most in need* … community college students! In writing this book, we realized the benefits accrued by involving others in the process of writing this text. This allowed for stimulating conversation which emphasized the importance of collaboration. The by-products of these rewarding conversations were: constructing and reconstructing conceptual models; challenging other perspectives, as well as our own; and envisioning new ideas/approaches focused on meeting the vision and mission of the community college.

We would like to acknowledge: Rose Penrose for her arduous work in editing the initial manuscripts of each chapter. Her optimism and tenacious dedication to reviewing this text was admirable; Brason Lee for editing the majority of chapters within. His critical lens served to improve successive versions of these chapters; Jian-zhong (Joe) Zhou for providing access to CSUS library resources; Debra Fleming for locating literature sources to be used in the book; Jenny Leung, Neel Jadia, and Betty Ronayne for providing technical support at various stages of this project; Juan Carlos González for reviewing the *Leadership Development* chapter; Peter Lang Publishing and Chris Meyers for working with us on this book; and Dr. Christopher M. Brown II for seeing the potential of this scholarly contribution to leadership in community colleges.

We would also like to thank the numerous community college leaders who contributed case studies to this book. Their insight, responsiveness, dedication, selfless commitment to community colleges, and willingness to share their "story" was commendable. We have no doubt that these cases will resonate with existing leaders in that they portray the numerous, complex and challenging issues facing community colleges, while gaining insight to resolving these dynamic scenarios. Case study authors included: (1) Case Study 1, President Edna Baehre and Vice President of Public Relations Patrick Early, Central Pennsylvania's Community College, "Accommodating Displaced Workers"; (2) Case Study 2, President Edna Baehre, Vice President of Student Affairs & Enrollment Management Winnie Black, and Campus Vice President Stuart Savin, Central Pennsylvania's Community College, "Student Friendly Campus Services"; (3) Case Study 3, President Edwin Massey, Indian River State College, "Leadership in Transition"; (4) Case Study 4, President Eduardo J. Marti, Queensborough Community College, "Funding Remediation Efforts"; (5) Case Study 5, President Mark G. Edelstein, Lakes Region Community College, "The Problem Student"; (6) Case Study 6, President & Superintendent Francisco Rodriguez, Mira Costa Community College, "When Language and College Policies Collide"; (7) Case Study 7, President Cynthia Azari, Fresno City College, "College Influences"; (8) Case Study 8, Former President Jim Riggs, Columbia College, "Facilitating Student Behavior"; (9) Case Study 9, President Gayle Hytrek, Moraine Park Technical College, "Pressures of Fund Raising"; (10) Case Study 10, Chancellor Ned Doffoney, North Orange County Community College District, "An Athletic Scandal?"; (11) Case Study 11, President Karcen Nicodemus, Cochise College, "A House Divided"; and (12) Case Study 12, President Cathryn Addy, Tunxis Community College, "Converging Issues as an Opportunity for Change."

Dr. Nevarez

Closer to family, I would like to express my deepest appreciation to my wife Ana Nevarez for her invaluable support, to Gabriela, Carlitos, and Samuel who inspire and guide my journey. I would like to acknowledge and praise Luke Wood for his work ethic and dedication. His path towards being a great researcher is paved.

Luke

First and foremost, I would like to thank God, my loving wife Idara (for her patience and support), my daughter Mayen (for inspiration), my family (for their love and support), and Dr. Nevarez (for his belief in me). I would also like to thank several integral mentors in my life: Ernie Micheli, Pastor Clifford Mero, Dr. Cecil Canton, Dr. Lisa William-White, and Dr. Caroline Sotello Viernes Turner.

CHAPTER ONE

THE COMMUNITY COLLEGE VISION AND MISSION

This chapter focuses on clarifying, articulating, explaining, and examining the vision and mission of the community college, as well as its influence on the functions and operations of the institution. Focus is given to critically examining the role and changing nature of these concepts in leading today's community college. We also discuss the importance of leaders' role in integrating the values of the community college vision and mission within their everyday leadership practices.

When reading this chapter, consider the following questions:

- What are the vision, mission, functions, and operations of the community college? What are their core elements?
- What are the benefits, if any, for leaders who understand the vision, mission, functions, and operations of the community college?
- What factors influence the vision, mission, functions, and operations of community colleges? How do these factors play out in your own institutional context?

This chapter provides leaders with an overview of the mission of the community college. This mission has been portrayed by community college scholars in several ways. For instance, Levin (2000) notes that some scholars have focused on the curricular aspects of the community colleges (e.g., remediation, vocational education); some on its purposes (e.g., economic development, social mobility); whereas others on its role (e.g., workforce preparation, transfer). Similarly, Bogart (1994) stated that traditional discussions of the community college mission have focused on its "role, function, and purpose," terms that are often used interchangeably with the term "mission" (pp. 60–61). We delineate among these concepts, and present the community college mission as a distinct notion, which is interrelated with its vision, functions, and operations. Thus, this chapter will provide a discussion of four concepts related to the community college: (a) vision; (b) mission; (c) functions; and (d) operations. The vision, mission, functions, and operations (VMFOs) are explained through the presentation of the *Community College Core Principles Model* (see Figure 1). After explicating these concepts, we also will discuss their evolving nature. Prior to engaging in this discussion, it is important to consider why leaders should be attentive to the VMFOs, which define the ideals, structures, and direction of these institutions.

- *Identity.* The community college's mission forms the character and value set of the institution, and this in turn serves to drive the institution toward specific paths. These principles have evolved from the ambitions of the organization's past and current practices. Without an identity, institutions and its leaders succumb to the latest academic fads and neglect to maintain a unified focus, centered on academic success. For example, lengthy mission statements do not succinctly or clearly articulate the values of an institution. They are counterproductive and inhibit the constituents' ability to identify with the institution's mission. The primary implication of this phenomenon is that the constituents (e.g., faculty, staff) will not understand, support, or enact the core values of the mission.

- *Baseline Evaluation Measure.* Typically, evaluations are conducted to assess whether the functions and outcomes of an organization are in alignment with and progressing toward its identified vision, mission, and objectives. The mission of the community college provides a guidepost for leaders in examining whether or not these institutions are meeting the needs of their students. For example, one aspect of the mission of the community college is to serve the local community. This can be measured through the salaries accrued by graduates and whether or not they complete a certificate program or transfer to a four-year university. Thus, if leaders recognize that their institutions have low job-placement rates or transfer rates, this can serve as a signal to the institution's leadership that the mission of the organization is not being met. Thus, leaders should reconsider, modify and include new policies that address this area of concern.

- *Strategic Plan.* In its simplest form, a mission is the stated strategic plan of an institution. It speaks to the core elements that guide the institution; it is a roadmap for leaders to meet the changing needs of their local communities. The mission serves as a succinct plan, which allows all members of the organization to coalesce around the identified community goals. For example, leaders can use the mission as a strategic plan to inform the faculty, staff, students, and community about the long-term aspirations of the community college.

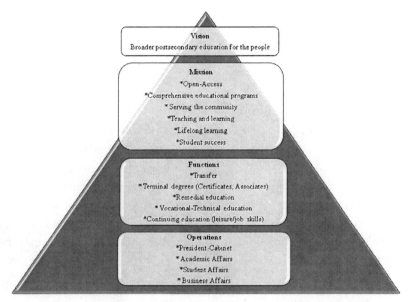

Note: Certain elements from Tillery & Deegan, 1985; Vaughan, 2006)

Figure 1 Community College Core Principles Model

It is important for leaders to be well versed in the VMFOs of the community college. Upon actualizing knowledge in their area, leaders will have a (a) firm foundation from which to influence the direction of their respective institutions; (b) platform to convey, inspire, and model behavior to their constituents; (c) tool to hold constituents accountable to the institution's VMFOs; (d) marketing plan, which can garnish financial resources (e.g., donations, grants) for the institution; (e) unified message describing the overall identity of the institution to external and internal community stakeholders (e.g., legislators, community members) and a clear rationale for how this will benefit the public; and (f) mechanism to drive change in accordance to its vision and mission.

Vision

A *vision* is the long-term aspiration of an institution. It guides the organization toward a desired outcome, which *should* be realistic and attainable. However, a vision in itself is limited, as it tells you where you want to be, and not how to get there. Thus, the vision is dependent upon the mission, as it specifies how the vision will be realized. Early two-year-college innovators in the 1800s and early 1900s had a twofold vision for these institutions: "they envisioned the formation of junior colleges not only to free the university for advanced study but also to encourage broader postsecondary education for the people" (Tillery & Deegan, 1985, p. 5). The first aspect of this vision never gained traction, as universities were reluctant to relinquish their general education function to two-year institutions. However, the vision of expanding postsecondary education has remained a core principle of these institutions throughout their tenure. In fact, the rapid growth of the community college can be attributed to this vision. From the progressivist movement of the nineteenth and twentieth centuries, to the open-access era of the 1960s and 1970s, to the numerous populations served by community colleges today, these institutions have worked arduously to expand postsecondary education, which has inspired community college constituents (e.g., students, faculty, staff, community members) to work toward realizing an ambitious visionary identity.

Mission

A *mission* indicates the core value-driven efforts undertaken by the community college to achieve its vision. More simply, it is the process in which a community college attains its long-term aspirations. As noted, the mission outlines the essential elements of a strategic plan by which all community college stakeholders (e.g., students, faculty, staff, community members) work collectively toward realizing the college's vision. Vaughan (2006) identifies the holistic attributes of the general community college mission: "serving all segments of society through an open-access admissions policy that offers equal and fair treatment to all students; providing a comprehensive educational program; serving the community as a community-based institution of higher education; teaching and learning; fostering lifelong learning" (p. 3).

Vaughan's five mission commitments illustrate how the vision and the mission of the community college are viewed as one. We have made a distinction between the two, in that the vision is the "what" and the mission is the "how." That being said, the core elements of his five mission commitments are the best representative articulation of the community college mission found thus far. As previously noted, the vision of the community college is to "encourage broader postsecondary education for the people." This vision indicates the ends desired by the community college, to expand postsecondary education as its primary value, which specifies what community colleges must achieve. Primarily,

Vaughan's mission components identify means as opposed to ends; thus, in addition to these five principles, we suggest that the community college mission also includes "aiding students in achieving their academic and career goals" or more succinctly, student success.

This final component of the community college mission provides for greater alignment with the initial vision of these institutions. It also emerges from the critique of community colleges that began in the last quarter of the twentieth century, which questioned whether access was equivalent to success (Cohen & Brawer, 2003; Richardson, 1987). Through our critique, we assert that the mission of the community college is to meet local community needs. In many ways, the six core elements of the community college mission (e.g., open access, comprehensive education programs, serving the community, teaching and learning, lifelong learning, student success) are interrelated. In fact, in order for the vision to be realized, they must be interconnected as each mission component should work collectively toward the unified vision of the organization. For example, providing open access to all individuals who seek a college-level education is one effective method for community colleges to serve the needs of their local communities. Likewise, comprehensive educational programming can also serve to meet the workforce preparation and intellectual development needs of local communities.

Further defining these six core elements of the community college mission will better enable leaders to see their interrelationship and whether the vision of the community college is being realized.

- *Open Access.* Open access refers to the core value of community colleges in providing college opportunities to all students who want to engage in postsecondary education, although the open access principle is being challenged in this current era. The value of open access was first conceptualized by progressivists in the mid to late 1800s. Progressivist leaders believed that education at all levels (e.g., elementary, secondary, postsecondary) should be open to all students. As noted by Vaughan (2006) open access "is a manifestation of the belief that a democracy can thrive, indeed survive, only if people are educated to their fullest potential" (p. 4). It was not until the 1960s that community colleges as a unified system embraced the "open-door" policy. During this time, the rising age of baby boomers; expansion of the nation's economy; the civil rights movement; increased public support for education; and expanding university infrastructure allowed community colleges to move toward truly becoming open access institutions (Cohen & Brawer, 2003; Kasper,

2002–03; O'Banion, 1989; Vaughan, 1983). Today, the impact of open access is seen in the widespread diversity of community college students by race/ethnicity, gender, age, socioeconomics, national origin, etc. This is of particular importance, considering many groups have historically been excluded and alienated from higher education.

- *Comprehensive Educational Programs.* Comprehensive educational programs refer to the wide array of programming offered by community colleges in order to meet the needs of the local communities in which they serve (Vaughan, 2006). While aiding students in completing their general education requirements and transferring to a four-year university remains a cardinal function of the community college, the institution also provides other functions. Programs such as remedial education, terminal degrees, vocational-technical education, and continuing education among other functions best illustrate the holistic aspect of its mission. No matter what educational/career goals students have, community colleges can serve as a venue for students to pursue and achieve their goals.

- *Serving the Community.* A core component of the community college mission is that of serving the needs of the local community. From their inception, community colleges have provided access to higher education for communities for which it has traditionally been out of reach. For example, Cohen & Brawer (2003) state that the rationale used to justify the establishment of Fresno Junior College in California was that the nearest institution of higher education was almost 200 miles away. Today, community colleges are situated within a reasonable drive of most communities. In addition to their physical locale, the mission of the community college is to provide academic programs and services, which meet the human, social, and cultural capital needs of their communities. In fact, this core component of their mission was a central factor for renaming junior colleges to community colleges, since they were both located in communities for the purpose of serving community needs.

- *Teaching and Learning.* Teaching and learning refers to the process by which students receive instruction and learn from the teaching given. It has been a core value of the community college mission since its inception. For example, nearly 59 percent of all full-time community college faculty teach 15 units or more per year (Digest of Education Statistics, 2008), nearly double that of many four-year research universities. This harkens back to the initial conception of the community college. Two-year-college leaders in the 1800s and early 1900s sought to eliminate the general education function of four-year universities and bestow this responsibility upon preuniversity institutions (e.g., junior colleges/high schools) in order for universities to focus on research (Cohen & Brawer, 2003; Ratcliff, 1994). To this day, teaching and learning have been the central focus of community colleges. The goal is not necessarily one of generating new knowledge (e.g., research), but providing access to knowledge (e.g., practical teaching and learning) for communities from which it has been elusive. The significance of the teaching and learning mission of the community college cannot be understated. It serves as an influential force in defining the purpose of community colleges.

- *Lifelong Learning.* Lifelong learning refers to the community college's commitment to the educational development of individuals throughout the span of their lives. As noted by Vaughan (2006), people have historically perceived education as "an activity a person engaged in for a certain number of years, and, when that person graduated, he or she would never return to the classroom" (p. 8). This perception has rapidly become outdated. Today, educational leaders know that technologies, skill requirements, academic requirements, and discipline-specific knowledge change rapidly. Thus, community colleges serve as a mechanism for individuals to attain the academic, career, and personal skills desired. On campuses today, working professionals and retirees as well as traditional college-aged students (i.e., 18- to 24-year-olds) attend for the varied programming offered at these institutions (e.g., professional/ job skill development, leisure activities, general education). Increasingly, community colleges are taking on the charge of educating nontraditional students (e.g., adult/returning students, students 25 years and older). This role is tied to the mission of community colleges in developing individuals throughout their life span. The demand for lifelong learning will increase as individuals need to be retrained to be competitive in the workforce.
- *Student Success.* A cardinal component of the community colleges mission is to aid students in achieving their academic and career goals. Students come into community colleges with diverse goals; attaining a terminal degree and transferring to a four-year university are among some of its core functions. This mission of aiding students in achieving their goals (i.e., student success), while intertwined with other concepts previously presented, focuses on the role of the community colleges in delivering success for

those who walk through its "open-door." While the 1960s and 1970s were characterized by access and *the right to fail*, from the 1980s until now, the community college has received increasing scrutiny for its inability to aid students in actualizing their goals (Cohen & Brawer, 2003; Richardson, 1987). Today, academic success has come to the forefront of priorities undertaken by college leaders, as the public demands a greater return on their investment and lawmakers focus on issues of accountability.

Functions

The *functions* of the community college refer to the methods by which its mission is achieved. If the mission is the "how," then the functions are the "actions" through which the "how" is achieved. The functions are informed by the vision and mission of the institution. It is the explicit ways in which they are carried out. As the mission of the community college has expanded over time, so too have the functions of the organization in moving the institution toward its broadening mission. We have identified four core functions of the community college: transfer, terminal degrees (e.g., vocational, technical, occupational certificates, associate degrees), remedial education, and continuing education (e.g., leisure, job skills). In many ways, these functions are interrelated.

Transfer

The transfer function of the community college refers to the organization's role in facilitating students' completion of general education requirements and transition from a two-year college to a four-year university. Generally, after completing the first two years of college-level coursework at a community college, students can transfer to a university at a junior-level class standing. There are three primary types of students who transfer from two-year to four-year institutions, those who (a) transfer after completion of an associate's of arts or science degree; (b) transfer with an applied associate's degree without coursework in the liberal arts; and (c) transfer and transition continuously between two-year and four-year institutions.

Transfer is an integral facet of the community college mission, one that has continued since the early years of the community college in 1901 (Townsend, 2001). And, it should be. Transfer is an attractive option for many students for several reasons: (a) students can attend more cost-effective community colleges for two years and save thousands of dollars before transferring to a four-year university; (b) they can be prepared socially, emotionally, and academically for success at a four-year university through tailored equal-opportunity programs; and (c) students can use transfer agreements (e.g., 2 + 2) as a mechanism to attain enrollment at top-notch institutions.

Although the transfer function is a primary motivation factor for students who attend community colleges, the majority of times, it is not realized. Among all students, 37.2 percent of students enter the community college with the intent to transfer, but only 28.9 percent of students transfer, and a mere 10.3 percent attain bachelor's degrees. When data is disaggregated by race, it is apparent that great disparities exist. For example, 21.6 percent of African Americans who enroll in two-year colleges expect to transfer to a four-year institution. However, only 3.1 percent of all African Americans successfully transfer and attain a bachelor's degree from a four-year institution (Hoachlander et al., 2003) (see Table 1).

Terminal Degrees

The terminal degree generally prepares students for direct entrance into the workforce. The terminal degree function of the community college (i.e., obtaining an associate's degree or certificate) has existed since its inception, though with different ends in mind. Eells (1941) notes that in 1900, President Harper of the University of Chicago (a central figure in the innovation of the two-year college) advocated for a bifurcated educational system before the National Educational Association in their annual meeting in South Carolina. In his speech, Harper stated that "weak" four-year universities could become two-year colleges. In these two-year institutions, "the student who was not really fitted by nature to take the higher work could stop naturally and honorably at the end of the sophomore year," he also stated that "many students whom might not have

Table 1 Two-Year-College Intention Rates vs. Bachelors Attainment Rates, 1995–96 to 2001.

	Intention (%)	Attained Bachelor's Degree (%)
White	24.1	7.1
Black	21.6	3.1
Asian	40.3	12
Hispanic	25.6	5.9
Male	28.2	10.5
Female	21.7	10

Note: The author notes that sample size was too small to report Native Americans.
Source: Hoachlander et al. (2003).

the courage to enter upon a four years' study would be willing to do the two years of work before entering business or the professional school" (p. 15).

Though Harper's comments illustrate elitist tendencies, it is clear that the terminal degree function of the two-year college was intentional among some of its earliest founders, though for early two-year college leaders, this undoubtedly included associate's degrees in classical fields. While some students will attain an associate's degree in arts or sciences as their highest degree, often, these students are not referred to as attaining a terminal degree. Why? Because these students have completed the coursework necessary to transfer to a four-year university. Community colleges of today have two primary types of terminal degrees: certificates and associate's degrees, both of which can be in vocational, technical, or occupational programs (Cohen & Brawer, 2003; Laanan, 2003). As noted by Cohen & Brawer (2003), the terms "terminal, vocational, technical, semiprofessional, occupation and career have all been used interchangeably" (p. 222). Thus, we are using the term "terminal" as an umbrella for all other associated concepts.

Students who are able to transfer with applied degrees transfer without a junior-class standing, thereby, leaving them with additional requirements upon deciding to transfer to a four-year institution. Community colleges have not been successful in aiding students toward terminal degree completion. For example, of the students who enter the community college only 9.7 and 15.7 percent attain a certificate or associate's degree respectively, in a seven-year time span (Hoachlander et al., 2003).

Remedial Education

Remediation of students is also a primary function of community colleges. Remedial education consists of academic programming, which provides students with instruction in basic skill areas (e.g., mathematics, reading, writing) in order to address and correct varied areas of academic ability. Cohen & Brawer (2003) state that "although some remedial work had been offered early on, the disparities in ability between students entering community colleges and those in the senior institutions [four year colleges] was not nearly as great in the 1920s as in recent years" (p. 23). They note that the need for remedial education became more evident in the 1960s when access to postsecondary education expanded.

There are many reasons why students may need to be remediated: (a) they received poor educational training at earlier levels of education; (b) they did not apply themselves at earlier levels of education; (c) they did not complete previous educational programming; and (d) some material has been forgotten. No matter the cause, large percentages of community college students (40 percent) need remediation in at least one subject area (e.g., reading, writing, mathematics) (U.S. Department of Education, 2001). This sentiment is shared by community college faculty. According to the Almanac (2008–09), 65.4 percent of community college faculty indicate that most of the students they teach lack the basic skills for college-level work. However, 92.1 percent state that they agree that their institution should offer remedial/developmental education.

As noted by Vaughan (2006), remediation is needed for students of all abilities, including many academically elite students. This is especially true since community colleges serve many returning students or students who were not adequately prepared in pre-K-12 education. Additionally, it is unclear who the remedial education students actually are, since there are no nationally normative assessments of community college remediation needs. In fact, in many instances, there are no statewide or even district-wide normative measures to determine who is, and who is not, a remedial student (Oudenhoven, 2002).

Notwithstanding, the implications for remediating community college students are plentiful: (a) teaching and learning needs to be tailored toward varied learning styles and abilities; (b) greater allocation of support services need to be allocated; (c) attainment rates for students who begin in remedial education are very low in comparison to nonremedial students; (d) remediation encompasses a wide range of students, those within a semester of entering college-level work and those with years of remedial work needed to begin college-level classes; and (e) high percentages of remedial students affect public perceptions of community colleges, questioning whether these colleges are truly institutions of higher learning. Remedial students are less likely to achieve success in the community college as compared to nonremedial students. For example, remedial math students are 15 percent more likely to drop out without a two-year degree and half as likely to complete a four-year degree in five years (Bettinger & Long, 2005).

Continuing Education

Downey, Pusser, & Turner (2006) define continuing education "as the range of programs and services that provide workforce training, adult basic education, academic transfer curricula, personal enrichment, and community outreach courses" (p. 75). Stated in a more succinct way, continuing education is an expansive aspect of the community college mission that covers educational offerings which are designed, in part or in totality, for those students who are either continuing their education after already achieving a degree or being in the workforce. As noted previously, the core concepts of the community college mission are interrelated. Continuing education overlaps with many core functions of the community college. However, it is a distinct aspect of the community college mission.

Adult and continuing education has been a staple of the community college mission since its early years. In the 1920s, leisure courses include a wide array of disciplines ranging from fine arts to mechanics. These offerings have allowed the community college to meet the varying academic, professional, and personal needs of their local communities (Witt et al., 1994). Continuing education programming can be both credit and noncredit in nature. As noted by Bailey (2002), there are several advantages for colleges to offer these programs, especially those which are noncredit: (a) they are easier to create and implement due to more limited accreditation requirements; (b) they can generate additional monies for colleges; and (c) when provided directly to businesses through contracts, they can generate political capital for the college.

Hoachlander et al. (2003) identified the main purposes for students who enroll in community college; they found that 16 percent enroll for personal enrichment and 23 percent for job skills. This indicates that nearly 40 percent of students enrolling in the community college are there for continuing education purposes. The high percentage of students enrolling in community colleges for continuing education is likely driven by the number of jobs held in a lifetime. According to the U.S. Department of Labor (2008), individuals born between 1957 and 1964 had "held an average of 10.8 jobs from ages 18 to 42" (p. 1). The implications of this phenomenon are that individuals will require additional work skills to adjust and succeed to new employment positions and settings. Thus, there is a continual demand for community college offerings to meet the needs of this student population.

Operations

The *operations* of the community college refer to the divisions and personnel within who carry out the functions of the institution. These operations are guided by the vision and mission of the college. In tying the VMFOs together, the vision is the "what," the mission is the "how," the functions are the "actions" through which the "how" is achieved, and the operations are the "who," the individuals charged with realizing the vision and mission of the organization. Wide variation exists in the governance structures of community colleges. For example, governing structures vary among small community college districts, large community college districts, multicollege districts, state community college systems, and university-controlled community college system (Cohen & Brawer, 2003). Bearing this in mind, there are four general divisions that exist within *most* community colleges. The organization of these divisions as presented here may differ from that of many community colleges; thus our goal was to provide a snapshot of a general organization structure.

President and Cabinet

The president serves as the presiding formal authority within the college. The president's role is to oversee the overall functions (e.g., public affairs, fundraising, business affairs) of the institution, in order to aid it in achieving its vision and mission. Presidents can do so by providing a supportive structure and environment that facilitate academic success. Presidential leadership is usually advised through a cabinet. Cabinets are comprised of executive-level university officials (e.g., vice presidents, provost) and senior staff who may have specialized expertise, which enhances decision making. For example, some cabinets include special assistants who may focus on issues such as equity and diversity, technology, planning, and legal affairs.

Academic Affairs

Academic affairs are usually headed by the college provost of academic affairs. This arm of the college coordinates and supports all academic operations and programming (e.g., faculty professional development, retention programs [1]), as well as the academic standards (e.g., direct instruction, distance education, continuing education) of the institution. Discipline-specific leadership is coordinated by academic/instructional deans and chairs who oversee the curricular operations of each division and report directly or indirectly to the provost or vice president of academic affairs. Faculty senates are usually an integral component of academic affairs and have great influence on all aspects of academic affairs (e.g., curricular standards, program development, academic policies, codes, and provisions).

Academic affairs also supervises retention-based programs, which are designed to support both the general student population and special student

---

[1] The institutional housing of retention programs varies by institution. Some institutions house these programs in academic affairs, some in student affairs. Either way, they are core operational aspects of both academic and student affairs.

populations (e.g., veterans, disabled, students of color) in achieving their academic and career goals. These efforts are primarily undertaken by the community faculty, of whom 83.1 percent report being strongly interested in the academic problems of students (Almanac, 2008–09). The curricular operations of academic affairs are improved by student affairs programs, which expand colleges' focus on holistic learning and the psychosocial development of students.

Student Affairs

Student affairs (or student services) refers to the conglomerate of campus operations which focus on the technical aspects of students' attendance (e.g., outreach, orientation, registration, enrollment, financial aid, assessment, counseling, judicial affairs); campus life operations of colleges, which encourage students social integration into the campus community (e.g., student government, student clubs and organizations, intramural and sanctioned athletics programs, housing); and practices which are viewed in the margins of academic and student affairs (e.g., service learning, retention programs, academic advising). Their charge is to create a student-centered campus environment which is welcoming to all students.

Ideally, the psychosocial support offered by student affairs complements the academic programming of colleges and vice versa. A balance between offering services and support, between student affairs and academic affairs, needs to be promoted in order to comprehensively teach the "whole" student. Unfortunately, the division of student affairs is often relegated to the periphery of institutional priorities, due to the perception that student affairs focuses on noncurricular issues. That being said, only 4.4 percent of community college faculty members believe that social activities are overemphasized.

Business Affairs

Business affairs or administrative affairs are umbrella terms that identify the divisions within colleges that focus on the technical aspects of running the daily operations of the institution. There are many areas which business affairs divisions usually oversee. They include (a) employee affairs or human resources (e.g., hiring, payroll); (b) institutional research, evaluation, and effectiveness; (c) institutional advancement (e.g., fund and resource development); (d) auxiliary organizations and entities (e.g., health centers, food services, bookstores); (e) office of the college counsel, which focuses on internal and external legal affairs; and (f) public and community affairs officers (e.g., external relations and marketing). Another primary role of business affairs is to ensure financial resources are accrued and dispersed throughout the institution. These resources provide support for students, faculty, administration and the overall livelihood of the institution. Business affairs is also the lead division responsible for internal auditing and financial accountability. It serves in an advisory capacity to the campus administration in determining funding reductions and responsible stewardship of campus resources.

Community colleges are experiencing a rapid paradigm shift. This in turn justifies a need to revisit the vision and mission of the community college to ensure the values within are congruent to meeting the ever-increasing needs of its constituents. Much of what is known about the nature, roles, functions, and operations of higher education is shifting, subsequently requiring a more skillful workforce than before. Funding, governance, diversity, accountability, faculty, institutional culture, and technology are evolving. These changes are mainly driven by the dire fiscal landscape and outlook of the nation with some states affected more than others. Several years ago, terms such as "furloughs" or more commonly "furlough Fridays," "stimulus funds," "employment exodus," and "financial exigency" were unheard of. Discussions of capping community college enrollments, widespread layoffs, and dramatic tuition hikes were unconscionable. Now these terms and discussions are commonplace, and their implications are played out in the daily operations and culture of these institutions.

Community colleges are at the forefront of this expanding financial crisis. Leaders must recognize and accept the monumental challenges facing these institutions. For example, one can predict that tuition will continue to increase, likely in a more exponential fashion. This is due to widespread reductions in state funding lines to these institutions; moreover, colleges are finding it necessary to become more self-sufficient through fundraising. In order for leaders to meet emerging challenges, they must deconstruct traditional policies and practices, which are incongruent with contemporary demands, thereby enabling leaders to construct approaches that are aligned with the new realities facing community colleges. In doing so, leaders can see this paradigm shift as an opportunity to better meet the expanding mission of the community college.

Change

Change in the VMFOs of the community college is affected through several sources (see Figure 2). An assessment of functional and operational outcomes of

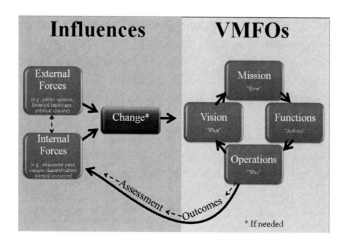

Figure 2 Community College Change Model

community colleges determines whether or not these institutions are actualizing their vision of creating "broader postsecondary education for the people" and mission of open access, comprehensive educational programs, serving the community, teaching and learning, lifelong learning, and student success. Upon having a comprehensive assessment of outcomes, external and internal groups use this information to enforce, modify, or change VMFOs in accordance with assessment results. Sometimes, there is a heightened influence on modification and change based upon external factors such as public opinion; the financial landscape; and the local, state, and national political climates. Change is also influenced by internal factors (e.g., attainment rates, campus climate/culture, internal resources), which address internal outcomes of these institutions.

It is of critical importance for community college leaders to fully comprehend the institution's VMFOs in order to develop, implement, and assess the effectiveness of structures, processes, and programs in place. In doing so, leaders need to ensure that elements pertinent to the college vision and mission are not treated in isolation but addressed in an interrelated manner. This is particularly important since each element has an impact on the whole. Understanding the mission of the community college can provide leaders with (a) a tool to drive their respective institutions in accordance with the community college's vision and mission; (b) a platform to gain credibility from peers and constituents; (c) the understanding of the institution needed to instigate change; and (d) a mechanism for marketing and gaining support for their respective community colleges. In sum, leaders need to live the vision and mission of their institutions within their everyday practices. Also, leaders must ensure that the mission of their individual institutions is relevant to the contemporary needs of their students and affiliates. The dividends of doing so will be priceless, in that their success will lead to greater institutional effectiveness, which ultimately will benefit students and all individuals affiliated with the institution.

Case Study

A case study is presented, which is designed to aid you in critically examining the VMFOs of the community college. When identifying resolution(s), be attentive to the interrelationship among these concepts, and the factors influencing their change.

President Edna Baehre,
Vice President of Public Relations, Patrick Early,
Central Pennsylvania's Community College,
Harrisburg, Pennsylvania

Accommodating Displaced Workers

As the community college for Central Pennsylvania, Harrisburg Area Community College (HACC) felt a strong need to respond to the recession of 2008–09. The college had responded in previous downturns by waiving tuition for displaced workers on a seats-available basis. However, it was recognized that this downturn was much steeper and more widespread and the college felt the need for a more systemic and planned approach. The overwhelming response to tuition waiver announcements by a few other community colleges in the state also argued for a planned and comprehensive approach. As a result, the college decided to approach the needs of dislocated workers on a very personal level.

Working with her cabinet, the college president established an economic response task force drawing expertise from departments throughout the college. There were representatives from academic affairs, noncredit/workforce training, student affairs, career services, financial aid, and public relations at the table. All were going to be involved in the process, and the college needed to tap into the expertise of each individual area. Conceptually, all of the needed expertise was at the table and those at the table would be responsible for implementing the program they would design.

The result was HACC's Targeted Retraining for Dislocated Workers (TRDW) program. More than a tuition waiver program, it is a comprehensive program in cooperation with the region's Workforce Investment Board (WIB) to evaluate displaced workers and place them in education and training programs—credit or noncredit—which would prepare them for jobs, which are still available despite the economic downturn.

Statement of the Problem

You are faced with a widespread crisis outside of your control. This is not a problem of your making, but the community expects you to respond effectively and quickly. At the same time, your response could have a long-term impact on your college's financial health and a lackluster or ineffective response—even though well-meaning—could hurt your reputation and ability to serve the community. What's more, the expertise needed to address the issue crosses many departmental lines and you will need help both designing a response and then implementing it. Finally, the college must balance the needs of each individual dislocated worker along with his or her expectations and the realities of the job market. How will you (1) collect the expertise needed to address the situation? (2) determine the resources needed to respond and the potential impact on the institution? (3) communicate the response both to the college community and the general public? (4) implement the solution while still moving forward with all of the day-to-day operations of the college? and (5) address the unique case management needs of each student while anticipating hundreds of dislocated workers seeking help from the college?

One of the first steps was to tap into the ongoing partnership with CareerLink (Pennsylvania's One Stop Centers under the Workforce Investment Act). Since that is already the enrollment point for jobless benefits, the college decided to make that the initial point of contact. As a result, dislocated workers go through a job exploration and self-assessment process, which matches student interest with their personal and financial needs.

After completing the CareerLink process, dislocated workers are referred to HACC for a one- to two-hour orientation where they get extensive information concerning college life; the dislocated worker credit and noncredit program options; and various financial options for education including all federal, state, and college-wide programs. Students leave the orientation with an individual step-by-step action plan to help them determine what to study, the steps they need to complete to be enrolled, and how to pay for it. If they do not qualify for Financial Aid or WIA dollars, the college can waive tuition or cover the cost of the program through a one-time allocation of $100,000 through the HACC Foundation.

Many of these students have never attended college and have been in the same job for a long time and require significantly more time and support than other students. They are being forced to face life-challenging situations. They don't know how long they will have unemployment, don't have working spouses, and don't have savings. All students apply for financial aid to ensure that they can get appropriate financial assistance. Students are made aware of their ability to apply for federal student loans in order to assist them with costs of books/supplies, transportation, and housing. They are also counseled about food stamps, child care, and other systems to support their living costs while going to school.

To help spread the word, the college set up a special web site and enlisted the resources of an outside call center as well as establishing a toll-free help line. Operators at the call center were given a basic script and were directed to take contact information and refer individuals to their local CareerLink office. They were also promised a comprehensive information packet within 48 hours of their calls. The college also launched a media relations effort, which attracted the attention and support of state legislators and local officials at every one of the five campuses.

Case Study Questions

In analyzing the response from the administrative team, consider the following questions: (1) what are the implications surrounding this case study and how it was addressed by the administrative team? and (2) what alternative or additional approaches can/must be undertaken to positively support HACC's Targeted Retraining for Dislocated Workers (TRDW) program?

References

Almanac (2008–09). *Opinions and attitudes of full-time faculty members, 2007–08.* Washington, DC: Chronicle of Higher Education.

Bailey, T. (2002). Community colleges in the 21st century: Challenges and opportunities. In P. A. Graham & N. G. Stacey (eds.), *The knowledge economy and postsecondary education: Report of a workshop* (pp. 59–75). Washington, DC: National Academy Press.

Bettinger, E. P., & Long, B. T. (2005). Remediation at the community college: Student participation and outcomes. *New Directions for Community Colleges, 129,* 17–26.

Bogart, Q. J. (1994). The community college mission. In G. A. Baker, III, J. Dudziak, & P. Tyler (eds.)., *A handbook on the community college in America: Its history, mission, and management* (pp. 60–73). Westport, CT: Greenwood Press.

Cohen, A. M., & Brawer, F. B. (2003). *The American community college* (4th ed.). San Francisco, CA: Jossey-Bass.

Digest of Education Statistics (2008). *Table 250. Percentage distribution of full-time faculty and instructional staff in degree-granting institutions, by type and control of institution, selected instruction activities, and number of classes taught for credit: Fall 2003.* Washington, DC: National Center for Education Statistics.

Downey, J. A., Pusser, B., & Turner, J. K. (2006). Competing missions: Balancing entrepreneurialism with community responsiveness in community college continuing education division. *New Directions for Community Colleges, 136,* 75–82.

Eells, W. B. (1941). *Present status of the junior college terminal education.* Washington, DC: American Association of Junior Colleges.

Hoachlander, G., Sikora, A. C., Horn, L., & Carroll, C. D. (2003). *Community college students: Goals, academic preparation, and outcomes.* Washington, DC: National Center for Education Statistics.

Kasper, H. T. (2002–03). The changing role of community college. *Occupational Outlook Quarterly,* 14–21.

Laanan, F. S. (2003). Degree aspirations of two-year college students. *Community College Journal of Research and Practice, 27,* 495–518.

Levin, J. S. (2000). The revised institution: The community college mission at the end of the twentieth century. *Community College Review, 28*(2), 1–25.

O'Banion, T. (1989). *Innovation in the community college.* New York: Macmillan.

Oudenhoven, B. (2002). Remediation at the community college: Pressing issues, uncertain solutions. *New Directions for Community Colleges, 117,* 35–44.

Ratcliff, J. L. (1994). Seven streams in the historical development of the modern American community college. In G. A. Baker III., J. Dudziak, & P. Tyler (eds.), *A handbook on the community college in America: Its history, mission, and management* (pp. 3–16). Westport, CT: Greenwood Press.

Richardson R. C. Jr. (1987). The presence of access and the pursuit of achievement. In J. S. Eaton (ed.)., *Colleges of choice: The enabling impact of the community college* (pp. 25–46). New York: Macmillan.

Tillery, D., & Deegan, W. L. (1985). *Renewing the American community college.* San Francisco, CA: Jossey-Bass.

Townsend, B. K. (2001). Redefining the community college transfer mission. *Community College Review, 29*(2), 29–42.

U.S. Department of Education (2001). National Center for Education Statistics, Postsecondary Education Quick Information System, "Survey on Remedial Education in Higher Education Institutions: Fall 1995," 1995; and "Survey on Remedial Education in Higher Education Institutions: Fall 2000."

U.S. Department of Labor (2008). *Number of jobs held, labor market activity, and earnings growth among the youngest baby boomers: Results from a longitudinal survey.* Washington, DC: U.S. Department of Labor.

Vaughan, G. B. (1983). Introduction: Community colleges in perspective. In G. B. Vaughan (ed.)., *Issues for community college leaders in a new era* (pp. 1–20). San Francisco, CA: Jossey-Bass.

Vaughan, G. B. (2006). *The community college story* (3rd ed.). Washington, DC: Community College Press.

Witt, A. A., Wattenbarger, J. L., Gollattscheck, J. F., & Suppiger, J. E. (1994). *American's community colleges: The first century.* Washington, DC: American Association of Community Colleges.

CHAPTER TWO

HISTORICAL LEGACY OF COMMUNITY COLLEGES

This chapter provides an overview of the history of the junior-community college with primary focus given to its origins. In doing so, this chapter will include the following: (a) an examination of social and philosophical forces that led to the development of the junior college; (b) an overview of the individuals who promoted its creation, specifically William Rainey Harper; and (c) a historical snapshot of the development of the junior/community college through seven periods.

When reading this chapter, consider the following questions:

- What social and philosophical forces spawned the development of the junior/community college? What evidence, if any, is there of these forces existing in your institution? How do these forces influence leadership practice?
- What can leaders learn from the success of William Rainey Harper? What can be learned from leaders and colleges that were not successful? How can this information be applied in your institution?
- What historical themes and trends are evident throughout the history of the community colleges? What implications do these themes and trends have for today's educational leaders?

At the dawn of the twentieth century, a unique set of higher education institutions emerged in the United States. From their origins as high school extensions and divisions of universities, they are now referred to as community colleges. The history of the community colleges is as diverse as the institutions themselves. Understanding their history will improve leadership in several ways, it will: (a) enhance leaders' understanding of the role community colleges have played in responding to the needs of an ever-changing society; (b) empower them with knowledge to avoid missteps taken by previous leadership; and (c) provide them with a framework of successful practices to model in current and future contexts.

As noted by Grandstaff & Sorenson (2009), leaders who understand history have an enhanced ability to lead; they state:

Today's world calls for strategic leaders to understand that history is far from irrelevant. It is something to use and leverage. The study of history can help leaders understand the nature of change and the consequences of being trapped in a parochial worldview. It provides leaders with a series of questions that, if properly developed and applied, will help them make good decisions by ferreting out what is important from what is not. (p. 96).

Social Forces Giving Rise to the Community College

Many competent scholars have disagreed over the most significant factor(s) leading to the development of the community college. As noted by Cohen & Brawer (2003), it is likely that a number of complex and interrelated forces contributed to its ideological justification, physical development, and exponential growth. This is not to say that some factors were likely more influential than others (e.g., public school official prestige, upper classes wishing to maintain their social position, alliance of the working and middle classes) (Cohen, 2001). For example, some have suggested that the lure of increased prestige for public school officials led to the development of the community college. This assertion suggests that public school superintendants/principals and teachers supported the development of the community college to assume the more esteemed designations of president and professor (see Cohen, 2001; Cohen & Brawer, 2003). While this incentive may have played a role in certain individuals' motivations to support the establishment of community colleges, the likelihood that an entirely new institutional behemoth was spawned, in totality or in part, for this reason seems improbable. Rather, we suggest four primary social forces that led to its rise: (a) interconnectivity of opportunity and education; (b) the German system of education; (c) industrial market needs; and (d) autonomous and localized educational practices. Prior to explicating these forces, a general foundation in the ideological standpoints of the populist and elitist movements may be helpful.

Philosophical Standpoints

The ideological underpinnings of the community college were motivated by the mutual aims of two social schools of thought. According to Witt et al., (1994), the elitist and populist movements of the late 1800s and early 1900s influenced the formation and development of the community college. These movements aligned to support the creation of the community college for their mutual benefit, but their motivations were based upon polarized worldviews. The populists were motivated by the ideal of freedom, which they saw as interconnected with that of opportunity, in particular, educational opportunity. As a result, populist leaders fought for the establishment of public schools at the elementary, junior, and high school levels. In doing so, they sought to create access to education for all people, not only those who were white, male, and wealthy. By the 1880s, populists had expanded their sights to higher education, demanding access to postsecondary education as well.

In contrast to the populists, Witt et al., (1994) note that the elitists (who were primarily comprised of university professors and presidents) were diametrically opposed to progressivism, preferring exclusivity rather than access. The elitists were proponents of the long-standing tradition, which restricted higher education from the general public and reserved it for the wealthy alone. This tradition dates back to the 1600s, when the first colleges and universities in the United States were founded for the purpose of providing a classical education to the privileged of colonial society. The success of the progressivists in expanding educational opportunities in precollegiate education resulted in the growing citizenry with a high school education. As the number of these graduates increased, the elitists moved to support the progressivists in order to maintain the intellectual and class separation of the educational system.

Interconnectivity of Opportunity and Education

As noted, the progressivists tied the notion and actualization of freedom to opportunity and subsequently to educational opportunity. The concept of educational opportunity became increasingly intertwined with that of financially accessible schooling (Griffith & Blackstone, 1945; Monroe, 1977; Witt et al., 1994). Monroe (1977) notes that during the time period between 1820 and 1850 public opinion became supportive of free, tax-sponsored public education. Post-Civil War, this resulted in the decline of tuition-based Latin schools and an increase in free public high schools. In general, this support was driven by a national ethos, "dedicated to the belief that all individuals should have the opportunity to rise to their greatest potential" (Cohen & Brawer, 2003). This opportunity was believed to be attainable through increased educational training for youth (Cohen & Brawer, 2003; Griffith & Blackstone, 1945). Specifically, this shift in American education was a result of a working- and middle-class union for free public education. This union offset the social stratification efforts of the upper class (Cohen, 2001). Evidence of the successful movement for free public secondary education was seen in the 1874 Kalamazoo ruling (Goldin, 2001; Monroe, 1977). The Kalamazoo ruling issued by the Supreme Court of Michigan mandated that public high schools be supported through taxation in a similar fashion as common schools (Goldin, 1999, 2001; Pedersen, 1987). Since many community colleges emerged from secondary educational institutions, this ruling was one basis for the alignment of the community college with free or low-cost public education (Monroe, 1977).

As successes in attaining free public schooling began to mount, the number of high schools around the country began to increase. As noted by Tillery & Deegan (1985), "the democratization of public school education...led to increasing completion rates from high schools," resulting in a rising number of high school graduates (Cohen & Brawer, 2003). As the belief in educational opportunity for the "commoner" seemed to be actualized in precollegiate education, the call to extend this opportunity to higher education was embraced by the public, which demanded greater societal equality (Cohen & Brawer, 2003). By the 1880s, it was clear that the increasing number of high school graduates was prompting immense demand for higher educational institutions; however, the sheer number of college-bound students was too great for the existing university structure (Cohen & Brawer, 2003; Tillery & Deegan, 1985). As noted by Cohen & Brawer (2003), demand for access to higher education continued to rise. By the early 1900s, the increasing public support of educational opportunity led to expansive growth in high school graduates seeking a college education. This set the stage for the development of the community college.

The German System of Education

A major factor, which influenced the establishment of the community college, was the birth of the American research university (Ratcliff, 1994; Tillery & Deegan, 1985). As noted, the traditional model of higher education provided that colleges and universities train upper-class students with a classical education. However, Witt et al., (1994) note that by the late 1880s, the German educational structure had begun to influence the thinking within the educational system in the United States. In the German structure, students continue their secondary education for about two years longer than the students in the United States in a school system called the gymnasium. During this time period, students complete their general education (the United States equivalent of grades 13 and 14). After the gymnasium, students may enter the workforce or move on to educational institutions with specialized foci.

In contrast to the American university, German higher education focused on research. Through this focus and structure, Germany made great advances in science and technology. This allowed the country to become the industrial beacon of Europe. The accomplishments of this educational structure were not lost upon higher education leaders in the United States (Hillway, 1958; Witt et al., 1994). Ratcliff (1994) states that in the late 1800s and early 1900s presidents of American universities became enamored with the German model of education. Gradually, this resulted in a shift within the American educational system to focus on research. According to Monroe (1977), the proponents of the German model thought that this model would enable universities to limit access to elite students who would be better suited for research and scholarship. This in turn, would allow institutions to prevent increases in unprivileged class enrollments. As a result, the move to separate the first two years of college from the latter two years became increasingly popular among elitists (Cohen, 2001).

Industrial Market Needs

As noted by Baker, Dudziak & Tyler (1994), the community college is a "social system because its internal functions and parts are affected by outside forces, and the institution in turn affects its external environment" (p. xii). They note that functions of this social system are seen in the development, growth, and responsiveness of the community college to meet the needs of the society. In the mid 1800s, the agricultural and mechanical industrialization of American society became prominent. As a result, the industrial markets required an influx of workers with advanced education beyond that provided in secondary schools (Cohen & Brawer, 2003; Griffith & Blackstone, 1945; Tillery & Deegan, 1985).

The need for vocational training in the agricultural and mechanical arts was recognized by the federal government, which resulted in the passage of two acts known as the Morrill Act of 1862 and the Morrill Act of 1890. In 1859, Justin Smith Morrill, the United States House representative from the state of Vermont successfully sponsored the first Morrill Act. Although vetoed by President Buchanan in 1859, the legislation was signed into law by President Lincoln on July 2, 1862. This act marked the federal government's first involvement in higher education. The Act allowed federal land to be sold and state governments to reap the monies derived from the sales for the establishment of colleges focused on agricultural and mechanical studies (Neyland, 1990; Redd, 1998; Sink, 1995).

On August 30, 1890, the second Morrill Act was signed into law by President Harrison. This Act allowed the sale of additional federal land for the purpose of establishing colleges with programs and additional facilities for research addressing the agricultural sciences and the mechanical arts (U.S. General Accountig Office, 1995; National Association of State Universities and Land Grant Colleges, 1995; Wolanin, 1998). The Morrill Acts are evidence of a growing philosophy that affirmed the need for "low cost college education for the common people [further evidence of the *interconnectivity of opportunity and education*] a college curriculum, which provided a nonsectarian, nonclassical education geared to the practical vocations and the applied sciences of engineering and technology in agriculture and industry" (Monroe, 1977, p. 6).

There is a link between the rise of the community college and its responsiveness to industry needs. Though the federal government had a very minimal role in the establishment of community colleges, the Morrill Acts addressed the need for a more complex educational system focused on both vocational training and classical education. This social force led, at least in part, to industries' support of the community college, likely due to the publicly sponsored training of its workforce. It also led to an increased recognition of the need for advanced vocational training, a mission taken on by the community college (Cohen, 2001; Cohen & Brawer, 2003).

Autonomous and Localized Educational Practices

The tradition of local control and support for education is another primary factor that gave rise to the community college. Undoubtedly, it is related to the *interconnectivity of opportunity and education* in that the purpose of local control is for greater local access. However, the drive for autonomous and localized education is based upon the desire to meet the specific needs of the local community. This focus is evident, even to the earliest periods in American education. Monroe (1977) notes that this tradition dates back to the Puritans who wanted all church members to have the ability to read the Holy Bible. For instance in 1647, the colony in Massachusetts Bay mandated that townships with 50 to 99 households establish reading schools. In larger townships of 100 households or more, grammar schools were established for the purpose of preparing youth for higher education. Monroe notes that by "1790, similar legislative provisions for the establishment of public elementary schools were adopted in most New England states" (p. 5).

Ratcliff (1994) identifies *seven streams of educational innovation* from which the community college was derived. Of these streams, one in particular pertains to the concept of local control and support. Ratcliff discusses the notion of *Local community boosterism, which he* refers to as the historical orientation of many colleges and universities in serving the needs of their local communities. If a community was in need of a college, members of the community banded together to build one. Additionally, if the community was primarily comprised of individuals with a certain denominational affiliation (e.g., Lutheran), then, the college that was built was associated with that denomination. In the case when the community was not associated with one denomination as a whole, then the college that was built was often public. Often, in these cases, a college was built by the local community that raised the money and literally constructed the colleges themselves (Ratcliff, 1994). The establishment of most community colleges began at the local level. Institutions were initiated in response to community educational needs. Eventually, their development and oversight occurred at the state level, but rarely at the federal level (Cohen, 2001). Clearly, the desire for autonomous and localized control of education was a primary factor in the development of the community college historically and its operations contemporarily.

It is important for leaders to understand that there are four social forces that influenced the development of the community college. Educational equity, preparing students for university-level study, responding to local market needs, and serving the needs of the local community are forces that permeate the mission of community college both historically and contemporarily. Institutions which aim to successfully serve their constituencies should model their programs, services, and personnel assessments around these four forces.

Intellectual Forebearers of the Community College

Many of the intellectual forebearers of the community college were heavily influenced by the German model of education. Henry P. Tappan, president of the University of Michigan from 1825 to 1863, was among the first to advocate the elimination of general education from the university (Cohen & Brawer, 2003; Monroe, 1977). Tappan and others suggested that general education should be provided by high schools and liberal arts colleges, and that the university should admit students entering their junior year of college (Medsker, 1960; Ratcliff, 1994). They maintained that the American university could not advance while being distracted with general education (Cohen & Brawer, 2003). In 1851, Tappan authored the book *University Education* (Hillway, 1958). In his book,

Tappan advocates the German university model, referring to it as "noble," "pure," and "complete." In contrast, he excoriated the lack of preparation that students in the United States had to engage in university life (Tappan, 1851). In addition to Tappan, many other presidents, scholars, and educational officials, especially those educated in Germany, supported the modeling of the German system (Ratcliff, 1994). These leaders include some of the following:

- *William Mitchell*—Mitchell was a trustee at the University of Georgia who submitted a plan in 1859 to eliminate the first two years of college for the institution due to students' lack of preparation for scholarly rigor (Cohen & Brawer, 2003). The plan was tabled by the board of trustees but never implemented (Witt et al., 1994).
- *William Watts Folwell*—Folwell became president of the University of Minnesota in 1869 (Bogue, 1950; Cohen & Brawer, 2003; Hillway, 1958; Medsker, 1960; Monroe, 1977; Ratcliff, 1994). In 1870, he proposed the Minnesota Plan, "a sweeping reorganization plan patterned after the German system"; however, faculty opposition prevented its implementation (Witt et al., 1994, p. 9).
- *Henry Simmons Frieze*–Frieze served as president of the University of Michigan (Ratcliff, 1994). His presidency spanned three terms that included 1869–1871, 1880–1882, and 1887–1888 (American Philosophical Society, 1890). Prior to his presidency, Frieze visited Germany as a professor and developed an "enthusiastic adoration" for the German model of education. As president, Frieze maintained previous efforts made by Tappan to implement this model at the University of Michigan (Angell, 1912).
- *Reverend J. M. Carroll*—Carroll was president of Baylor University during the economic crisis of 1894. During this period, many Baptist colleges were struggling financially. Carroll recommended that the smaller Baptist colleges in Texas and Louisiana eliminate the second two years of their curriculum, and suggested Baylor take on students in their third and four year of study (Ratcliff, 1994).

Of the leaders who were the most influential in developing the community college, William Rainey Harper is the most lauded. He also is widely described as the *Father of the Community College* (see Eells, 1941; Hillway, 1958; Ratcliff, 1986; Vaughan, 1983). Drawing heavily from the ideas of Folwell, Tappan, and others, Harper was an ardent supporter of the German education model. As such, he sought to eliminate the first two years of college from the university (Hillway, 1958; Ratcliff, 1986). According to Tillery & Deegan (1985), Harper and other early two-year college advocates "envisioned the formation of junior colleges not only to free the university for advanced study but also to encourage broader postsecondary education for the people" (p. 5). Likely, this dual focus appeased the interests of elitists and progressivists alike, making Harper more successful than his predecessors. Although his predecessors were unsuccessful in actualizing these policies, they served to lay the groundwork for Harper's success.

In 1891, Harper became the first president of the University of Chicago. Soon after, he made his intention to mold the university after the German model. In 1892, only one year into his presidency, Harper received approval from the Board of Trustees to split the university into two divisions. The upper division, comprised of the last two years of study, became known as the *university college*. The lower division, consisting of the first two years of study, was referred to as the *academic college*. In 1896, the names of the divisions were changed; the *university college* was changed to the *senior college*, and the *academic college* was renamed the *junior college* (Eels, 1941; Hillway, 1958; Monroe, 1977). As a result, Harper is credited with coining the name—*junior college* (Eels, 1941; Medsker, 1960; Tillery & Deegan, 1985).

In order to advance the idea of the *junior college*, Harper advocated its development to educational leaders. According to Eels (1941), Harper addressed the National Education Association in 1900, noting that more than 200 fiscally unstable four-year colleges could improve their standpoint by becoming junior colleges. In doing so, these colleges would simply provide general education courses and eliminate the last two years of study. Among other reasons, Harper argued that students with lower academic aptitude could respectably complete their studies after two years of college and enter the workforce.

Harper's recommendations were widely ignored by these colleges. As a result, Harper turned his efforts to the local Baptist colleges in the Chicago region. As a Christian and a Baptist, Harper attempted to use his influence to encourage local Baptist colleges to restrict their offerings to general studies. If a college opted to follow the German model, Harper noted that provisions would be created for students' college-level work to be accepted by the University of Chicago. This is evidence of early efforts to establish junior college to university transfer agreements. Despite his efforts among college leaders, Harper's most notable successes occurred with high schools. Harper was responsible for supporting the establishment of the Lewis Institute in Chicago, Illinois, in 1896, and the Bradley Polytechnic Institute, now Bradley University, in Peoria, Illinois, in 1897. However, chief among his accomplishments is Harper's role in supporting the establishment of Joliet Junior College in Chicago, Illinois, in 1901, as an extension to Joliet High School (Eby, 1927; Monroe, 1977; O'Banion, 1989).

Leaders examining the unsuccessful campaigns to implement the German model by Tappan, Folwell, and others, as opposed to the success of Harper, can glean an important lesson. Harper, unlike his predecessors, was able to bridge divergent educational philosophies. He brought stakeholders from opposing positions to the table and sought commonalities rather than differences. This resulted in the successful division of the University of Chicago and played an influential role in the founding of multiple junior colleges. Like Harper, leaders today must use common interests to guide organizational change, community involvement, and student success.

Seven Periods of Development and Expansion

Despite the aforementioned challenges, the junior college continued to develop. What follows is an examination of its rise throughout the twentieth century and into the millennium. A review of literature and emergent themes from select decades illustrates six primary periods of development, which include: (a) the Origins Period from 1901 to 1920; (b) the Maturation Period from 1920 to 1940; (c) the Credence Period covered 1940 to 1960; (d) the Equal Opportunity Period 1960 to 1980; (e) the Accountability and Assessment Period dating 1980 to 2000; and (f) the Millennial Period 2000 to present. Figure 1 presents definitive moments in the history of the community college. Each moment will be described throughout the presentation of the six periods and throughout this chapter. Leaders should consider several themes, which permeate the following periods: (a) the responsive mission of the community college to regional, state, and national needs; (b) chronic funding shortages; (c) increasing institutional

Harper begins Junior College at the Univ. of Chicago	Joliet Junior College founded	American Association of Junior Colleges founded	Asheville decision	Serviceman's Readjustment Act (GI Bill)	Harry Truman's Commission on Higher Education	Eisenhower Committee on Education
1892	1901	1920	1930	1944	1947	1956

Figure 1 Definitive Moments of the History of the Community College

growth; (d) increasing student diversity (e.g., race/ethnicity, gender, age, enrollment status); and (e) dedication to educational opportunity.

The Origins Period, 1901–1920

We termed the period between 1901 and 1920 as the *Origins Period*, since it was the initial period of development for the community college (See Figure 2). While private two-year colleges such as Decatur Baptist College in Texas and Lasell Junior College in Massachusetts predate the founding of Joliet Junior College (Cohen, 2001; Eels, 1941; Hillway, 1958), Joliet is hailed as the oldest public two-year college in existence (AACC, 2009a; Cohen, 2001; Kasper, 2002–03; Monroe, 1977; Tillery & Deegan, 1985). Joliet began offering college-level coursework in 1900, but provided a comprehensive curriculum by 1901. While Harper is credited for influencing the expanded curriculum offered at Joliet, it was the leadership of J. Stanley Brown, then superintendent of Joliet High School and fellow Baptist, who made Harper's dream come to fruition (Griffith & Blackstone, 1945; Monroe, 1977).

The founding of the junior college was a monumental accomplishment. As such, it has been hailed by scholars for being "distinct" and "unique" (Cohen, 1969; O'Banion, 1989; Ratcliff, 1994; Tillery & Deegan, 1985). Despite its exceptionality, like most grand efforts, its development in the early 1900s was modest and slow-paced (Baker et al., 1994). Griffith & Blackstone (1945) attribute its slow development to many primary factors, which include: (a) a belief that innate academic ability limited the number of students who could compete successfully

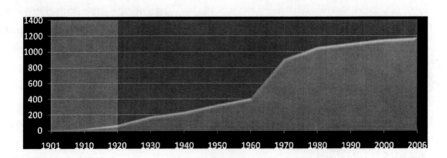

Figure 2   Total Number of Community College Institutions in the Origins Period
Source: Phillippe, K. A. & Sullivan, L. G. (2005). *National Profile of Community Colleges: Trends & Statistics.* Washington, DC: American Association of Community Colleges. American Association of Community Colleges (2009). *Fast Facts.* Washington, DC: Author.

at the collegiate level, which resulted in a widely held perception that too many students were being educated at higher levels; (b) a related belief and perception that too many institutions of higher education were in existence at the time; (c) another opinion that tax monies should be dedicated to elementary and secondary education until the enrollment pipeline was prepared for junior colleges; (d) a philosophical conflict over whether public or private entities should be sponsoring vocational education; and (e) the observation that attrition rates were just as high in junior colleges as they were in university education.

Data presented by Koos (1924) indicates that by the first decade of the twentieth century, 27 junior colleges were established. This included colleges such as: Goshen Junior College in Indiana (1901); the University Preparatory School and Junior College in Oklahoma (1904); and Fresno Junior College in California (1910) (Morsch, 1971; Ratcliff, 1986). As noted by Ratcliff (1986), these early colleges were "philosophically committed to equal-access, equal opportunity education...offer[ing] both vocational and transfer curricula" (p. 15). This philosophy was responsive to local communities' concern that universities were inaccessible to the general public, particularly due to their distance from students' home communities and lack of financing (Brossman & Roberts, 1973). For example, Cohen & Brawer (2003) state the justification for Fresno Junior College was that "there was no institution of higher education within nearly two hundred miles of the city" (p. 19). They note that similar rationale was used to justify the development of other junior colleges.

Medsker (1960) states that many of the first junior colleges were not officially sanctioned operations. State-level legislation guiding their definition, roles, and operations came slowly. Often, these processes were made difficult by public fear of their competition with other postsecondary institutions and apprehension of tax hikes. In 1907, California State Senator Anthony Caminetti sponsored legislation authorizing high schools to provide college-level coursework (Cohen, 2001). This legislation served as a model for the establishment of junior colleges throughout the country (Cohen & Brawer, 2003). The primary method used to develop colleges during this period was to extend the high school curricula to the 13th and 14th grades. These curricular offerings eventually led to the development of junior colleges (Brossman & Roberts, 1973).

In 1915, junior colleges also were initiated in the states of Minnesota and Washington (Cohen, 2001; Morsch, 1971). By 1916, sixteen high schools in California were providing junior college curricula. A year later, the state established guidelines for their operations, structure, and admissions (Morsch, 1971). Also, during this year, the Kansas and Michigan legislatures authorized the founding of junior colleges. As in California, colleges in Kansas, Michigan, Missouri, Minnesota, and Washington were extensions of high schools (Cohen, 2001; Cohen & Brawer, 2003; Morsch, 1971). According to Ratcliff (1994), the first two decades of the twentieth century resulted in large expansions in elementary and secondary school enrollments. This in turn led to rapid growth in the junior college. As more schools were constructed, especially junior high schools, new space allowed for more college program offerings in secondary institutions.

In 1917, the Smith-Hughes Act was implemented. Sponsored by Senator Michael Hoke Smith and Representative Dudley Mays Hughes, this act provided federal funds for public high schools and colleges for vocational education in the agricultural and industrial fields (Eels, 1941; Tegene et al., 2002). Smith-Hughes funding was not intended for junior colleges. However, since the vast majority of junior colleges were appendages of high schools, the Act "had the unintended effect of fostering career training in American junior colleges" (Witt et al., 1994, p. 103).

The Maturation Period (1920–1940)

We refer to the period between 1920 and 1940 as the *Maturation Period*, as the community college gained legitimate status as an educational entity through the formation of a national representative body known as the American Association of Junior Colleges and through advanced accreditation (see Figure 3). By the 1920s, 74 community colleges had been established in the United States. By the end of the decade, this number would more than double, reaching 180 institutions by the 1930s (Phillippe & Sullivan, 2005). It was during this period that

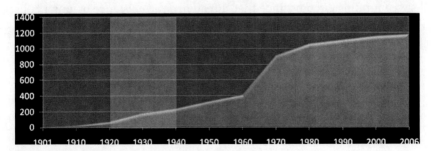

Figure 3 Total Number of Community College Institutions in the Origins Period
Source: Phillippe, K. A. & Sullivan, L. G. (2005). *National Profile of Community Colleges: Trends & Statistics.* Washington, DC: American Association of Community Colleges. American Association of Community Colleges (2009). *Fast Facts.* Washington, DC: Author.

junior colleges began to emerge as separate entities from secondary schools. For example, in 1921, California enacted legislation that permitted the development of junior college districts; these districts were separate from high school districts (Cohen, 2001). Within six years of the authorization, California junior colleges were a blend of high school extensions, college divisions, and autonomous entities. With this in mind, Cohen & Brawer (2003) state:

> Indicative of the inchoate nature of the institution in its early years, in 1927 California had sixteen colleges organized as appendages of the local secondary schools, six as junior college departments of state colleges, and nine organized as separate junior college districts (p. 19).

From 1917 to 1929 most regional accreditation associations developed standards specific to junior colleges (Eels, 1931). This provided important legitimacy to these institutions. However, the greatest milestone of this period occurred on June 30th and July 1st of 1920 when 34 public and private junior college leaders met in St. Louis, Missouri. This meeting led by Dr. George Zook, then the United States Commissioner of Education, resulted in the establishment of the American Association of Junior Colleges (AAJC). The purpose of the organization was to provide a platform to discuss issues concerning junior colleges and to create a cohesive national voice for the movement (AACC, 2009b; Eels, 1941; Vaughan, 1983). It has served this role since its founding.

Despite advancements in the number, organization, and legitimacy of these institutions, student enrollments remained low (Kasper, 2002–03). Additionally in many states, junior colleges faced opposition. Primarily, this opposition came from public officials' resistance to increasing tax dollars for, or sharing tax funds with junior colleges. This resulted in chronic funding shortages in many junior colleges, a funding circumstance that threatened the existence of junior colleges in the 1930s. Examples of state opposition to the establishment of junior colleges include the following:

- In 1925, junior colleges in the State of Washington operated without financial backing from the state government, a condition which would not be rectified until the 1940s (Morsch, 1971). In 1929, Governor Roland Hill Hartley vetoed legislation to authorize state funding to three junior colleges. He "described the state's expenditures on education as excessive" and noted that there was a need to lower taxes (Pedersen, 1987, p. 49).
- In 1927, a proposal was submitted to Baltimore Mayor William Frederick Broening for the establishment of a junior college in the Baltimore

school system. The proposal requested $100,000 to fund the initial expenditures. The request was immediately refused by Mayor Broening who believed that the college was too expensive. In 1928, another attempt to establish a junior college also was rejected at the mayoral-level (Pederson, 1987).

- In 1928, Ohio Attorney General Edward Turner prohibited the establishment of public junior colleges. He noted that local school boards, in which most junior colleges arose, were never granted authority to establish colleges or provide postsecondary education offerings (Pederson, 1987).

Moreover, the existence of many junior colleges was challenged by the financial turmoil of the depression (Pedersen, 1987). For instance, attempts to increase tax levies in Wyoming to support the development of junior colleges failed in the state legislature, stalling junior college development for years. Monroe (1977) notes that growth in the number of junior college institutions continued during the depression era. Despite the immense financial pressures of the era, junior colleges still managed to respond to the needs of their communities. In doing so, Kasper (2002–03) explains, many "began to provide job training programs as a way to ease widespread unemployment" (p. 15). Though not all states provided funding to junior colleges at that time, the depression reduced funding for the ones that did. Funding reductions coincided with increased growth in student enrollments, severely affecting the ability of many states to establish new junior colleges (Tillery & Deegan, 1985). For some colleges, the depression era presented an unbearable challenge. One example of this phenomenon occurred in 1936, when a junior college in Maywood, Illinois, was disestablished due to insufficient funding after only a year of operation (Griffith & Blackstone, 1945). The historic Crane Junior College (in Chicago, Illinois), then the largest in the nation (Pederson, 1987), also closed in the 1930s; though it reopened later in a different form (Monroe, 1977).

In 1930, a landmark ruling in North Carolina had a national impact on public funding for junior colleges. Beginning in 1927, the Board of School Commissioners in Asheville, North Carolina, had operated a publicly funded junior college. Though the college did not provide extensive offerings, it did provide business and clerical coursework (Wiggs, 1987). Local residents attended the college free of charge, and no tax increases were imposed. A local citizen named Zimmerman sued the Board, stating that they did not have the authority to operate a college using tax dollars without approval from the state legislature.

Both the County Superior Court in Buncombe and the State Attorney General affirmed Zimmerman's claim that Asheville's operations were unconstitutional (Pederson, 1987; Tollefson, 2009). Upon appeal of the decision, the state Supreme Court supported the "School Commissioners' right to establish and operate a junior college. Yet…this right did not empower the commissioners to impose any additional tax in support of the college above the minimum local levy specified in the state's foundation program" (Pedersen, 1987, p. 50). Wiggs (1987) presents the Asheville decision in the same light as the 1874 Kalamazoo ruling, which provided public high schools the ability to receive public support in a similar fashion as common schools. Pederson (1987) notes that even the prominent junior college scholar Leonard Koos believed that the Ashville decision was akin to the Kalamazoo ruling. In contrast, Pederson states:

> The Asheville decision clearly set the junior college apart from elementary and secondary schools as an inferior class of institutions with no primary claim on local tax revenues… [During the depression] the application of this principle in such states as Iowa, Kansa, and Illinois resulted in the forced closure of a great many junior colleges (p. 50).

Despite varying perceptions on the benefit or difficulties that this ruling presented, it clearly set a legal precedent and public tone for supporters and detractors of the junior college.

The Credence Period (1940–1960)

We have termed the period between 1940 and 1960 as the *Credence Period*, since the junior college gained national credibility from the Truman and Eisenhower administrations (see Figure 4). By 1940, 238 junior colleges had been established, and by the end of the decade nearly 100 more institutions would be created (Phillippe & Sullivan, 2005). Despite this fact, some junior colleges continued to be disestablished due to funding shortages (e.g., Maine Township Junior College in Des Plaines, Illinois) (Griffith & Blackstone, 1945). In 1945, student enrollments in junior college began to surge (Eaton, 1994). Exponential increases in student enrollment after 1944 are attributed to the passage of the G.I. Bill also known as the Servicemen's Readjustment Act of 1944 (Cohen, 2001; Cohen & Brawer, 2003; Vaughan, 1983). Vaughan (1983) notes that prior to the G.I. Bill, attending college "was largely viewed as a privilege and not a right" (p. 5). However, upon the passage of the G.I. Bill, this belief began to change as World War II veterans were given funding for college tuition and for their cost of living (Cohen & Brawer, 2003; Eaton, 1994; Vaughan, 1983).

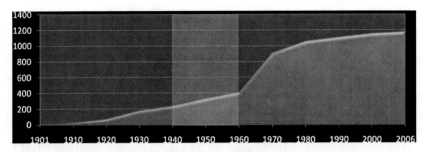

Figure 4 Total Number of Community College Institutions in the Credence Period
Source: Phillippe, K. A. & Sullivan, L. G. (2005). National Profile of Community Colleges: Trends & Statistics. Washington, DC: American Association of Community Colleges. American Association of Community Colleges (2009). Fast Facts. Washington, DC: Author.

In 1947, junior colleges benefited greatly from a report released by the Truman Commission on Higher Education. Established on July 13, 1946, the commission was chaired by George Zook, who had led the first meeting of the AAJC nearly three decades earlier. Its membership was composed of educational, religious, and civic leaders (Quigley & Bailey, 2003). The commission's findings indicated that nearly 50 percent of the nation's population was capable of and would benefit from participation in at least 14 years of education (Medsker, 1960). The commission also found that only 16 percent of 18- to 21-year-olds were enrolling in college, thus indicating a massive void in college-going rates among the general population (Monroe, 1977). As a result, the commission recommended massive expansion in the number of junior colleges. The commission also indicated that the mission and activities of existing and future colleges be expanded to meet the needs of their communities (Gleazer, 1994; Medsker, 1960). In fact, "the commission used the term community college to describe these locally controlled institutions" (Vaughan, 1983, p. 6). This term would gain increasing popularity in the coming years, illustrating the unique mission of the junior college to respond to local community demands. By the 1950s, the term junior college began to be used less in reference to general education divisions at private universities and private two-year colleges. Increasingly, the term community college became used in reference to public two-year institutions (Cohen & Brawer, 2003). Reflecting on this change, the American Association of Junior Colleges was renamed as the American Association of Community and Junior Colleges in 1972 (AACC, 2009b).

At the end of the 1950s and the beginning of the 1960s, the community college began presenting itself as both an open-door and comprehensive institution (O'Banion, 1989). This meant that previous program offerings, which were often myopic in nature, were expanded to meet the educational needs of a greater number of students (Gleazer, 1994). This increase resulted in providing courses in alternative time formats (e.g., early morning, evening) (Tillery & Deegan, 1985). As a result, the number of nontraditional students (e.g., older students, part-time students) began to increase, as did the popularity of the institutions themselves (Medsker, 1960). In particular, rising student enrollment has been attributed to the growing number of veterans from the 1950s and 1960s. Veterans from World War II, Korea, and Vietnam continued to take advantage of government funding for school (Brossman & Roberts, 1973).

As the number of veterans in the community college increased, so did the federal government's support of the institutions. Between the 1950s and 1960s, the community college benefited from a number of legislative acts, including: the National Defense Act of 1958, the Higher Education Facilities Act of 1963, the Vocational Education Act of 1963, the Higher Education Act of 1965, and the Vocational Education Act of 1968 (Monroe, 1977). However, it was in 1956 that the community college received praise from another presidential administration. President Eisenhower had created a Committee on Education Beyond the High School charged with examining the status of postsecondary education in the United States. This committee released a report hailing the importance of the community college and noting the important role that it could continue to play in creating educational opportunities to higher education (Medsker, 1960; Monroe, 1977). Between the Truman Commission and the Eisenhower Committee, the government had made clear the importance of the American community college.

The Equal Opportunity Period (1960–1980)

We refer to the period between 1960 and 1980 as the *Equal Opportunity Period* due to the exponential growth experienced in the community colleges, especially from nontraditional student populations (e.g., minority students, adult students, low-income students) (see Figure 5). By the 1960s, the number of community colleges in the nation had increased to 412 (Phillippe & Sullivan, 2005). This is attributed to: (a) the rising age of baby boomers; (b) the expansion of the nation's economy; (c) increased public support for education; and (d) a university infrastructure that was unable to respond to the increased demand for higher education (Cohen & Brawer, 2003; Kasper, 2002–03; Vaughan, 1983). As noted by Cohen (2001):

> By the 1960s state plans were mushrooming across the nation, leading to a period of tremendous expansion with some 50 new colleges opening each year. Half the states in

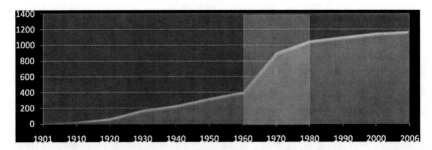

Figure 5 Total Number of Community College Institutions in the Equal Opportunity Period
Source: Phillippe, K. A. & Sullivan, L. G. (2005). *National Profile of Community Colleges: Trends & Statistics*. Washington, DC: American Association of Community Colleges. American Association of Community Colleges (2009). *Fast Facts*. Washington, DC: Author.

the nation were commissioning studies, writing master plans, passing legislation, and building toward statewide systems of community colleges (p. 6).

Coinciding with the increasing number of new colleges being established were the number of outreach, branch, and extension centers providing programs and services. All these expansions supported the open access efforts of these institutions. These efforts resulted in increasing educational access and opportunity for students of color and nontraditional student populations, (O'Banion, 1989), especially as "educational opportunity became interwoven with the civil-rights movement" (Richardson, 1987, p. 28). Richardson (1987) explains that in the 1960s and 1970s, community colleges were defined by their access to postsecondary education, though not necessarily by their success in aiding students' academic achievements. The policy of admitting students without regard to their academic skill level and without providing services to support their success was referred to as *the right to fail*. In this era, disastrously high attrition rates permeated the community college as students enrolled in classes without proper preparation or support once enrolled (Tillery & Deegan, 1985).

In the 1970s, community college growth continued on an expansive trajectory, increasing to over 1,058 institutions by the end of the decade (Phillippe & Sullivan, 2005). Lawmakers and higher education leaders predicted decreases in community college enrollment due to the declining importance and degree attainment in secondary education (Gleazer, 1994; Ratcliff, 1994). However, community college enrollment increased, which was attributed to: (a) increased parental support for higher education; (b) students seeking to avoid the Vietnam draft; and (c) increased enrollment of nontraditional students (e.g., immigrants, mothers) (Kasper, 2002–03; Ratcliff, 1994).

During the latter part of 1970s, the open access *right to fail* philosophy became scrutinized. According to Tillery & Deegan (1985) many educators believed that "the claims and public rhetoric of the community colleges of this period exceeded their achievements" (p. 16). Richardson (1987) states that many educational leaders became critical of academic offerings that lacked alignment, coherence, and structure; as a result, leaders began to change their discourse around access to include discussions around success as well (Richardson, 1987). Community colleges responded by placing an emphasis on resources and support services/programs for students (Tillery & Deegan, 1985).

The Accountability Period (1980–2000)

The period between 1980 and 2000 is described as the *Accountability Period* due to the increased public scrutiny of community college success that took place during this era (see Figure 6). This heightened climate of accountability reverberated through all public institutions as a result, at least in part, of the Government Performance and Results Acts, which required government entities to begin setting, measuring, and holding entities accountable for results. The rapid growth experienced by community colleges during the 1960s and 1970s leveled out during the 1980s and 1990s, though increases were experienced. During the Accountability Period, community colleges began to refocus their efforts on transfer, lifelong learning, economic improvement, and student services (Baker, Dudziak, and Tyler 1994; Eaton, 1994). Community colleges also expanded the delivery of their educational offerings in order to meet the needs of a growing number of nontraditional students. In doing so, they offered:

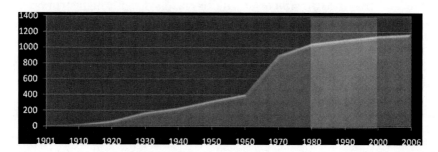

Figure 6 Total Number of Community College Institutions in the Accountability Period
Source: Phillippe, K. A. & Sullivan, L. G. (2005). *National Profile of Community Colleges: Trends & Statistics.* Washington, DC: American Association of Community Colleges. American Association of Community Colleges (2009). *Fast Facts.* Washington, DC: Author.

"evening and weekend colleges, special programs, on-site instruction, and credit for experience" (Eaton, 1994, p. 33). Despite these efforts, the community college reputation was under fire during the 1980s. On one hand, the colleges were criticized for not adequately serving underrepresented communities, not providing a venue for academic excellence, and not supporting social/economic mobility (Eaton, 1994). On the other hand, they were disparaged for focusing too much on social support and services, and for placing too much emphasis on serving underrepresented communities (Richardson, 1987). Due in part to the public scrutiny of their success, lawmakers began reducing funding to and eliminating programs of community colleges. These cuts overlapped with federal reductions to student aid programs (Vaughan, 1983).

As experienced in the 1970s and 1980s, the growth of the community college in the 1990s was more tempered, though increases did occur. In the 1990s, 47 more institutions were added, bringing the total number of institutions to 1,155 by the beginning of the millennium (Phillippe & Sullivan, 2005). Phillippe & Patton (2000) indicate that discussions regarding the appropriate extent to which remedial education services should be offered were widespread in the community college during the 1990s. There was a rise among students enrolling with remediation needs during this period, which coincided with rampant funding issues. They note that funding issues presented significant barriers to maintaining low-cost education, especially since "no new taxes and downsizing government obligations" were common during this time (p. 21). As lawmakers sought increased accountability from community colleges, funding began to be tied to success rates (e.g., graduation, persistence). These success rates failed to account for the variety of students (e.g., full-time, part-time, high school dropouts) that the community college serves.

While this era was challenging for community colleges, there were significant legislative acts passed, which advanced their mission. For example, in 1992 the Scientific and Advanced Technology Act was passed. This act provided an opportunity for community colleges to establish a collaborative partnership with the National Science Foundation (NSF) to advance technological education. Six years later, the Hope Scholarship and Lifetime Learning Tax Credit was enacted, this act encouraged the lifelong learning mission of the community college by providing a tax credit for the first two years of education. In this same year, the Workforce Investment Act was established. This act set the stage for community colleges to become further linked with the local business industry to advance workforce development. As indicated by this act, the local focus of community colleges continued to be reinforced by educational leadership, policymakers, and the community (Vaughan, 2006). Cohen & Brawer (2003) further explain that during the 1970s, the term "junior college" was gradually replaced by the term "community college," with the latter referring to both private and public two-year institutions. As a result, in 1992, the American Association of Community and Junior Colleges (AACJC) changed its name to the American Association of Community Colleges (AACC) (AACC, 2009b).

The Millennial Period (2000 to present)

By the time the community college entered the *Millennial Period*, it had set its place as a dominant and integral force within the nation's postsecondary educational system. In 2001, the public community college celebrated its 100 year anniversary since the founding of Joliet Junior College in 1901. Since the founding of Joliet, the movement has grown to nearly 1,200 institutions serving more than 11.7 million students (AACC, 2009).

Phillippe & Sullivan (2005) report that the service regions of community colleges have expanded; there is an institution, extension center, or branch located within a reasonable proximity to every community in the nation. The maturation of the Internet also has presented opportunities for community colleges to offer hybrid and online courses. In line with the evolving role of these institutions, the millennium period brought with it potential changes to the core mission of community college. In particular, the move to offer bachelor's degrees at the community college has been and continues to be a point of sharp debate. Widespread support for this initiative is unlikely, at least in the current future. As seen in this brief historical overview "community colleges have a long history of resilience and innovation that will allow them to make the leadership transition and find effective solutions for contemporary and future challenges" (p. 6).

There is a potential for continued advocacy as community colleges evolve in the twenty-first century. For example, in July of 2009 the Obama administration announced a new plan to support community colleges around the country in graduating five million more students by the year 2020 (Biden 2009). The administration is set to provide nine billion dollars in federal grants to these institutions in order to aid them in reaching this goal. However, in harkening back to the accountability period, this funding will come with accountability measures, including benchmarks for degree completion, preparation of graduates for the workforce, and career placement (Field, 2009). For fuller description of current and emerging trends in the community college, see Chapter 12 on *Emerging Trends*.

Conclusion

Leaders reading this brief overview of community college history should note two important points. First, the funding problems experienced in community colleges today are situated within a historical legacy of underfunding. Providing access and success under these circumstances is difficult, but attainable. Leaders should continue to seek increased funding levels from state government, local bond measures, and fundraising efforts. However, major increases in funding are unlikely to come. As a result, leaders must constantly assess their programs, services, and personnel to ensure that they are meeting their maximum potential. With assessment measures imbedded within the culture of institutions, leaders can make informed decisions regarding the expansion, continuation, revision, or elimination of resources. Secondly, the community college has a historical focus on access and opportunity. However, as noted by increased public scrutiny and decreased legislative favor in the 1980s and 1990s, leaders must recognize that access without student achievement and support services is a failure. If community colleges continue to define themselves as institutions for opportunity, then deplorable persistence and graduation rates among specific population groups must be addressed swiftly and through collaborative efforts among students, staff, faculty, community members, and so on.

Case Study

Below we present a case study, which requires leaders to be mindful of the content presented in this chapter when resolving the following case. In particular, leaders should consider several themes which permeated the periods presented in this chapter: (a) the responsive mission of the community college to regional, state, and national needs; (b) chronic funding shortages; (c) increasing institutional growth; (d) increasing student diversity (e.g., race/ethnicity, gender, age, enrollment status); and (e) dedication to educational opportunity.

President Edna Baehre
Vice President of Student Affairs &
Enrollment Management, Winnie Black
Campus Vice President, Stuart Savin
Harrisburg Area Community College
Harrisburg, Pennsylvania

Student-Friendly Campus Services

Background

Harrisburg Area Community College (HACC) is a multicampus institution comprised of five physical campuses and a virtual campus across Central Pennsylvania. HACC is the oldest community college in PA, established in 1964. As the college grew over time, it also expanded into the surrounding areas in the late 1980s. Responding to community requests, the college expanded its reach by starting educational centers that eventually became official campuses. These expansion campuses are located in Lancaster, Lebanon, Gettysburg, and York. These regional campuses have grown substantially and now make up almost half the enrollments and staff of the whole college. Expected enrollments for fall 2009 are 23,000 ± credit students.

Like any organization, functional areas grow and develop structures, processes, and policies to meet perceived needs within the resources available at the time. At the original campus in Harrisburg, Student Affairs and Finance (areas such as student accounts, registration, cashiering, advising, and counseling) slowly grew and developed into departments of their own. This new configuration has been common in America's colleges for the last 30 years. However, there have always been discussions across many colleges questioning separation of these areas and the possible redundancy of services, or possible barriers to serving students.

In the case of HACC, the original campus in Harrisburg developed with separate areas for student accounts, registration, cashiering, advising, and counseling. Staff from these departments reported to different divisions in the organization including Student Affairs and the Finance areas. Likewise, over time the credit and the noncredit operation also had developed separate but related structures with staff also reporting to two different divisions. It was a complicated structure, but for many years this worked relatively well. However, as the regional centers started to develop and then grow into full-fledged campuses, the services were provided out of one area. This was largely due to the smaller infrastructure of the locations and staff resources, but the result was a one-stop experience for students. Data also showed that when it came to registration-related activities students of the regional campuses were more likely to use technology for many of their needs. Later, as the regional campuses grew, each one started to imitate the original organizational and structural model from the Harrisburg campus.

Statement of the Problem

Within a few years it started becoming clear that the more a regional campus moved towards the existing big-campus model, the further they became removed from the one-stop servicing opportunities for students. The smaller regional campuses began to question the need to grow in the same direction. Staff observed that completely separated services for each area was becoming cumbersome, redundant, and fragmented not only for the students, but for internal communications and operations as well. Students would have to go to one area to register, go to another building if it was noncredit, and another area if it was a financial aid question or a student accounts question, and to yet another area for routine information questions. Frustrations abounded for students and staff alike. Student services and finance staffs at all campuses began conversations to explore possible options that could address these concerns. It became clear that the organizational model and the one-stop approach by the regional campuses should be replicated at each campus, including the Harrisburg Campus.

The campus vice presidents and the college-wide vice president of student affairs and enrollment management set out to develop the concept of a one-stop-styled area at each campus, which would cross over the student affairs, financial, credit, and noncredit services. The philosophical underpinning is to create a seamless service experience where all the general needs of the students can be met in a Welcome Center. The focus is on developing front-line services to better meet the information and service needs of the students, and empower staff to make informed decisions to help the students (see Figure 7).

Questions to consider: (a) how do you effect change and shift culture in an organization with over 40 years of a "cherished" tradition? (b) how can internal structures and processes be aligned without a complete physical redesign of the facilities—a very expensive proposition? (c) how can a one-stop experience facilitate the information and service needs of students? (d) how can consistency of information and service be achieved across all campuses by all staff? and (e) how should the administration approach implementing one-stop centers?

The diagram below can serve as a foundation for addressing the above questions.

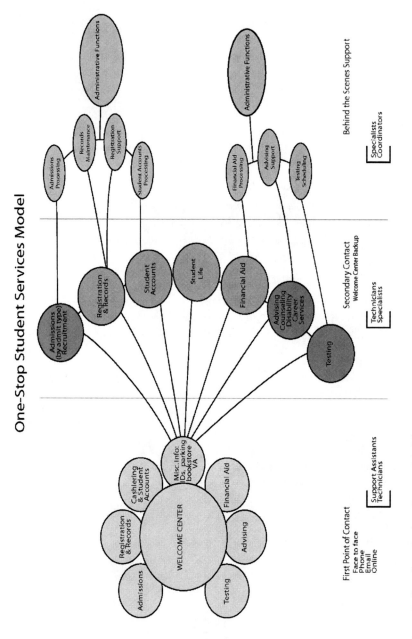

Figure 7 One-Stop Student Services Model

References

AACC (2009a). About community colleges. Washington, DC: American Association of Community Colleges. Retrieved August 28, 2009, from: http://www.aacc.nche.edu/AboutCC/Pages/default.aspx.

AACC (2009b). Who we are. Washington, DC: American Association of Community Colleges. Retrieved August 28, 2009, from: http://www.aacc.nche.edu/About/Who/Pages/default.aspx.

American Philosophical Society (1890). Proceedings. Philadelphia, PA: American Philosophical Society.

Angell, J. B. (1912). Selected Addresses. New York: Longmans, Green, and Co.

Baker, G. A., III, Dudziak, J., & Tyler, P. (1994). A handbook on the community college in America: Its history, mission, and management. Westport, CT: Greenwood Press.

Biden, J. (2009, July 21). Community colleges are crucial. The Sun News. Retrieved August 3, 2009, from: http://www.thesunnews.com/158/story/990694.htm.

Bogue, J. P. (1950). The community college. New York: McGraw-Hill Book Company.

Brossman, S. W., & Roberts, M. (1973). The California community colleges. Palo Alto, CA: Field Educational Publications, Inc.

Cohen, A. M. (1969). Dateline '79: Heretical concepts for the community college. Beverly Hills, CA: Glencoe Press.

Cohen, A. M. (2001). Governmental policies affecting community colleges: A historical perspective. In B. K. Townsend & S. B. Twombly (eds.), Community colleges: Policy in the future context (pp. 3–22). Westport, CT: Ablex Publishing.

Cohen, A. M., & Brawer, F. B. (2003). The American community college, 4th Edition. San Francisco, CA: Jossey-Bass.

Eaton, J. S. (1994). The fortunes of the transfer function: Community colleges and transfer 1900–1990. In G. A. Baker III, J. Dudziak, & P. Tyler (eds.), A handbook on the community college in America: Its history, mission, and management (pp. 28–40). Westport, CT: Greenwood Press.

Eby, F. (1927). Shall we have a system of public junior colleges in Texas? Texas Outlook, 20, 22–24.

Eells, W. B. (1931). The junior college. Boston, MA: Houghton Mifflin.

Eells, W. B. (1941). Present status of the junior college terminal education. Washington, DC: American Association of Junior Colleges.

Field, K. (2009, July 29). For community colleges, federal aid would come with strings attached. The Chronicle of Higher Education. Retrieved August 3, 2009, from: http://chronicle.com/article/For-Community-Colleges-Aid/47493/?utm_source=at&utm_medium=en.

Gleazer, E. J. II. (1994). Evolution of junior colleges into community colleges. In G. A. Baker III, J. Dudziak, & P. Tyler (eds.), A handbook on the community college in America: Its history, mission, and management (pp. 17–27). Westport, CT: Greenwood Press.

Goldin, C. (1999). A brief history of education in the United States. Cambridge, MA: National Bureau of Economic Research.

Goldin, C. (2001). The human capital century and American leadership: Virtues of the past. Cambridge, MA: National Bureau of Economic Research.

Grandstaff, M., & Sorenson, G. (2009). Strategic leadership: The general's art. Vienna, VA: Management Concepts.

Griffith, C. R., & Blackstone, H. (1945). The Junior College in Illinois. Chicago, IL: The University of Illinois Press.

Hillway, T. (1958). The American two year college. New York: Harper and Brothers.

Kasper, H. T. (2002–03). The changing role of community college. Occupational Outlook Quarterly, 14–21.

Koos, L. V. (1924). The junior college. Minneapolis, MN: University of Minnesota.

Medsker, L. L. (1960). The junior college: Progress and prospect. New York: McGraw-Hill Book Company, Inc.

Monroe, C. R. (1977). Profile of the community college. San Francisco, CA: Jossey-Bass.

Morsch, W. (1971). State community college systems: Their role and operation in seven states. New York: Praeger Publishers.

National Association of State Universities and Land Grant Colleges. (1995). The land-grant tradition. Washington, DC: National Association of State Universities and Land Grant Colleges.

Neyland, L. W. (1990). Historically Black Land-Grant Institutions and the development of agriculture and home economics, 1890–1990. Washington, D.C: Economic Research Service, Agriculture and Rural Economics Division.

O'Banion, T. (1989). Innovation in the community college. New York: Macmillian Publishing Company.

Phillippe, K. A., & Patton, M. (2000). National profile of community colleges: Trends and statistics (3rd ed.). Washington, DC: American Association of Community Colleges.

Phillippe, K. A., & Sullivan L. G. (2005). National profile of community colleges: Trends and statistics (4rd ed.). Washington, DC: American Association of Community Colleges.

Pedersen, R. (1987). State government and the junior college, 1901–1946. Community College Review, 14(4), 48–52.

Quigley, M. S., & Bailey, T. W. (2003). Community college movement in perspective: Teachers College responds to the Truman Commission. Lanham, MD: Scarecrow Press, Inc.

Ratcliff, J. L. (1986). Should we forget William Rainey Harper? Community College Review, 13, 12–19.

Ratcliff, J. L. (1994). Seven streams in the historical development of the modern American community college. In G. A. Baker III, J. Dudziak, & P. Tyler (eds.), A handbook on the community college in America: Its history, mission, and management (pp. 3–16). Westport, CT: Greenwood Press.

Redd, K. E. (1998). Historically black colleges and universities: making a comeback. New Directions for Higher Education, 102 (1), 33–43.

Richardson, R. C. Jr. (1987). The presence of access and the pursuit of achievement. In J. S. Eaton (ed.)., Colleges of choice: The enabling impact of the community college (pp. 25–46). New York: Macmillian Publishing Company.

Sink, J. D. (1995). Public policy and America's land-grant educational enterprise: The unique West Virginia experience. The Journal of Negro Education, 64(1), 6–14.

Tappan, H. (1851). University Education. New York: G.P. Putnam.

Tegene, A., Effland, A., Ballenger, N., Norton, G., Essel, A., Larson, G., & Clarke, W. (2002). Investing in people: Assessing the economic benefits of 1890 institutions. Washington, DC: U.S. Department of Agriculture, Economic Research Service.

Tillery, D., & Deegan, W. L. (1985). Renewing the American community college. San Francisco, CA: Jossey-Bass.

Tollefson, T. (2009). Community college governance, funding, and accountability: A century of issues and trends. Community College Journal of Research & Practice, 33(3-4), 386-402.

U.S. General Accounting Office (1995). Land-grant college revenues. Gaithersburg, M.D: U.S. General Accounting Office.

Vaughan, G. B. (1983). Introduction: Community colleges in perspective. In G. B. Vaughan (ed.), Issues for community college leaders in a new era (pp. 1–20). San Francisco, CA: Jossey-Bass.

Vaughan, G. B. (2006). The community college story (3rd ed.). Washington, DC: Community College Press.

Wiggs, J. L. (1987). A legacy in search of a mission: The tension of governance, finance and planning in North Carolina's community colleges. *Community College Review*, 14(4), 19–29.

Witt, A. A., Wattenbarger, J. L., Gollattscheck, J. F., & Suppiger, J. E. (1994). American's community colleges: The first century. Washington, DC: American Association of Community Colleges.

Wolanin, T. R. (1998). The federal investment in Minority-Serving Institutions. *New Directions in Higher Education*, 102(1), 18–32.

CHAPTER THREE

LEADERSHIP AND LEADERSHIP THEORY

This chapter will focus on leadership and leadership theory in relation to the community college. The following areas will be addressed: (a) differences, and commonalities between leadership and administration; (b) an examination of leadership styles (e.g., authoritarian, transactional, transformational); (c) an overview of primary leadership theories (e.g., trait theory, behavioral theory, contingency-situational theory); and (d) a presentation of leadership approaches (e.g., bureaucratic leadership, democratic leadership, political leadership).

When reading this chapter, consider the following questions:

- What are the benefits of theory? How can theory be used to guide leadership practices?
- How are the concepts of leadership and administration defined? What are the differences and commonalities among these concepts?
- What are the primary leadership styles, theories, and approaches addressed in this chapter? What are the differences and commonalities among these concepts? What are the benefits and drawbacks of each concept?

Leadership in the community college is complex and dynamic. Leaders must address the changing needs of the students they serve with fluctuating resources; tenuous relationships with faculty; financial uncertainties; ever-changing community needs; external stakeholder demands; and shifting federal, state, and local support. In light of these challenges, leaders need to exemplify sound leadership (e.g., working toward institutional stability, creating a climate of success, fostering positive relationships among constituents) in a climate that is seemingly unpredictable. Although experience is a worthy component in guiding the decision-making process, it is a limited approach to leading these complex institutions. While experiential knowledge should be highly valued by leaders, it can be enhanced by knowledge of theory. In approaching leadership from a practical and theoretical framework, leadership is advanced through a holistic approach to leading community colleges.

Most leaders do not use theory as a tool to guide the decision-making process. There are several reasons why this occurs: (a) many leaders are unfamiliar with theory for a multitude of reasons, including: they did not learn theory in their prior academic preparation, and those who did learn theory, did not apply it; thus, the information learned was not retained; (b) many leaders perceive (and sometimes rightfully so) that theories are too abstract, general, and not applicable to the practical realities of community college leaders; and (c) they do not fully comprehend how theory can inform and guide their leadership practice. While many leaders do not use theory to shape their leadership practice, many benefits await leaders who do. These include:

- *Understand.* Theories enable leaders to better understand the complexities of factors and actions which contribute to issues faced by community college leaders. Upon leaders gaining a comprehensive knowledge base of a variety of theories (e.g., leadership-member exchange theory, trait leadership theory, behavioral leadership theory, bureaucratic leadership theory), their understanding of the dynamics surrounding a particular issue is enhanced in a multiplicity of domains (e.g., psychological, environmental, political, social).

- *Organize.* Leaders who understand and know how to employ theory are able to use it as a tool to organize the various elements involved with particular issues. In doing so, it allows them to conceptualize and construct a holistic view of a phenomenon and the intricacies of issues impacting it. In essence, it enables them to mentally erect a visual depiction of a problem.

- *Predict.* Leaders who understand theory are better able to predict trends, actions, and behaviors of people internal and external to the institutions in which they serve. In a volatile environment of accountability, dwindling fiscal resources, and heightened public scrutiny of educational institutions, the ability of leaders to predict and envision the actions of others is paramount.

- *Consider.* Leaders who understand the complexities of the issues they face (as informed by theory), and can predict their trajectories, are better able to consider the implications of various trends. By understanding these trends, leaders can conceptualize new or shifting trajectories which are best for themselves, their departments/subunits, and the institutions that they serve. By observing trends, leaders can better understand which policies, personnel, and structures can facilitate a positive outcome.

- *Collaborate.* Leaders who understand theory can predict outcomes, understand their implications, and commit to establishing collaborations across institutional constituents that will allow leaders to garnish resources, political support, and buy-in. Upon building collaboration, leaders gain the institutional and stakeholder confidence needed to enact policies, practices, and structures that can help resolve the issue(s).
- *Control.* Leaders who are able to engage in the aforementioned steps are better able to control, manage, and direct outcomes. This ability: (a) empowers leaders with a sense of reassurance in their leadership ability; (b) situates leaders as credible authorities in the leadership structure; and (c) provides them with the ability to influence other players, policies, and structures internal and external to the institution. The ability to control outcomes is an advantage for leaders personally as well as the institutions that they serve.
- *Assess.* Issues are dynamic in nature; thus, the usage of theories should be dynamic as well. Leaders must become reflective practitioners, constantly assessing whether: (a) the dynamics of an issue are being addressed by the theory employed; (b) theory needs to be refined to address certain situations; and (c) existing theories are relevant in addressing the intricacies of issue(s). Leaders should understand that new theories are constantly developed which better address the current and emerging realities of a given situation.

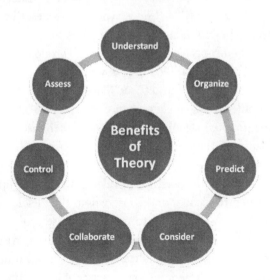

Figure 1 Benefits of Theory

Leadership is a broad concept; as such, it has been defined in a number of ways which emphasize different aspects of its nature. For example, take these popular definitions of leadership:

Northouse (2007) defines leadership as, "a process whereby an individual influences a group of individuals to achieve a common goal" (p. 3).

Hogg & van Knippenberg (2003) defines leadership as "a relationship in which some people are able to influence others to embrace, as their own, new values, attitudes and goals, and to exert effort on behalf of, and in pursuit of, those values, attitudes and goals" (p. 1).

House & Associates (1999) notes that the core concept, which ties together most definitions of leadership, is influencing "others to help accomplish group or organizational objectives" (p. 12).

Gini (1998) defines leadership as "a power-and value-laden relationship between leaders and followers/constituents who intend real change(s) that reflect their mutual purpose(s) and goal(s)" (p. 365).

Hughes, Ginnett, and Curphy (1995) define leadership as "a social influence process shared among all members of a group" (p. 43).

Bennis (1959) defines leadership as "the process by which an agent induces a subordinate to behave in a desired manner" (p. 6).

While the aforementioned definitions vary, there are some common themes that are integral to each perspective on leadership. For instance, each definition involves four primary parts: (1) A *leader*, who is also described as an "agent" (Bennis, 1959), who (2) *exerts influence*, which can be social, political, and hierarchal in nature, on (3) *other people*, also described as "groups" (Northouse, 2007), "others" (House & Associates, 1999; Hogg & van Knippenberg 2003), "followers or constituents" (see Hughes Ginnett, & Curphy, 1995), and "subordinates" (Bennis, 1959) in order to (4) *produce change* in "values," "attitudes" (see Hogg & van Knippenberg, 2003), "goals" (Gini, 1998; Northouse, 2007), "purposes" (Gini, 1998), "objectives" (House & Associates, 1999), and "behaviors" (Bennis, 1959). We have two critiques to the core concepts identified among these definitions of leadership. First, leadership insinuates a relationship of inspiration, which occurs between the leader and those whom they lead. Leaders use their language, actions, and overall being to motivate those around them. Second, effective leadership inspires those within the organization to go beyond contractual or obligatory goals, and actualize excellence in attaining goals not yet realized. As such, bearing these four components of leadership in mind as well our critique, we define leadership as "leaders influencing and inspiring others beyond desired outcomes."

Leadership is juxtaposed with the concept of administration. Often used as synonyms, these terms are vastly different. Administration speaks to a top-down (or autocratic) notion of leadership in which one individual dictates and controls the operations of an organization or group. What drives administrators is attention to rules, regulations, processes, policies, law, bylaws, strategic plans, and other established institutional protocol. Often the influence placed on these documents supersedes aspects of collegiality, shared responsibility, and valuing the input of others (Razik & Swanson, 1995). Administrators are task oriented, focusing on the day-to-day operations of the institution; they are keen to ensure that constituents within the institution are playing out their roles and responsibilities according to their contractual obligations. With this in mind, we prefer Olsen's (2005) definition of administration; he states that: "Administration is based on the rule of law, due process, codes of appropriate behavior and a system of rationally debatable reasons" (Olsen, 2005, p. 5). Table 1 illustrates the different connotations and views of leadership and administration.

Each concept (i.e., leadership, administration) within itself has its strengths; however, when used in tandem, organizational effectiveness is enhanced. The concepts of leadership and administration when taken together provide community college leaders with a holistic approach to leading their institutions. This is accomplished by leaders supporting the foundational institutional structures while allowing the organization to be fluid. For example, when a leader's decision-making process is anchored on strictly adhering to administrative protocol, the organization suffers. Change is denied since leaders are more influenced by rules and regulations than the need to change policies, structures, and personnel in their organization to improve its effectiveness. Likewise, leaders keen on change may not provide a foundational structure of support for their institution. This

Table 1 Differences between Leadership and Administration

Leadership versus Administration	
Collaborative	Controlling
Conceptual/Visionary	Task oriented
Inspiring others	Directing others
Transforming	Maintaining the status quo
Shares Gratification	Self-gratification
Responsible for faults	Displaces fault

can lead to misguided practices, ambiguity, lack of a unified vision, and overall institutional instability. A critical balance of both leadership and administration is needed by leaders in order for their organizations to be effective.

A wide range of leadership styles exist (e.g., instructional, participatory, servant leadership, distributive). Consider the following three general leadership styles: authoritarian, transactional, and transformational leadership.

Authoritarian. Authoritarian leadership emphasizes control. It is a top-down hierarchical approach to leading where a clear reliance on the "chain of command" is followed. Control drives this leadership style in that authoritarian leaders use rules and regulations as an "objective" means to maintain power and influence over others as well as to drive others toward goal attainment. For example, an authoritarian leader in a community college is one who implements an organizational mission; changes a university logo; and/or builds a recreational center without seeking consensus, buy in, or input from faculty, staff, students, and the local community (Guthrie & Schuermann, 2010).

There are benefits and drawbacks to this leadership approach. Benefits include: (a) the ability to drive an institution towards a stated goal in a time of crisis (e.g., a military leader brought into a community college institution as president in order to ensure accreditation status is maintained, a business leader hired as a vice president of finance for the purpose of reversing losses, creating efficient practices, and fundraising); (b) allegiance to the organization. They seek excellence through the implementation of accountability measures which address the "bottom-line." Drawbacks of this leadership style include: (a) leaders isolating constituents through an overemphasis on control; (b) the creation of an environment that lacks collegiality and fails to value the contributions of all stakeholders; and (c) lowered morale among faculty, staff, and administration due to feelings of being isolated and undervalued.

Transactional. Transactional leadership refers to an exchange between the leader and those whom they lead. In this exchange, followers are rewarded for their commitment and goal attainment. The leader recognizes needs of the followers (e.g., financial) and attempts to meet their interests. In exchange, followers work towards organizational objectives. The follower–leadership relationship is based upon a contingent award system; money for performance. When leaders and followers are satisfied with the exchange, a sense of mutual cooperation and trust is established and sustained. This cooperation and trust ultimately benefits the organization. In this approach to leadership, the award (e.g., monetary, promotions, power) is the motivating factor in behavior, actions, and dedication of the followers to the organization (Nguni, Sleegers, & Denessen, 2006).

Several benefits to this leadership approach are apparent; (a) interests of the followers are met by the leader; (b) organizational goals, objectives, and interests are met; and (c) followers and leaders are content with the dyad relationship. Drawbacks to this manner of leadership include: (a) followers will often maintain the status quo, never going beyond the contractual obligations required of them; (b) leaders' expectations are unlikely to be exceeded; and (c) the value and importance of the award can only serve to motivate workers for a short period of time.

Transformational. Transformational leadership is the act of empowering individuals to fulfill their contractual obligations, meet the needs of the organization, and go beyond the "call of duty" for the betterment of the institution. Leaders inspire, motivate, and appeal to followers through an array of skills and behaviors which communicate: (a) their value to the institution; (b) the potential of their contribution; and (c) high expectations in accordance with a supportive environment. Transformational leaders serve as role models to others, emulating the characteristics, behaviors, and actions which they seek from all members of their organization. This set of behaviors and actions serves to guide constituents towards individual and institutional success, beyond what is expected of them. Transformational leadership is comprised of three primary elements: (1) a team-approach; (2) an emphasis on follower empowerment; and (3) a comprehension of change within oneself and in the organization. There are three primary aspects of a transformational leader. First, transformational leaders are motivational. They inspire those around them to achieve the highest standards possible. Second, transformational leaders intellectually challenge themselves and others in envisioning an organization that surpasses its current form. Third, these leaders provide individualized attention and support to each member of the institution (Bass & Avolio, 1994; Howley & Howley, 2007; Nguni, Sleegers, & Denessen, 2006).

The benefits of transformational leadership are: (a) these leaders improve the bottom-line; this occurs as employees regularly surpass expectations; (b) morale is increased through leaders' efforts to fully integrate followers into the core functions of the institution; and (c) institutional commitment is advanced as contributions of followers are authentically valued and considered integral to driving the decision-making process. The challenges of transformational leadership are: (a) leaders can be easily burned out considering the enormous amount of personal attention, energy, and investment they need to focus on inspiring, motivating, and meeting the personal needs of institutional affiliates; (b) high expectations without the proper support structure in place can adversely impact institutional effectiveness; and (c) followers of transformational leaders can become exhausted from high expectations, going beyond the call of duty, and extensive personal investment. This tends to be the case when transformational leaders do not sustain a high level of consistency, motivation, support, and empowerment of their followers.

Leadership Theories

The study of leadership and leadership theory provides conceptual bases for describing various leadership behavior, orientations, and a framework for evaluating leadership styles and approaches. While leadership theories provide a template on leadership approaches based on research, leadership styles are patterns of behaviors and actions used by leaders to influence individuals and the overall direction of the institution. There are hundreds of definitions that encompass leadership and many classifications of theories, styles, and approaches. Our discussion focuses on a select few (e.g., trait theory, behavioral theory, contingency theory) with coverage focusing on the broad fundamental concepts underpinning each of these theories and approaches. In doing so, we realize that we are not doing justice to the intricacies that describe and distinguish theoretical frames and styles. What follows are classifications of prominent theories and approaches used to describe leadership behavior. These are:

Trait theory. This classification of theory is focused on an individual's physical, social, and personal characteristics. The presupposition driving this theory was based on an either/or approach to leadership. That is, some individuals were genetically predisposed to having the leadership abilities and attributes to lead. Biological traits, such as height, race/ethnicity, gender, and perceived intelligence were attributes used to determine leaders' potential, ability, and effectiveness. More importantly it served to identify and select those viewed as prime candidates to assume leadership roles. This theory, in its focus on biological traits, has been used to exclude and discriminate against individuals that did not possess the biological traits defined by this theory. Although this theory has been refuted in general, the usage of this theory can be found in myriad instances. For example, based on a cursory review of popular leadership books, which define leadership effectiveness, one quickly finds a step-by-step laundry list of leadership abilities and attributes consistent with the trait theory. The theory is also popular considering its constructs are clear and concise, versus other leadership theories, which are sometimes convoluted and difficult to comprehend. The trait theory's sole focus on an individual's genetic makeup makes no allowance for contextual factors (e.g., access to resources, cultural, social, economic capital, institutional equity issues). The current literature on the trait theory does not dismiss the importance of contextual factors, but makes the claim that both contextual factors, as well as attributes need to be considered in defining effective leadership (Guthrie & Schuermann, 2010).

Behavioral Theory. Behavioral theory focuses on actions and interactions between leaders and their constituents. It also addresses the effects these interactions have on the productivity, attitudes, confidence, and satisfaction of followers (White & Lippitt, 1990). Leaders' styles of leadership vary greatly, ranging from overly controlling and dominating to laissez-faire; this is informed by a variety of factors: (a) prior experience of leaders with authority (e.g., parents, law enforcement, school officials); (b) their overall leadership style (e.g., autocratic, democratic); (c) psychosocial disposition; (d) formal/informal leadership training; (e) the generation to which they belong; (f) belief system (e.g., religious/spiritual, political affiliation); and (g) personal and career aspirations. There are two general areas of behavioral theory. The first is centered on the behavior of the leaders in relationship to goal attainment. For example, increasing graduation rates by five percent may be an institutional goal. In utilizing a behavioral approach, the leader will allocate resources, expertise, and policies focused on realizing that goal. In examining efforts of the leaders toward this goal, those using a behavioral paradigm will focus on the actions and behaviors that the leader undertook toward achieving the desired outcome. The second aspect of behavioral theory focuses on the importance of building, sustaining, and enhancing interpersonal relationships that lead to enhanced efforts in reaching a common goal. For example, in reaching the five percent graduation rate increase, the focus is to enhance interpersonal relationships among colleagues as a means to facilitate goal attainment. Although leaders have a tendency to fall within one of these two dimensions, elements of both are needed in order to lead effectively (Guthrie & Schuermann, 2010). That is, in reaching a particular goal, leaders ought to pay attention to the task at hand, while facilitating relationship building.

Contingency-Situation Theory. Leadership is contingent upon contextual factors. Thus, contingency-situation theory focuses on the role of multiple factors in contributing to the manner in which leaders should approach a given situation in order to achieve a desired outcome. In essence, this is a "matching-approach" to leadership, in that the skills, abilities, and disposition of the leaders need to be aligned to the situational context. Unlike trait and behavioral theory, contingency theory does not rely upon one lens; rather, it is informed by a multiplicity of contextual factors (e.g., organizational makeup, skills of individuals within the institution, political dynamics within the institution, values held by members of the institution, leadership styles) (House, 1971; Blake & Mouton, 1978). Smith & Peterson (1988) identified "three situational factors that influence leader effectiveness: (a) the quality of leader–subordinate relations, (b) the leader's position power, and (c) the degree of task structure" (p. 52). In other words, in addition to behavior relations, contingency theory also can focus on issues of credibility and the intricacies of the tasks needed to address an issue. Thus, by recognizing multiple factors, contingency theory is arguably a more robust method of addressing, viewing, and understanding leadership.

Leadership Perspectives on Organizational Processes

There are three main approaches that scholars have employed to describe leadership perspectives on organizational processes. These approaches are: (a) the bureaucratic approach; (b) the democratic approach; and (c) the political approach. An explication of these approaches follows:

Bureaucratic Approach. Administrators who use the bureaucratic approach view leadership through the lens of existing rules, policies, regulations, and protocols. When guiding documents do not exist or are unclear, administrators assume the responsibility of making an autocratic determination of what should be done and create new policies/procedures to address the issue in the future. The bureaucratic approach is very mechanistic in nature, an assembly-line approach to leading institutions. As noted by Bass (1985), "the guiding principle here is that human beings can be programmed in the same ways as machines through a careful analysis and planning of job design and organizational structure" (p. 2).

Administrators employing the bureaucratic approach control the behavior and actions of their followers through five primary mechanisms: (1) They place high importance on the hierarchical structure, undertaking micromanagement of employees through close supervision, monitoring, and authoritative directives. (2) They utilize and rely on the hierarchical structure for communication, where a top-down approach is employed. Comments, concerns, and issues from lower levels of the hierarchy must properly adhere to the chain of command. (3) They approach situations through the usage of established policies, protocols, strategic plans, duty rosters, bylaws, and other guiding documents; standards of expectations are set. These standards serve as the guiding force in directing individuals towards a certain organizational structure. In essence, these processes serve to establish the organizations' culture and climate. (4) Explicit protocol is established, emphasized, and reinforced. This protocol serves to control and coordinate behavior. (5) As the organization grows and becomes more complex, the creation of new administrative positions increases. Thus, in order to control and gain "a hold" of new issues and unexpected challenges, administrators respond by adding to the administrative bureaucracy (Jackall, 1988; Weber, 1947).

The benefits of the bureaucratic model include: (a) Clear understanding of roles, responsibilities, and expectations of all institutional affiliates makes ambiguity nonexistent, where explicit and clear rules and regulations guide organizational behavior. (b) Accountability is paramount to personal, departmental, and organizational success. Thus, an institutional structure of efficiency is maintained. (c) Coordination of efforts and resources is maximized. This is of particular importance in a large, complex, and dynamic institution (such as the community college). There are drawbacks of overrelying upon a bureaucratic model, which include: (a) followers' feel that their input, recommendations, expertise, thoughts, and perceptions are not valued or sought out; (b) morale is compromised due to the impersonal relationships between employee and employer; and (c) disinterest from employees is manifested due to the mechanistic nature of duties and responsibilities.

Democratic Approach. Democratic leaders assume a human relations approach to leading. In this approach, stakeholders, followers, and concerned parties are involved in mutually addressing and resolving issues and challenges that may arise. In essence, this approach is characterized by a "shared-authority model." For example, if a vice president/dean of institutional research at a community college wanted to improve assessment and evaluation of faculty, they would involve multiple stakeholders in the process, as opposed to articulating these efforts on their own. They would bring officials and stakeholders representing faculty from various departments, staff who will assist in collecting the data, administrative officials who work with accreditation agencies, among others to address the issue in a collaborative manner. Involving institutional members in the decision-making process encourages a team approach that is given the responsibility of making final decisions (Cunningham & Cordeiro, 2006; Tannenbaum & Schmidt, 1958). To be clear, democratic leadership varies from that of the bureaucratic model due to the rationale for input. In a bureaucratic organization, committees, task forces, and planning councils are established to advise a senior-level administrative official. In the democratic approach, they are created to seek valued input from stakeholders and to arrive at a mutually agreeable decision with senior-level administrators.

There are three general benefits of the democratic approach: (1) leaders' respect, trust, and equitable treatment of followers are reciprocal and permeate the social fabric of the organization; (2) as the organization grows and becomes more complex, confidence is placed in the followers' decision-making abilities; thus, their contributions increase organizational effectiveness; (3) employee morale increases as their input, expertise, and experience is valued through leaders' incorporation of followers as "members of the team." Drawbacks to democratic leadership include: (a) a lengthy and cumbersome decision-making process since input from various stakeholders is valued; (b) organizational ambiguity when leadership is distributed without clear guidelines and procedures; and (c) followers who become disenchanted without a strict set of guidelines, protocol, and rigid structure.

Political Approach. The political approach does not adhere to specific decision-making structures, rather it utilizes any structure (e.g., bureaucratic, democratic) to gain influence over others. The political approach is not necessarily concerned with how actions will impact the entire organization, but rather, how actions will: (a) play out in the subunit in which the leader resides; (b) affect key issues, operations, and structures of importance to the leader; and (c) impact the leader personally. Political leaders maneuver resources, people, and policies to advance their goals. They capitalize and maximize on unclear procedures, ambiguity, and uncertainty; in doing so, they use rules, regulations, policy, and law as "tools" to achieve their desired ends. For these leaders "negotiation, coalition formation, and political gains are the keys to understanding life in such structures" (Hoy & Miskel, 2005, p. 112). During times of turmoil and crisis, political leaders use their power to configure the organization in a manner that influences their power. This can lead to the development of informal organizations within organizations. Political leaders are typified as being highly critical thinkers, viewing issues, phenomenon, and challenges multiple steps in advance. As such, they are astute at predicting outcomes, behaviors, and actions of organizations, departments, and those who reside within. In general, they employ an advanced understanding of factors which contribute to personal and organizational motivations. Political leaders rely upon formal and informal mechanisms of power to accomplish established goals. Often, political leaders are idealistic, driven by the principles, values, and morels to which they adhere.

There are several benefits to political leadership: (a) leaders can better advocate for the allocation of resources that maintain and enhance the vitality of their respective subunits and the institution; (b) political leaders usually emerge around ideological standpoints; thus, these standpoints compete and can contribute to positive organizational change; and (c) implementation of a leader's decision is enhanced through networks of support, which can expedite their initiation (Bass, 1985; Hoy & Miskel, 2005). Drawbacks to political leadership include: (a) fractured and divisive organizations that arise from the excessive power of political camps, often the case when political leadership advances beyond the professional level to personal vendettas, wars, or contempt; (b) compromised efficiency when interests collide and fail to align with the vision and mission of the organization, making progress become stagnant; and (c) a decline in morale and job satisfaction when those who refuse to participate in the political leadership or are not equipped to do so, become ostracized, alienated, or maligned. Community colleges are highly political organizations and such pressures can take a psychological toll on employees.

A Unified Approach

When used in isolation, the bureaucratic, democratic, and political approaches are rife with ineffectiveness due to their narrow focus in leading highly complex, dynamic, and evolving institutions. Although at times institutional success is seen, it is often temporary. As shown, each approach (e.g., bureaucratic, democratic, political) bears its own advantages and disadvantages. Often, disadvantages are a result of over-usage of one particular approach. Leadership effectiveness calls for multiple approaches. Thus, leaders should employ: (a) a bureaucratic approach, which focuses on rules, regulations, protocols, organizational hierarchy, and authoritarian rule; (b) a democratic approach that centers on an inclusive and shared decision-making model; and (c) a political approach utilizing political tactics to gain institutional influence, power, and control. Independent of each situation that arises, leaders should use all three approaches as a guide for indentifying, implementing, and assessing practices.

At the end of this chapter, we present the Nevarez-Wood Leadership Inventory. This inventory is designed as a tool (to be used in conjunction with other tools) to aid leaders in examining their usage of the three leadership approaches. Leaders are encouraged to use this inventory to assess their strengths and areas in need of improvement. Ideally, leaders should strive to reach a balanced score among the three leadership approaches. This will allow leaders to employ a balanced set of skills and knowledge to address issues and phenomena they face.

Case Study

In this chapter, we have described a multiplicity of leadership theories, styles, and approaches. We ended with a description of three primary leadership approaches (e.g., bureaucratic, democratic, and political), which should be integral to leaders' repertoire. Below, we present a case study requiring leaders to exhibit knowledge of the material provided in this chapter. Leaders engaging in this case study should be cognizant of their own leadership approaches (per the Nevarez-Wood Leadership Inventory). Leaders should use the three approaches as a framework for identifying a resolution to the case.

President Edwin Massey
Indian River State College
Fort Pierce, Florida

Leadership in Transition

Background

Campbell Community College (CCC) is a comprehensive community college that serves regional and statewide educational and workforce needs by offering certificate programs, associate, and selected baccalaureate degrees. CCC has five campuses and had a 2007–08 unduplicated headcount of 34,149 students, 12,098 full-time equivalent (FTE), served by 685 full-time and 1,181 part-time employees, including 180 full-time faculty. The multicultural student population is 55 percent female and 45 percent male. CCC is located in a progressive community experiencing diversification of the economy through the attraction of various biotechnology, alternative energy, digital media, marine, and agricultural research institutes. CCC is currently a highly ranked community college at the state and national level and is recognized for its state-of-the-art facilities and innovative programs of study. A review of the college's history reveals that this was not always the case.

Campbell Community College inaugurated its third president in 1990. The new president inherited several challenges including a highly critical state audit, enrollment problems, and fiscal issues. For the next 10 years this administration focused on corrective actions to strengthen the policies, procedures, reporting structure, and internal controls. To accomplish these enhancements the president practiced a no-nonsense, top-down, tough leadership approach that cleaned up most of the issues he inherited. CCC became a very fine institution as measured by conventional indicators in every category: transfer, graduation, placement, and licensure rates; perfect financial audits; top state test scores; outstanding accreditation results; and exceptional employee satisfaction survey results. By the year 2000, the college had clearly established a solid reputation for being a really *good* institution.

During the spring of 2000 the president assembled his Executive Council for a series of planning/visioning workshops. Cognizant of the growth the college was undergoing in programs, students, facilities, land acquisition, and new employees, the president voiced concern that growth could result in losing touch with the people and the most important resource...the culture. Even though the college had evolved into *a good institution* he felt strongly that change must take place before the college could ever reach its full potential. Upon closer review it became evident that this instinct was right on target as certain traditions and other customs were starting to disappear. The president realized that only through the culture would people be able to reach their full potential.

Questions to Ponder:

- What was that "instinct" the president felt?
- Is listening to that gut level feeling an important part of leadership and why?
- Explore intuition and the role it plays when leading an institution or a department

Statement of the Problem

Later that spring, the president invited an outside consultant to conduct focus groups with college employees to check the pulse of the institution. Over several days the college community participated in small informal groups discussing openly, and in confidence, any issue, concern, or perception they wanted to talk about. The consultant summarized this feedback in a report that identified several recurring themes and issues. It became apparent that some employees had strong feelings about certain issues that they were not comfortable talking about because they did not want to "rock the boat." These issues included: communication, chain of command, technical support, staffing levels, training for employees, career development, compensation, and recognition.

There were some unspoken rules exposed in the report that included: fear of making mistakes, unnecessary processes and procedures, and barriers that had been formed. Behavior was guided by terms such as: only good news travels up; it has got to be perfect; watch out for the "higher ups"; and "we don't do it that way here." While the intent behind the employee feedback was about improvement, the report captured underground issues that seemed to have been percolating for a long time. No one was more pained by this feedback than the President. He read and re-read the report and after several weeks came to realize some profound realities about the culture of this College. The feedback from the report revealed that even good institutions can harbor old habits resulting in a complacent culture that prevents the college from reaching its full potential.

- As a leader, what steps would you take to alter the leadership style of this college that would result in a culture that allowed the college to reach its full potential?

Other questions to consider:

- How do issues define a college culture?
- What did these particular issues say about the culture of this College at that time?
- What actions should a President employ when faced with issues such as these?
- Who should be involved in moving the institution to the next level?
- What is the role of the leadership in creating the college culture? What is the role of the employees?

Nevarez–Wood Leadership Inventory

The Nevarez–Wood Leadership Inventory (NWLI) is designed to aid leaders in assessing the leadership approaches, which guide their practice. The inventory offers an opportunity for leaders to assess their approaches in three primary areas: bureaucratic leadership, democratic leadership, and political leadership. Begin by reading each statement below. For current leaders, reflect upon your typical actions. Be sure to consider what your actions are, not what you would like them to be. For aspiring leaders, conceptualize how your actions in formal and informal settings (e.g., school, home, extracurricular activities) may translate into the leadership approach(es) most likely to be used. Mark the appropriate response.

Key: 1= Not True; 2= Seldom True; 3=Occasionally True; 4= Somewhat True; 5=Very True

1. I strongly adhere to the chain of command.	1	2	3	4	5
2. I involve as many others as possible in decision making.	1	2	3	4	5
3. I follow rules and regulations to the "T."	1	2	3	4	5
4. I consider myself a maverick.	1	2	3	4	5
5. I believe collaboration achieves better results.	1	2	3	4	5
6. I believe decisions should always be made in concert with others.	1	2	3	4	5
7. I see rules as "tools" to achieve my goals.	1	2	3	4	5
8. I have set stringent procedures and protocols for my staff.	1	2	3	4	5
9. I enjoy working with others.	1	2	3	4	5
10. Leadership is like a game of chess.	1	2	3	4	5
11. I am astute at predicting the actions and behaviors of others.	1	2	3	4	5
12. I use hierarchy as a mechanism of control.	1	2	3	4	5
13. I use a team approach in making decisions.	1	2	3	4	5
14. I closely direct, monitor, and supervise my staff.	1	2	3	4	5
15. I think about my actions multiple steps in advance.	1	2	3	4	5
16. I believe building relationships is an important aspect of leadership.	1	2	3	4	5
17. I use my leadership position to build potential in others.	1	2	3	4	5
18. I believe explicit protocols must always be in place.	1	2	3	4	5
19. I use the interests of others to my advantage.	1	2	3	4	5
20. I usually make decisions on my own.	1	2	3	4	5
21. I have an unofficial coalition/team within my organization.	1	2	3	4	5

Scoring

To score your responses, do the following: (1) add up your responses for questions 1, 3, 8, 12, 14, 18, 20. This is your total bureaucratic leadership score; (2) sum your responses for questions 4, 7, 10, 11, 15, 19, 21. This your political leadership score; (3) add up your responses for questions 2, 5, 6, 9, 13, 16, 17. This is your democratic leadership score.

Total scores: Bureaucratic Leadership____Political Leadership____ Democratic Leadership____

Interpreting Your Score

This assessment tool is one tool among many that can help guide you in determining the leadership approach(es) you use most often. Compare your score on each item (bureaucratic leadership, political leadership, democratic leadership). Ideally, leaders should have scores that are relatively even across all three approaches. Continue to emphasize your strengths as indicated by your score. More importantly, you should consider improving your usage of approaches in your lowest score area(s). Refer back to Chapter 3 on *Leadership and Leadership Theory* to better understand the intricacies of each leadership approach. To enhance your training in specific leadership approaches, see Chapter 11 on *Leadership Development in the Community College*. Leadership development must be constant given the rapidly changing nature of the profession. If you scored low in one or more leadership approach(es), you should consider the following action items:

Bureaucratic Leadership

- ❖ Be more task-oriented.
- ❖ Be more explicit in your expectations of others.
- ❖ Be more attentive to rules, regulations, policies, and protocol.
- ❖ Be more mindful of organizational hierarchy.
- ❖ Hold organizational affiliates accountable.

Political Leadership

- ❖ Contemplate the implications of your actions in the decision-making process.

❖ Anticipate behaviors, actions, and strategies used by others.

❖ Use policies, regulations, and protocol to advance your personal and organizational agenda.

❖ Form or affiliate yourself with formal/informal coalitions and networks.

❖ Use crises as an opportunity to leverage your personal and organizational goals.

Democratic Leadership

❖ Be more mindful to include others in the decision-making process.

❖ See collaboration as an advantage, rather than a disadvantage.

❖ Inspire organizational affiliates.

❖ Validate the contributions of others.

❖ Allow a space and time for varied ideas, inputs, and approaches.

References

Bass, B. M. (1985). *Leadership and performance beyond expectation.* New York: Free Press.

Bass, B. M., & Avolio, B. J. (1994). *Improving organizational effectiveness through transformational leadership.* Thousand Oaks, CA: Sage.

Bennis, W. G. (1959). Leadership theory and administrative behavior: The problem of authority. *Administrative Science Quarterly, 4,* 259–260.

Blake, R. R., & Mouton, J. S. (1978). *The new managerial grid.* Houston, TX: Gulf.

Cunningham, W. G., & Cordeiro, P. A. (2006). *Educational leadership: A problem-based approach* (3rd ed.). Columbus, OH: Pearson.

Gini, A. (1998). Moral leadership and business ethics. In In G. R. Hickman (Ed.)., *Leading organizations: Perspectives for a new era* (pp. 360–371). Thousand Oaks, CA: Sage Publications.

Guthrie, J. W., & Schuermann, P. J. (2010). *Successful school leadership: Planning, politics, performance, and power.* Boston, MA: Allyn & Bacon.

Hogg, M. A., & van Knippenberg, D. (2003). Social identity and leadership processes in groups. In M. P. Zanna (Ed.). *Advances in experimental social psychology* (pp. 1–52). San Diego, CA: Academic Press.

House, R. J. (1971). Path goal theory of leader effectiveness. *Administrative Science Quarterly, 16*(3), 321–339.

House, R. J. & Associates (1999). Cultural influences on leadership and organizations. *Advances in Global Leadership, 1,* 171–233.

Howley, A., & Howley, C. (2007). *Thinking about schools: New theories and innovative practice.* Mahwah, NJ: Lawrence Erlbaum Associates, Inc.

Hoy, W. K., & Miskel, C. G. (2005). *Educational leadership and reform.* Greenwich, CT: Informational Age.

Hughes, R. L., Ginnett, R. C., & Curphy, G. R. (1995). *What Is leadership?* In J. T. Wren (ed.). *The leader's companion: Insights on leadership through the ages* (pp. 39–44). New York: Simon and Schuster.

Jackall, R. (1988). *Moral mazes: The world of corporate managers.* New York: Oxford University Press.

Nguni, S., Sleegers, P., & Denessen. E. (2006). Transformational and transactional leadership effects on teachers' job satisfaction, organizational commitment, and organizational citizenship behavior in primary schools: The Tanzanian case. *School effectiveness and school improvement: An international journal of research, policy and practice,* 17(2), 145–177.

Northouse, P. G. (2007). *Leadership: Theory and practice.* Thousand Oaks, CA: Sage Publications.

Olsen, J. P. (2005). Maybe it is time to rediscover bureaucracy? *Journal of Public Administration Research and Theory* 16 (1): 1–24. Retrieved September 4, 2009, from: http://www.arena.uio.no/publications/working-papers2005/papers/wp05_10.pdf

Razik, T & Swanson, A. (1995). *Fundamental concepts of educational leadership and management.* Englewood Cliffs, NJ: Simon and Schuster.

Smith, P. B., & Peterson, M. F. (1988). *Leadership, organizations, and culture: An event management model.* London, UK: Sage Publications.

Tannenbaum, R., & Schmidt, W. H. (1958). How to choose a leadership pattern. *Harvard Business Review,* 36(2), 95–101.

Weber, M. (1947). *The theory of social and economic organizations.* Translated by T. Parsons. New York: The Free Press.

White, R., & Lippitt, R. (1990). Leader behavior and member reaction in three "social climates." In J. Hall (Ed.), *Models for management: The structure of competence* (2nd ed.). (pp. 146–172). The Woodlands, TX: Woodstead Press.

CHAPTER FOUR

ACHIEVEMENT GAP AND
THE ROLE OF COMMUNITY COLLEGES

This chapter examines the community college achievement gap. In doing so, we present: (a) the P-12 influence on the community college achievement gap; (b) the personal and social benefits of postsecondary education; (c) persistence research and models; (d) the community college achievement gap model, which identifies factors directly influencing two-year-college achievement disparities; (e) minority male initiatives; and (f) the guiding steps for community college leaders to address the achievement gap through the presentation of the Achievement Gap Action Model.

When reading this chapter, consider the following questions:

- What P-12 factors directly influence the community college achievement gap?
- What are the personal and social benefits of attaining a postsecondary education?
- How might your work in addressing the achievement gap be informed by persistence research?
- How do the factors described in the community college achievement gap model relate to and inform your own institutional context?
- What steps do you believe institutions should take in addressing the achievement gap? How might these actions be informed by the Achievement Gap Action Model described in this chapter?

The achievement gap permeates every sector of the educational system. Community colleges are not immune to this phenomenon. For the purposes of this chapter, we define the *community college achievement gap*—as pervasive success disparities among students on academic performance indicators (i.e., rates for enrollment, remediation, retention/persistence, graduation, and transfer).

K-12 Influence on the Community College Achievement Gap

Generally, success disparities begin in the early grades (K-6) and persist, usually widening, throughout the academic pipeline (e.g., elementary, secondary, post-secondary) as indicated by fewer and fewer individuals attaining degree-holder status. For example, assessment test scores in Math and English among African American, Native American, and Hispanic students in the 8th and 12th grade reveal significant disparities among the performance of these students in comparison to White and Asian/Pacific Islander students.[1] Low academic performance in reading and math (see Table 1) hinders student academic success and has a direct effect on graduation rates and higher education goals (Grigg, Donahue, & Dion, 2007; Lee, Grigg, & Dion, 2007a, 2007b). As illustrated in Table 1, low achievement in math and reading has implications for graduation rates. It is particularly revealing for minority students. For example, only 6 percent of African Americans and Native Americans and 8 percent of Hispanics are at or above proficient in 12th-grade mathematics. This has significant implications for high-remediation needs for students entering the community college.

Nationally, graduation rates for four-year public high school students vary by race/ethnicity (KewalRamani et al., 2007; Levin et al., 2007). In 2005–06, the four-year graduation rates for high school students were as follows: African

Table 1 National Assessment of Educational Progress Scores in 2005, by Race/Ethnicity

Percent at or above proficient	Asian/Pacific Islander	White	American Indian/ Alaskan Native	Hispanic	Black
8th Grade reading	40%	39%	17%	15%	12%
12th Grade reading	36%	43%	*	20%	16%
8th Grade math	47%	39%	14%	13%	9%
12th Grade math	36%	29%	6%	8%	6%

Source: U.S. Department of Education, National Assessment of Education Progress. * In cases where data is missing on a specific subgroup, the source of the data has indicated that the populations examined were too small for data to be reported.

---

[1] Data regarding the academic achievement of Asian Americans hides the realities of educational achievement for all Asian subgroups. According to Ngo and Lee (2007) "Although the racialization of Asian Americans lumps all Asian groups in the United States into a singular, high achieving category, an examination of disaggregated data by ethnic groups reveals striking differences" especially among many Southeast Asians groups that score comparable to other students of color (p. 419).

Americans 59.1 percent; Hispanics 61.4 percent; Native Americans 61.8 percent; Asian Americans 89.9 percent; and Whites 80.69 percent (Stillwell & Hoffman, 2009). Disparities are further seen when data is disaggregated by gender. For example, in 2001 male graduation rates by race/ethnicity were as follows: 70.8 percent for Whites; 72.6 percent for Asian Americans; 42.8 percent for African Americans, 48 percent for Hispanics; and 47 percent for Native Americans (Orfield et al., 2004).

High school graduation rates inevitably affect collegiate enrollment rates. For example, 80.6 percent of white students graduated from high school in 2005–06; of these 68.5 percent enrolled in a two- or four-year college the following fall. While 59.1 and 61.4 percent of African American and Hispanics graduated from high school in 2005–06, of which 55.5 and 57.9 percent, respectively, enrolled in colleges the following fall (Stillwell & Hoffman, 2009) (see Figure 1).

Though 73.2 percent of students graduate from high school (Stillwell & Hoffman, 2009), similar success rates are not seen at the collegiate level. As students progress through the pipeline, fewer degree holders are evident at each successive level (e.g., associate's, bachelor's, master's, doctoral) (see Figure 2). For example, in 2005 Hispanics represented 13.7 percent of all high school graduates, 11.3 percent of all associate's degree holders, 7.2 percent of all bachelor's degree recipients, 5.5 percent of all students possessing a master's degree, and 3.4 percent of all those with doctoral degrees. Similar declines in representation at successive levels of education are seen for Blacks and Native Americans. In contrast,

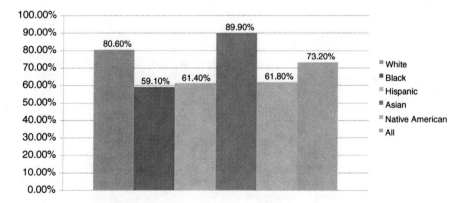

Figure 1 High School Student Graduation Rates, 2005–06
Source: Stillwell, R. & Hoffman, L. (2009). *Public school graduates and dropouts from the common core of data: School year 2005–06; A first look.* Washington, DC: National Center for Education Statistics. Note: Calculated from freshman entrance to high school completion in a normal time frame.

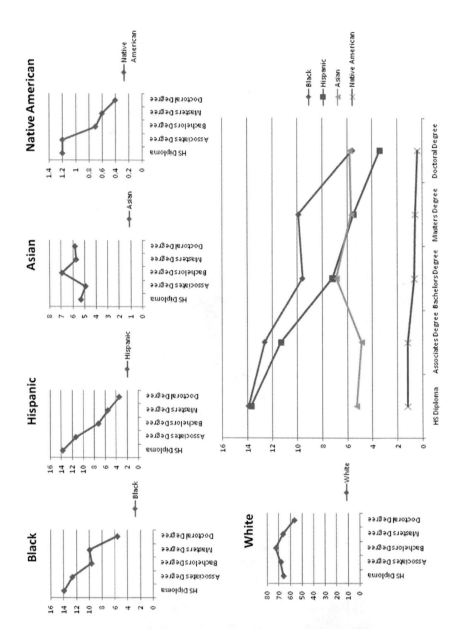

Figure 2 Percentage representation of racial/ethnic groups at successive degree levels, 2005–06
Source: U.S. Census Bureau, (2008). Note: Figures for whites are not presented in the larger chart for visual clarity of trend lines. It is clear that their representation far exceeds that of other groups.

the percentage of Asian Americans at successive levels of education illustrates an upward trend. This is particularly noticeable from high school to bachelor's degree recipients (U.S. Census Bureau, 2008).

This phenomenon can also be conceptualized and understood as a pyramid (see Figure 3). This pyramid illustrates successive stages in the academic pipeline. It highlights major points of attrition, which occur during transitional periods from one educational level to the next (e.g., middle school to high school and high school to college).

For those who continue through paths of higher degree attainment, added challenges intensify and impact their success (e.g., increased academic expectation levels, delayed gratification for earnings, adaptation to the college environment). This results in significant decreases in the percentage of individuals acquiring higher level degrees. For example, the U.S. Census Bureau (2008) reports the percentage of the U.S. population by highest degree earned, see Table 2. They note that approximately 65.9 percent of the U.S. population possesses a high school diploma, 30.9 percent for whom this is their highest degree. Thirty five percent hold at least a two- or four-year degree (8.2 percent and 17.8 percent for whom the associate or bachelor's degrees were the highest degree earned). Of these, approximately 9 percent hold at least a master's or professional degree (6.6 percent and 1.3 percent for whom the master's or professional degrees were the highest earned). Of the entire population, only 1.1 percent have earned doctoral degrees (see Figure 3).

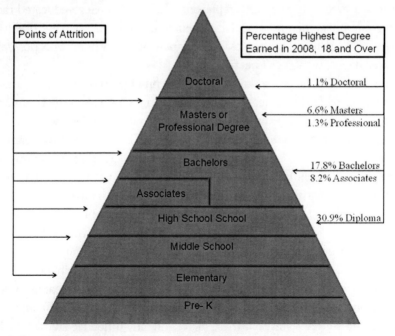

Figure 3 Points of Attrition
Source: U.S. Census Bureau (2008). Current Population Survey, Annual Social and Economic Supplement.

Table 2 Educational Attainment of the Population 18 Years and Over, by Age, Sex, Race, and Hispanic origin, 2008

	Less than high school	Some high school	High school graduate	Some college	Associates	Bachelors	Masters	Professional	Doctoral
All	5.0 %	9.1%	30.9%	19.6%	8.2%	17.8%	6.6%	1.3%	1.1%
Black	4.0%	14.1%	34.9%	21.4%	8.0%	12.1%	4.0%	0.5%	0.5%
Hispanic	19.3%	17.5%	30.1%	15.4%	5.7%	8.3%	2.4%	0.6%	0.2%
White	5.1%	8.5%	31.0%	19.5%	8.3%	18.1%	6.7%	1.3%	1.0%
Asian	5.7%	5.4%	19.1%	14.3%	6.4%	30.2%	12.8%	2.6%	3.1%

Source: U.S. Census Bureau (2008). Current Population Survey, Annual Social and Economic Supplement. Note: Data on Native Americans not reported in detailed tables.

Stated more simply, if there were 100 total high school graduates, 35 would graduate from college with at least an associate's degree, nine would achieve master's or professional degrees, and one would receive a doctorate. Disparities in the highest degree conferred are evident when disaggregated by racial/ethnic group, as illustrated in Table 2. In sum, 35 percent of the nation's population possess at least an associate's degree, with 55.1 percent of Asian Americans possessing an associate's degree or higher. This represents the largest college-educated racial/ethnic group in the nation, especially when compared to 25 percent of African Americans; 17 percent Hispanics, and 35 percent of Whites who possess an associate's degree or higher (see Table 2).

The mission of the community college is to provide (a) open access to education; (b) comprehensive educational programming; (c) serve to the community; (d) teaching and learning; (e) lifelong learning; and (f) student success. These institutions are to be commended for their efforts in: (a) enrolling nearly half of all undergraduate students in higher education; (b) creating opportunities for underrepresented populations, which traditionally have not had access to higher education; (c) preparing a skilled workforce by enhancing employment skills and certifying students in various fields (e.g., health, technical fields); and (d) providing a platform for students to transfer into a four-year university. Community colleges, however, face significant challenges in ensuring that students experience success. These efforts are complicated by widespread inadequate academic preparation in the P-12 system, which is further exacerbated by lower levels of education of the parents, lower socioeconomic status (SES), and so on. National data substantiates that these factors directly influence student achievement. For example, Figure 4 illustrates that students who are socioeconomically

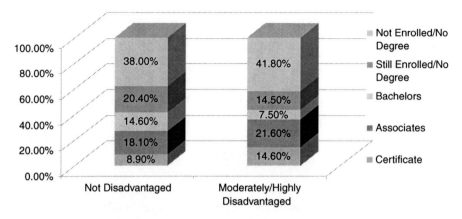

Figure 4 Highest Degree Earned of Students Starting in Two-Year Institutions, 2001
Determined by a socioeconomic diversity index that includes parental income as a percentage of the 1994
federal poverty level, parental education, and the proportion of the student body at the student's high school
that was eligible for free or reduced-price lunch. U.S. Department of Education (1996–2001). National
Center for Education Statistics, Beginning Postsecondary Students Longitudinal Study (BPS:96/01).

disadvantaged by federal standards (see footnote of Figure 4) are more likely to
receive certificates and associate's degrees rather than earn a bachelor's degree.
Data further indicates this group of students is more likely to stop pursuing their
degree(s) and discontinue their enrollment in college.

Personal and Public Benefits of Postsecondary Education

If it were not for the existence of community colleges, many students would
not have access to higher education. In serving these students, community colleges are challenged to: (a) remediate a large percentage of students; (b) retain
students by providing them with a supportive structure which facilitates their
success; and (c) prepare students for the workforce and/or advanced studies at
four-year universities. Although these challenges are daunting and difficult to
overcome, much can be gained in their efforts to educate a large percentage of
the nation's postsecondary students. Personal and public benefits also can be
accrued as a result of degree completion in higher education (see Table 3).

Faculty, parents, and community members often encourage young adults
to enroll and complete higher education by simply stating, "go to college, it is
important!" Often this statement is not substantiated through the identification of actual benefits accrued by college graduates. Table 3 notes many benefits

Table 3 Postsecondary Education's Personal and Public Benefit

Public benefits	Individual benefits
Reduces individual reliance upon social services	Provides increased career mobility
Increases local, state, and federal tax base	Promotes to become a critical consumer
Increases likelihood of civic engagement	Increases social and professional network
Reduces crime rate	Increases job skills (e.g., writing, presentation skills)
Increases philanthropy	Increases exposure to varying cultural contexts
Increases adaptability to workforce needs	Increases professional credibility
Promotes greater cultural awareness and affirmation	Enhances earning potential
Increases workforce satisfaction	Enhances job attainment and security

Note: Data presented is based upon a variety of sources (see Futrell, 1999; Levinson, 2007, Vernez & Mizell, 2001), as well as authors views and experiences.

gained when individuals achieve a higher education. The benefits are plentiful. For the individual, graduates are more likely to be employed and earn a higher salary than someone without a higher education. A college graduate is likely to have greater career mobility since a degree gives an individual the opportunity to be more marketable. The social benefits are numerous; individuals with a college degree tend to be involved in civic engagement opportunities at higher rates as compared to those without a higher education. This is mainly due to their work flexibility and exposure to these avenues. Society also benefits by individuals not depending on social services (e.g., welfare, unemployment benefits). This is due to their high employment rate and adequate earnings in comparison to nondegree holders (Futrell, 1999; Levinson, 2007, Vernez & Mizell, 2001).

Persistence Research

As a precursor to identifying factors that affect the achievement gap in the community college, it is important to understand the work of the scholars Spady (1970), Tinto (1975), and Bean and Metzner (1985), whose models and research are pervasive in the field of retention, attrition, and persistence studies. Their research can provide community college leaders with: (a) a framework for understanding factors that affect student success in postsecondary education; (b) a theoretical/research-based foundation for examining the complexities of these issues; (c) the ability to understand the premises that shape persistence models; (d) a conceptual framework for critiquing thought processes and assumptions behind persistence research; and (e) the knowledge necessary to determine whether these models are congruent to the realities of students or whether new models need to be created that are more attuned to the barriers facing student success.

The first model was developed by William Spady (1970), who constructed *An Empirical Model of the Undergraduate Dropout Process*. This model was informed by Durkheim's (1951) theory of suicide. Durkheim's theory suggested that individuals who did not integrate socially and intellectually into society were more likely to commit suicide. Spady refers to these social and intellectual needs as collective affiliations and moral consciousness, respectively. In equating suicide to dropping out of college, Spady uses Durkheim's work to create the concepts of normative congruence and friendship support, concluding that students who do not integrate intellectually and socially into institutions of higher education are less likely to succeed (Spady, 1970).

Spady influenced the work of Vincent Tinto, whose research on college student departure, retention, and persistence is by far the most commonly used framework for persistence research (Hausmann, Schofield, & Woods, 2007). Tinto (1975, 1987, 1988, 1993) states that student attrition should be viewed from a longitudinal perspective, as it is a process in which social and academic systems are interacting with the individual. These interactions result in the constant modification of academic objectives and dedication to the institution. Tinto's model addresses the academic and social integration of students into institutions of higher education, suggesting that greater integration is associated with greater commitment to the institution, which in turn, leads to a higher likelihood of completion.

Bean and Metzner's (1985) model of nontraditional student attrition was a response to the research of Spady (1970) and Tinto (1975) as well as other scholars who focused on the persistence factors of traditional college students. According to Bean and Metzner (1985), nontraditional students include those who commute to school, work part-time, are older than traditional college-aged students, and racial/ethnic students. As noted by Bean and Metzner (1985), the "chief difference between the attrition process of traditional and nontraditional students is that nontraditional students are more affected by the external environment than by the social integration variables affecting traditional student attrition" (p. 485). Bean and Metzner's (1985) model of nontraditional student attrition focuses on the role of four factors. The authors assert that background variables, environmental variables, academic variables, and social integration variables all play a role in the attrition of nontraditional students. Of these factors, environmental variables are the primary focus of the model, which is a major divergence from Tinto's model.

Community College Achievement Gap Model

Based on the work of the aforementioned scholars as well as more contemporary research by scholars of community college persistence (e.g., Cejda, and Hagedorn and Cepeda,), we developed the *Community College Achievement Gap Model* (presented later in this chapter). This model provides a comprehensive overview of the various factors which directly and indirectly affect the achievement gap at the community college. The model focuses on factors affecting the success of racial/ethnic and gender student groups. However, leaders should be cognizant of achievement gap disparities that are seen among many other groups (e.g., social status, class, region of origin, language ability). Each of these areas, as well as others, should be understood and addressed by leaders. Achievement gap indicators, as depicted in the center of Figure 7, illustrate the primary areas in which achievement disparities are seen among students. These indicators are impacted (negatively or positively) by background, personal, institutional, and social factors as well as macro-level support for the institution. The indicators include remediation, persistence, graduation, and transfer rates. These achievement indicators are best viewed in context to student success rates at the precollegiate level and the quality of the education received. What follows is an explication of community college achievement gap indicators.

Remediation is a major factor influencing academic success among community college students. A large percentage of community college entrants require some level of remediation. This is especially relevant in the "gatekeeper" subject areas of reading, writing, and mathematics. According to the U.S. Department of Education (2001), 40 percent of all students enrolling in public two-year colleges need remediation in multiple subject areas (e.g., reading, writing, mathematics). This rate is nearly double that of public four-year universities, which provide remediation to 21 percent of their students in these areas. A notable subject area in need of remediation at the public two-year college is mathematics, where a third of students, 32 percent, are in need of remediation (See Figure 5).

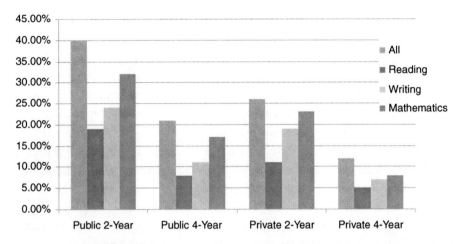

Figure 5   Remediation Rates for Reading, Writing, Mathematics by Institutional Type, 2000
Source: U.S. Department of Education (2001). National Center for Education Statistics, Postsecondary Education Quick Information System, "Survey on Remedial Education in Higher Education Institutions: Fall 1995," 1995; and "Survey on Remedial Education in Higher Education Institutions: Fall."

This data presents implications for community colleges in multiple areas since: (a) substantial resources must be allocated to provide high levels of remediation to students; (b) remediation needs directly influence student confidence in their ability to excel academically; (c) the time to complete a degree is often slowed down due to additional course requirements; (d) remediation requires curriculum and instruction to be congruent with students' learning needs; and (e) high remediation levels affect public perception and scrutiny of community colleges, leaving their institutional reputation and prestige in question. More positively, it places community colleges at the forefront of providing educational opportunities for students with a broad range of academic abilities.

Community colleges have been criticized for not retaining students at adequate levels. In particular, first year *persistence/retention* rates are of particular concern, considering a high percentage of community college enrollees drop out in the first year. Retention rates can be deceiving when taking into account longitudinal data, which indicates that few students graduate or transfer from community colleges in two years. The accuracy of persistence data is further complicated by the *"stop out" phenomenon,* where students enroll sporadically throughout their academic career. Accuracy also is impacted by federal requirements, which require students to declare their intent to receive a terminal degree (e.g., certificate, associate's degree) in order to receive financial aid, therefore, encouraging nondegree students (i.e., those seeking job skills, leisure activities, loan deferral, access to college services) to inaccurately declare degree status for the purpose of acquiring financial support.

Even when leaders account for the lack of preparation for college-level education and inaccuracies in how persistence rates are measured, the community college is struggling to meet its goal of facilitating the academic success of students. National data on student *graduation* rates from the community college illustrates inconsistencies across racial/ethnic and gender groups. Across all racial/ethnic groups, the lowest graduation rates are seen among Black, Hispanic, and Native American students at 16.5 percent, 18.7 percent, and 21.8 percent, respectively. When this data is disaggregated by gender, it is apparent that graduation rates for male students are lower than females. For example, African American males graduate at a 16.2 percent rate, Hispanic males at a 17.3 percent rate, and Native American males at a 19.2 percent rate while females graduate at a higher rate of 16.7 percent, 19.8 percent, and 23.8 percent respectively. White and Asian males graduate at higher rates, 25.2 percent and 23.4 percent, yet they lag behind their female peers who graduate at a rate of 27.8 percent and 27.1 percent respectively.

All male graduation rates are contrasted with that of female graduation rates, which are higher for every racial/ethnic group as illustrated in Figure 6 below.

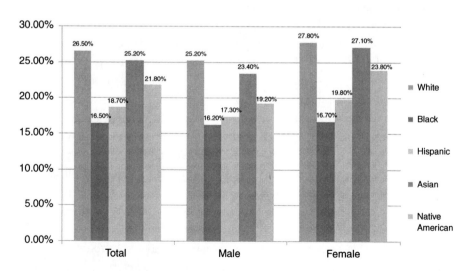

Figure 6 Public Two-Year-College Graduation Rates by Race/Ethnicity, 2002
Source: U.S. Department of Education (2000). National Center for Education Statistics, Integrated Postsecondary Education Data System (IPEDS), Graduation Rates component. Note: Graduation rate based upon completion in 150% normal time (3 years).

Graduation rates, however, are only one measure of student success. Attainment rates,[2] which examine the percentage of students who achieve any degree (e.g., certificate, associate's, bachelor's), after enrolling in the community college are also an important measure of student success. In all, 35.7 percent of students who enroll in a public two-year college will attain some degree[3] in a seven-year period. However, disparities in attainment rates are seen by racial/ethnic affiliation. Of Asian American students, 38.9 percent who enroll in a public two-year college will attain a degree. This percentage is slightly lower for White students at 38.1 percent. The lowest degree attainment rates are seen for Black and Hispanic students, at 26 percent and 29.5 percent (Hoachlander et al., 2003).

One of the primary reasons that students enroll in the community college is to *transfer* to four-year colleges and universities. With the exception of certain programs which facilitate students' transition into four-year institutions (e.g., Puente, MESA, EOPS), this core function of the community college is often not realized. Hoachlander et al., (2003) reporting on 2001 transfer and baccalaureate degree attainment data from the National Educational Longitudinal Study (NELS) for students entering postsecondary education in the 1995–96 school year, indicate that 37.2 percent of the students who begin at a public two-year institution expect to transfer to a four-year college/university. When disaggregated by race, 60.7 percent of Asian Americans indicated that they expect to transfer. In contrast, African Americans were the least likely to expect to transfer at only 27.5 percent. Transfer expectation rates for White and Hispanic students were 37.3 and 38 percent, respectively.

Though nearly 40 percent of public two-year college students indicate their intentions to transfer, only 28.9 percent succeed in meeting their goal. For those who transferred, 10.3 percent attained bachelor's degrees. White students were the most successful in this process, at 12 percent. Percentages are smaller for other racial/ethnic groups—7.1 percent for Asian Americans, 3.1 percent for African Americans, and 5.9 percent for Hispanics. In sum, 37.2 percent of students enter the community college with the intent to transfer, 28.9 percent of students transfer, and 10.3 percent attain bachelor's degrees. When data is disaggregated by race, it is apparent that greater disparities exist.

---

[2] Rates are for 1995–96 beginning postsecondary students who first enrolled in a public two-year college according to the highest degree attained by 2001.
[3] This report uses degree to encompass both certificates and associate's degrees. In contrast, the authors have made a distinction between the two in this chapter and in others.

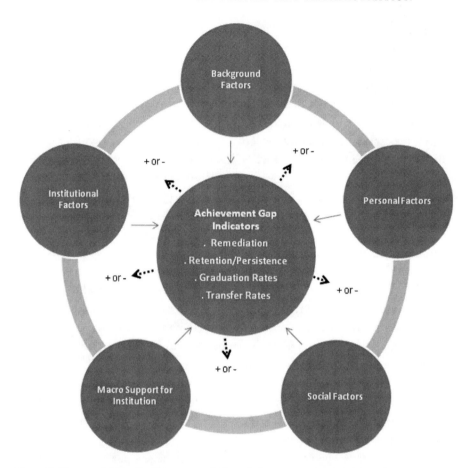

Figure 7   Nevarez & Wood's Community College Achievement Gap Model

Two lines of thought are generally used to explain the educational status of community college students in relation to access, retention, and completion. These include personal and institutional factors. In accordance with these two factors, theoretical frameworks have been developed to explain student success (e.g., An Empirical Model of the Undergraduate Model of Nontraditional Student Attrition). Although these explanations provide insights to various student and institutional factors that influence academic success, they are incomplete. The model above is inclusive of additional factors that lend themselves to a greater understanding of how all factors are interconnected and have either a positive or negative influence on the achievement indicators, which in turn, influence academic success. A description of achievement gap indicators, based upon a comprehensive review, follows:

- *Background factors* include characteristics associated with students' personal, social, and economic status, previous academic performance, as well as their parental socioeconomic status and level of education (among other variables). For example, in general, as their parental income, parents' level of education, and high school GPA increase, so do enrollment, persistence, graduation, and transfer (EPGT) rates of the students.
- *Personal factors* include academic habits, political savvy, confidence, and motivation of the students, among additional variables. Typically, increasing student's academic/personal confidence, educational goal commitment, academic motivation, attendance, study habits, and political astuteness is associated with increased EPGT rates.
- *Social factors* include social integration of the students into the campus setting, typified by their relationships, networks, and involvement in the fabric of the campus environment. Generally, students who establish relationships with faculty, staff, and peers, and involve themselves in campus activities (e.g., athletic commitments, student clubs/organizations, student government) are more likely to be committed to the institution. This is often associated with higher levels of academic success as personal, psychological, and relational needs of the students are met.
- *Macro-level support for the institution* includes the status of institutional resources as affected by campus revenue streams and funding from federal and state governments, local industry, and alumni. Fiscal resources allow institutions to meet student needs in multiple ways, among them: (a) academic prevention and intervention programs; (b) professional development for faculty; (c) increased instructional resources (e.g., technology); (d) the ability to attract quality institutional researchers, faculty, staff, and leaders; and (e) the extension of branch campus programs and resources.
- *Institutional factors* focus on issues related to the campus culture and climate, sense of belonging of the students to the campus, financial support for students, and campus diversity. For example, when institutions create an inclusive, supportive, and positive campus environment, it facilitates student success. Institutional student inclusiveness leads to: student success, increase of involvement in extracurricular activities, and an environment that facilitates that cognitive and affective development of students.

While the aforementioned factors contribute to student achievement in a general context, we encourage leaders to become acquainted with scholarly literature which provides conceptual and empirical information on persistence and academic success research specific to student groups by racial/ethnic and gender affiliation. In general, see the work of scholars such as Linda Hagedorn, Rita Cepeda, Brent Cejda, Tatiana Melguizo, and Athena Perrakis. For work specific to African Americans see Hagedorn, Maxwell, & Hampton (2001–02), Mason (1998), Perrakis (2008); Asian Pacific Americans see Makuakane-Drechsel & Hagedorn (2000); and Hispanic/Latinos see Cejda & Rhodes (2004), Cejda & Short (2008), Hagedorn & Cepeda (2004), Hagedorn et al., (2007), Laden, Hagedorn, & Perrakis (2008), Melguizo (2009).

Minority Male Initiatives

Minority Male Initiatives (MMIs)—refer to a wide variety of entities (e.g., private organizations, individual campuses, districts, nonprofit organizations), which provide a platform for dialogue, research, and direct action (e.g., conferences, workshops, speaker series, retention programs) to increase the persistence and graduation rates of minority male students. Bobb (2006) in discussing Black Male initiatives (a type of minority male initiative) notes that they bear several core functions in common: "(1) identify the obstacles to Black male college admission and retention; (2) devise and support programmatic interventions to mitigate those obstacles; and (3) to provide a small annual budget to accomplish goals one and two" (p. 43). He notes that these initiatives struggle against anti-affirmative action efforts, which affect their overall success. Despite barriers to their success, MMI's are extremely important to improving discourse on the unique barriers male students of color face in the community college. They bring together stakeholders (e.g., counselors, faculty, researchers, outreach staff, administrators) who are concerned about the issues facing these students. These individuals work collectively through programming, hosting conferences, and by enhancing student services to address the holistic needs of these students for the purpose of improving student learning and personal development. We will examine two examples of MMI's.

An MMI is seen in the Maricopa Community Colleges in Arizona. In the Maricopa Minority Male Initiative (MMMI) faculty, staff, and administrators from all ten district colleges meet to discuss critical issues facing minority male students on their respective campuses. The MMMI has three primary goals: (1)

to improve enrollment and continuation rates of male students of color; (2) to link male students of color to campus support services and resources in their first semester of attending a district college; and (3) to transform campus cultures to foster welcoming environments of success for these students. In order to accomplish these goals, the MMMI is currently engaged in a large-end qualitative study of minority males on each district campus. Through focus groups, preventions and interventions are being designed to aid students' in their success. In addition to research, the MMMI hosts summits for minority males. These summits feature speakers who discuss issues facing minority male students and approaches undertaken to promote academic success. The MMMI emerged from existing district efforts at the campus level. Examples include the Gateway Community College's Minority Male Leadership Group and Estrella Mountain Community College's (EMCCs) Minority Male Forums. Though not necessarily part of the MMMI; a notable effort in the district is the development of the Men of Color Association (MOCA) at EMCC. MOCA is a student association that provides support for minority males based on Maslow's Hierarchy of Needs. Physiological needs are met through the provision of food prior to each meeting. Safety needs are addressed both physically and environmentally through closed conversations, which provide a "safe space" for honest discussion. Love/belonging needs are met through the creation of internal bonds (counselor and student-to-student). Esteem is addressed through a group mantra that vocalizes affirmations of respect, empowerment, knowledge, brotherhood, and integrity. Self-actualizing occurs through critical examinations of issues facing minority communities, with a focus on males of color.

Another example of an MMI is the African American Male Educational Network and Development (A²MEND). A²MEND is a nonprofit organization composed of African American male administrators. The organization urges members to employ their skills as researchers and practitioners of education to facilitate institutional change within the community college. Based upon what they describe as a "moral responsibility" to the African American community, A²MEND members are urged to work for the betterment of African Americans in the community college, with an emphasis on African American males, in multiple capacities (e.g., student, faculty, administrators) (A²MEND, 2009). As a result, A²MEND has several core operations: (1) A mentor/mentee program— where African American males receive mentorship from African American male administrators. This program has two tracks, one for students (i.e., the Student Mentor Program) and another for professionals (i.e., the Professional Mentor Program). (2) A scholarship program—designed to provide African

American students with assistance in paying for tuition/fees, course materials (e.g., books), and cost-of-living expenses. (3) The African American male summit—which brings together African American males (e.g., faculty, students, administrators) to discuss issues facing African American males in the community college, as well as strategies to improve their condition in education. Conferences feature four strands focusing on students, faculty, student service professionals, and administration. They provide strategies to improve the status of these individuals in the areas of policy, instruction, student issues, and support services.

Minority/Low-Income Initiatives

Achieving the Dream Initiative (ADI)—"is a multiyear national initiative to help more community college students succeed. The initiative is particularly concerned about student groups that traditionally have faced significant barriers to success, including students of color and low-income students" (Achieving the Dream, 2005, Para. 1). This initiative realizes the varied functions of community colleges, which include, for example, terminal degrees, transfer, remedial education, and continuing education. The initiative realizes the complexities involved in meeting the multiple goals of member institutions and serves as mutual partners in facilitating the success of students. This is done for three primary reasons: (1) to ensure that community colleges are efficiently educating students so that they graduate in a timely manner and institutions that fail to promote the timely success of students will be drained of resources needed to support new students; (2) to use data effectively for the purpose of improving fiscal planning, particularly important for community colleges considering their limited access to funds, resources, and services; and (3) to promote equity by providing a platform to share data on student success, access, and persistence strategies and practices, through transparent discussions about the overall status of the community colleges and efforts to improve institutional practices. For these institutions, change based upon data evidence is supported and welcomed. In sum, the purpose is to develop an institutional culture that addresses the achievement gap in higher education. The initiative is comprised of 102 total institutions in 22 states, including 98 colleges and 4 universities (Hart, 2009). Participating colleges have high percentages of low-income and minority students. ADI seeks to create educational equity through: (a) a student-centered approach to education; (b) data/evidence-driven decision making; (c) the concepts of equity and excellence. In order to do so, the initiative provides: grants to help colleges in collecting data and using data to conceptualize, develop, and implement strategies to aid student success. The ADI works with its member institutions to collect data which can be used to design innovative practices and strategies for addressing the achievement gap (Achieving the Dream, 2007). The primary tool that drives this initiative is the usage of longitudinal data collection to account for the status of students in respect to enrollment, retention, and completion.

In order for underserved student initiatives to be successful, several points must be taken into consideration by community colleges leaders and initiative affiliates.

- *Funding.* Funding varies from initiative to initiative. In general, the larger the initiative (e.g., national, statewide) the larger the funding associated with the initiative. Additionally, the entities and sponsors that support and fund these initiatives determine the effectiveness of their programming. A precursor to funding is dependent upon the perceived or actual, effectiveness of the program, based upon evidence of success.
- *Leadership.* The reputation, political capital, and social networks of the individuals leading these initiatives determines their success. In general, most of these initiatives are short lived; those which persist have four things in common that relate to the success of their leadership: (a) they have built a strong leadership capacity; (b) they use data to inform practice; (c) they have funders, supporters, and members who have an invested interest in the success of the initiative; (d) they have institutionalized support within the structure of the institution or partner institutions.
- *Assessment–Evaluation.* Initiatives have three components; discussion, research, and action. It is critical that before the action component takes place that preventions and interventions are designed based upon research results from the campuses the initiatives serve. In addition, assessment must take place throughout the duration of programming and services, which are the result of the initiative. These assessments must be used for an overall evaluation to determine whether the initiative actions should be revised, modified, expanded, or eliminated.
- *Maturation.* As previously stated, the majority of initiatives are short lived. In order to be successful, these initiatives must be given time for maturity and refinement (i.e., after assessment). Leaders and initiative

affiliates must not become dismayed if initial results illustrate lack of success. Rather, they must use these results to refine their efforts.

- *Research based.* Initiatives must base their efforts upon current research, specific to minority males in the community colleges. Oftentimes, these initiatives are informed by research on four-year university students. While certain practices apply to both two-year and four-year institutions, differences do exist. In the community college context, students, funding, structure, faculty, services, and resources are different at the four-year university, thus, leaders must design and implement practices and strategies that address the unique realities of students in the community colleges.

Guiding Steps for Addressing the Achievement Gap

Greater efforts are needed in order for community colleges to address achievement disparities among students. Community college leaders can be aided by adhering to the following steps: (1) *identify* challenges, barriers, underlying problems, external/internal influences, and factors that contribute to the academic achievement gap; (2) *understand* these issues through dialogue with constituents (e.g., students, community members), needs assessments (e.g., campus climate, educational experiences of the students), and analysis of trends to understand the context in which these issues occur; (3) *design* prevention and intervention programs/services, and institutional policies and practices to address the varying issues facing students; (4) *implement* and institutionalize these programs, services, policies, and practices as core functions of the college; (5) *assess* the overall effectiveness of these efforts through multiple approaches (e.g., qualitative, quantitative, mixed-methods); and (6) *revise* these efforts in accordance with assessment results (e.g., eliminate, recreate, modify, expand). These steps are illustrated in the following model (see Figure 8).

The community college achievement gap exists and its prolongation is influenced by a variety of internal and external factors as exemplified by this chapter's content. This in turn, challenges community colleges leaders to engage in efforts to identify and implement practices and policies that deliberately decrease the achievement gap. Leaders cannot afford to take a business-as-usual approach to leadership, especially in consideration of the wide disparities that exist among students. Leaders must begin to take bold actions, engage in difficult conversations, and solicit widespread support from stakeholders in their efforts to conceptualize

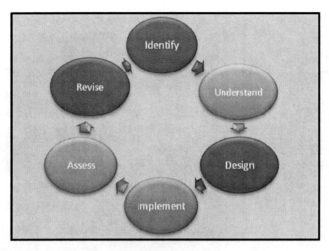

Figure 8 Achievement Gap Action Model

new practices, yet to be realized. Clearly, current leadership practices continue to perpetuate stagnant change and often declines in academic achievement among community college students.

Case Study

A case study is presented, which is designed to aid you in a critical examination of indicators affecting the achievement gap. When identifying resolution(s) be attentive to the interplay among various factors (e.g., social, background, personal, environmental, macro-level support for the institution) impacting the achievement gap in examining the following scenario.

President Eduardo J. Marti
Queensborough Community College
Bayside, New York

Funding Remediation Efforts

Background

Queensborough Community College is one of 22 units of the City University of New York (CUNY.) The University serves over 200,000 students and offers programs ranging from the associate's to the PhD The six community colleges of CUNY are the only colleges operating under an "Open Admissions" policy. In the fall, 2008, Queensborough Community College enrolled 13,752 degree students, 7,270 (61.6 percent) were full-time. The college offers 12 transfer (AA or AS) programs, 20 career degree programs (AAS), and 10 certificate programs. The college participates in the CUNY College Now program that provides college-level courses to high school students. This program enrolls the majority of the nonmatriculated (1,948) students. The six-year graduation rate for the fall '02 cohort was 26.2 percent.

Queensborough is a diverse campus; its ethnic population breakdown is as follows: 26 percent White, 27.8 percent Black, 22.5 percent Hispanic, 0.35 percent Native American, and 24.4 percent Asian. The student/faculty ratio is 17.5:1. Student learning at Queensborough is supported by learning communities, honors courses, student research programs, service learning projects, and required writing intensive courses.

CUNY requires all students entering the community colleges to take three types of tests: placement tests for incoming freshmen, exit tests from students completing remediation or workshops, and the CUNY Proficiency Exam (CPE), which is required for graduation. *The COMPASS Reading Test* measures reading comprehension. Students are given several readings that may be practical or drawn from prose fiction, the humanities, social sciences, or natural sciences. The exam asks students to determine implicit meanings, to draw conclusions, and to make comparisons and generalizations. The readings are like those commonly assigned in first-year courses in college. This is an untimed, multiple choice, and computer-based test.

The Writing Sample assesses the student's writing skills based on sample writing. Students are given a choice of two questions, and are asked to write an organized, focused essay. The essay questions are similar to one another in the following way: each one describes a choice that a person in a position of authority must make between two alternatives. The writer is asked to advise the authority on the best choice and explain why the group should agree with the writer's position. The writing sample is scored by two trained readers, using a six-point scale. For each passage you will be asked a set of multiple-choice questions.

The COMPASS Mathematics Test is designed to measure students' knowledge of a number of topics in mathematics. The test is organized into four sections: numerical skills/pre-algebra, algebra, college algebra, and trigonometry. Numerical skills/pre-algebra questions range from basic math concepts and skills (integers, fractions, and decimals) to the knowledge and skills that are required in an entry-level algebra course (absolute values, percentages, and exponents). Placement into CUNY's required basic math courses is based on results of the numerical skills/pre-algebra and algebra sections. The test covers progressively advanced topics with placement into more advanced mathematics or mathematics-related courses based on results of the last two sections of the test.

Students who do not demonstrate sufficient proficiency must take a remedial course. All students registered in their college's top-level course in Reading, Writing, or ESL will take the test(s) at the end of the semester. Students who do not pass the test(s) will not be able to begin college composition (Freshman English) until they pass. Likewise, no student may be placed in a college-level mathematics course who has not passed or been exempted from the COMPASS Mathematics Test. More than one-half of all incoming freshmen require at least one remedial course.

Learning Communities are groups of students who take two or three classes together. The classes may be designed around a unifying theme or, as in the case of courses in specialized majors, based on courses that reinforce the special needs or requirements of the students. Students in the first or second semester at Queensborough and whose placement test results make them eligible for English 101 can join a Learning Community. Students in need of Basic Skills courses in Reading or Writing, or in need of MA-005, can take advantage of the Learning Communities for Basic Skills students and the linked courses for Basic Skills students.

The Collective Bargaining Agreement between CUNY and the Board of Trustees provides a measure of parity to the faculty members within all units of the University. However, the Agreement also requires all faculty members to hold a PhD or the equivalent for a tenure-track position. Individuals hired at the Instructor rank must complete the PhD or equivalent within 5 years. Lecturers can be granted a Continuous Employment Contract after 5 years of service; 58 percent of the 304 full-time faculty members hold a doctorate. Faculty members are evaluated on their teaching, college service, and publications for promotion and tenure. For the last 5 years, the president of the college has been encouraging empirical pedagogical research by recognizing it for promotion and tenure.

Statement of the Problem

The College received a $500,000 grant from a foundation to perform empirical studies on the effectiveness of learning communities. The study calls for random assignments of students into two groups (learning communities and individual courses). Upon registration, students will be asked to either enroll in a designated learning community or choose to take the same courses in separate sections. Those who choose to take individual courses will be compared with those who are taking the same course but in a learning community. The groups will be compared using rubrics of student learning outcomes, retention rates, and student satisfaction. While participation in a learning community is strictly voluntary, students must provide informed consent. Questions to consider: (1) how can this money be used to improve student learning outcomes, retention rates, and student satisfaction? (2) what stakeholders (e.g., administrators, faculty, staff, community members) and departments should be involved; and in what capacity? and (3) what assessment and evaluation measures should be put into place?

References

Achieving the Dream (2005). About achieving the Dream: Overview. ADI. Retrieved August 28, 2009, from: http://www.achievingthedream.org/aboutatd/default.tp

Achieving the Dream (2007). Success is what counts. ADI. Retrieved August 28, 2009, from: http://www.achievingthedream.org/docs/SUCCESS-counts-FINAL-11.6.pdf

A²MEND (2009). *About: Our mission, our vision, our goals.* San Bernardino, CA: Author. Retrieved August 28, 2009, from: http://a2mend.org/about.html

Bean, J. P., & Metzner, B. S. (1985). A conceptual model of nontraditional undergraduate student attrition. *Review of Educational Research, 55*(4), 485–540.

Bobb, K. (2006). The paradox of black male initiatives. *Diverse Online* (March 23), 10, 43.

Cejda, B. D., & Short, Matt (2008). Influencing the college attendance rates of Hispanics in Texas. *Community College Journal of Research and Practice, 32*(4), 347–361.

Cejda, B., & Rhodes, J. (2004). Through the pipeline: The role of faculty in promoting associate degree completion among Hispanic students. *Community College Journal of Research and Practice, 28*(3), 249–262.

Durkheim, E. (1951). *Suicide.* New York: The Free Press.

Futrell, M. (1999). The challenge of the 21st century: Developing a highly qualified cadre of teachers to teach our nation's diverse student population. *Journal of Negro Education,* 68(3), 318–334.

Grigg, W., Donahue, P. L., & Dion, G. (2007). *Nations report card: 12th grade reading and mathematics 2005.* Washington, DC: National assessment of educational progress, U.S. Department of Education, Institute of Education Sciences and the National Center for Education Statistics

Hagedorn, L., & Cepeda, R. (2004). Serving Los Angeles: Urban community colleges and educational success among Latino students. *Community College Journal of Research and Practice* (March), 28(3), 199–211.

Hagedorn, L. S., Chi, W., Cepeda, R., & McLain, M. (2007). An investigation of critical mass: The role of Latino representation in the success of urban community college students. *Research in Higher Education,* 48(1), 73–91

Hagedorn, S. L., Maxwell, W., & Hampton, P. (2001–02). Correlates of retention for African-American males in the community college. *Journal of College Student Retention,* 3(3), 243–263.

Hart, R. (2009). *Twenty community colleges in seven states join national student success initiative.* Achieving the Dream. Retrieved August 28, 2009, from: http://www.achievingthedream.org/Portal/Modules/f62bff99-dbc8–47ef-9633–7be78ade27bf.asset?

Hausmann, L. R. M., Schofield, J. W., & Woods, R. L. (2007). Sense of belonging as a predictor of intentions to persist among African American and white first-year college students. *Research in Higher Education,* 48(7), 803–839.

Hoachlander, G., Sikora, A. C., Horn, L., & Carroll, C. D. (2003). *Community college students: Goals, academic preparation, and outcomes.* Washington, DC: National Center for Education Statistics.

KewalRamani, A., Gilbertson, L, Fox, M., & Provasnik, S. (2007). *Status and trends in the education of racial and ethnic minorities (NCES 2007–039).* Washington, DC: National Center for Education Statistics, Institute of Education Sciences, U.S. Department of Education.

Laden, B. V., Hagedorn, L. S., & Perrakis, A. (2008). Dónde están los hombres? Examining success of Latino male students at Hispanic-Serving community colleges. In M. Gasman, B. Baez, & C. S. V. Turner, (eds.). *Understanding minority serving institutions* (pp. 127–140). New York: State University of New York Press.

Lee, J., Grigg, W. S., & Dion, G. S. (2007a). *The nation's report card: Mathematics 2007.* Washington, DC: National Assessment of Educational Progress, U.S. Department of Education, Institute of Education Sciences and the National Center for Education Statistics.

Lee, J., Grigg, W. S., & Dion, G. S. (2007b). *The nation's report card: Reading 2007.* Washington, DC: National Assessment of Educational Progress, U.S. Department of Education, Institute of Education Sciences and the National Center for Education Statistics.

Levin, H., Belfield, C., Muennig, P., & Rouse, C. (2007). *The costs and benefits of an excellent education for all of America's children.* Retrieved August 20, 2009, from: *http://www.prepkc.org/assets/files/resources/Leeds_Report_Final_Jan2007.pdf*

Levinson, M. (2007). *The civic achievement gap: Circle working paper 51.* College Park, MD: The Center for Information and Research on Civic Learning and Engagement.

Makuakane-Drechsel, T., & Hagedorn, L. (2000). Correlates of retention among Asian Pacific Americans in community colleges: The case for Hawaiian students. *Community College Journal of Research and Practice* (September) 24(8), 639–655.

Mason, H. P. (1998). A persistence model for African American male urban community college students. *Community College Journal of Research and Practice,* 22(8), 751–760.

Melguizo, T. (2009). Are community colleges an alternative path for Hispanic students to attain a bachelor's degree? *Teachers College Record*, 111(1), 90–123.

Ngo, B., & Lee, S. J. (2007). Complicating the image of model minority success: A review of southeast Asian-American education. *Review of Educational Research, 77*(4), 415–453.

Orfield, G., Losen, D., Wald, J., & Swanson, C. (2004). *Losing our future: How minority youth are being left behind by the graduation rate crisis.* Cambridge, MA: The Civil Rights Project at Harvard University.

Perrakis, A. I. (2008). Factor promoting academic success among African American and White male community college students. *New Directions for Community Colleges, 142*, 15–23.

Spady, W. G. (1970). Dropouts from higher education: An interdisciplinary review and synthesis. *Interchange, 1*, 64–85.

Stillwell, R., & Hoffman, L. (2009). *Public school graduates and dropouts from the common core of data: School year 2005–06; A first look.* Washington, DC: National Center for Education Statistics.

Tinto, V. (1975). Dropouts from higher education: A theoretical synthesis of recent research. *Review of Educational Research, 45*(1), 89–125.

Tinto, V. (1987). *Leaving college: rethinking the causes and cures of student attrition* (2nd Ed.). Chicago, IL: The University of Chicago Press.

Tinto, V. (1988). Stages of student departure: Reflections on the longitudinal character of student leaving. *Journal of Higher Education, 59*(4), 438–455.

Tinto, V. (1993). *Leaving college: Rethinking the causes and cures of student attrition* (2nd Ed.). Chicago, IL: University of Chicago Press.

U.S. Census Bureau, (2008). Current population survey, 2008 annual social and economic supplement.

U.S. Department of Education, National Center for Education Statistics (1996/01) Beginning Postsecondary Students Longitudinal Study (BPS:96/01).

U.S. Department of Education (2001). National Center for Education Statistics, Postsecondary Education Quick Information System, "Survey on Remedial Education in Higher Education Institutions: Fall 1995," 1995; and "Survey on Remedial Education in Higher Education Institutions: Fall 2000."

U.S. Department of Education (2006). National Center for Education Statistics, Integrated Postsecondary Education Data System (IPEDS), Spring, Graduation Rates component.

Vernez, G., & Mizell, L. (2001). *GOAL: To double the rate of Hispanics earning a bachelor's degree.* Santa Monica, CA: RAND.

CHAPTER FIVE

ETHICAL LEADERSHIP
AND DECISION MAKING

This chapter presents the concept of ethics as it relates to leadership in the community college. Focus is given to: (a) the importance of knowing the codes of ethics, which govern the profession of community college leadership; (b) using multiple ethical paradigms (e.g., ethic of justice, ethic of critique, ethic of care, ethic of profession); and (c) employing ethical decision-making models.

When reading this chapter, consider the following questions:

- What are the codes of ethics or "standards of practice" that guide your profession? How can you become better acquainted with these codes? What are their limitations?
- What are the multiple ethical paradigms? Which paradigm(s) do you adhere to? Why is it important to incorporate all four into your leadership practice?
- What are ethical decision-making models? What are the steps that these models have in common? How can these models be used to improve ethical decision making in the community college?

Change, in many ways, defines the primary challenge of leadership in this era. The maturation of the Internet has led to an increase in hybrid/online course offerings and greater accessibility to information. The influence and growing effect of regional economies and globalization has resulted in heightened competition in public and private sectors, as old markets become contested with new opposition. Increasing national diversity of race/ethnicity, gender, class, and so on has coincided with rising student diversity, requiring changes to programs, policies, and services to meet emerging student needs. Growing economic turmoil has challenged postsecondary institutions to serve more students, with greater accountability and fewer resources. Responding to constant change and evolving with a rapidly shifting social landscape while maintaining the community colleges mission of access has been the challenge, call, and opportunity of community college leaders for more than a century. Due to the increasingly complex nature of leadership in these institutions, long work hours, high levels of stress, elevated expectations, and slow-moving bureaucracies, leaders are challenged to make "right," and often difficult, decisions on a daily basis. Thus it is crucial that community college leaders possess a clear understanding of the ethical dilemmas that arise in this rapidly changing environment.

There are plenty of examples of business leaders (e.g., Kenneth Lay, Bernie Madoff) and political leaders (e.g., Richard Nixon, John Edwards) who, in their roles as leaders, faced such challenges and made poor choices. These leaders engaged in unethical behavior because they did not weigh the consequences of the ethical dilemmas they encountered. They made decisions and acted based on what was expedient rather than what met the highest ethical standard. Consequently, such actions have elevated public scrutiny of all leaders, highlighting the need for an increased focus on the intersection of ethics and decision making by community college leaders, as well (Sullivan, 2001). Community colleges are not precluded from this phenomenon. Recent events occurring in community colleges further highlight the need to advance ethical behavior among community college leaders. Below, are some examples of these incidents from *The Chronicle of Higher Education* [1]

> The Board of Trustees at Barton County Community College has fired its president... because of a scandal during his administration that led to the federal indictment of three former basketball coaches at the Kansas institution...The three former coaches... face federal charges that include fraud, embezzlement, and theft. They are accused of participating in a scheme to use false academic credentials to improperly obtain federal and work-study grants for men's basketball players. They are also alleged to have falsified work records that allowed the players to be paid for work they did not do (Wills, 2005).

> The former president of Mississippi's Holmes Community College was convicted this month on two counts of embezzlement after being charged with using college funds to buy car tires and having employees do work at his home in preparation for a wedding there (Wu, 2006).

> [Professor X] says El Camino administrators, led by the president...fired him from his post as an associate professor teaching automobile repair in February because he

---

[1] These excerpts are presented without individuals' names.

drew attention to allegedly unethical practices at the college. Among other things, his suits accuse the two-year college of enrolling students who do not exist or who aren't actually taking courses. His suits say the practice is part of a scheme to attract more state and federal funds, keep classes open despite low enrollment, and grant favors to colleagues (Reynolds, 1998).

The president of Edward Waters College resigned last month, after the governing board learned that he had falsified credentials on his resume, a college official said. [President X] claimed that he had a master's of business administration from Stetson University and a doctorate from the University of South Florida. The college's Board of Trustees hired him as interim president in April 1993 and unanimously appointed him president of the historically black college in February 1994. The trustees discovered that he had faked his credentials after anonymous fliers appeared on the campus accusing him of lying about his background (Wanat, 1996).

While these instances of possible fraud, embezzlement, theft, and falsification of records illustrate clear breaches of ethical behavior, many of the ethical dilemmas that challenge leaders are much more complex. Ethical dilemmas are not always cases of whether law is being violated, though sometimes they are, or instances where the "right" action is clear, though occasionally, they can be (Maesschalck, 2004); they are multifaceted in nature, confounded with uncertainty, and dynamic. For example, an individual insinuating, but never asserting, that they have more academic credentials than they actually do is not breaking the law, but their motives are questionable, which breaches trust and can be construed as unethical; whereas, spending money on expenses which are clearly defined as personal, not business, is both against the law and violates ethical codes of conduct. A person who suggests that the extent of a relationship is more meaningful than in actuality for self-promotion is falsifying the record. While it is not illegal, it violates the trust of colleagues and peers. Increasing professional perks to make up for salary reductions or furloughs violates the code of ethics and the law.

Vaughan (1992) states that ethical dilemmas are a direct result of the interactions of the community colleges with various components of the society. He states that challenges emerge from: (a) corporate leaders, who desire the college to serve their needs before others; (b) special interest groups, who demand educational offerings which meet the needs of their respective groups; (c) politicians who pressure community college leaders to hire family and friends; (d) four-year universities who advocate that two-year colleges change their programming to fit their standards; and (e) lack of resources, which necessitates that some areas receive more attention than others. These issues produce circumstances ripe for unethical behavior. Thus, a need for holding leaders accountable through direct and indirect oversight is needed. This can be accomplished in multiple ways: (1) requiring all leaders to report regularly to an individual (e.g., vice president, president) or entity (e.g., board); (2) semiannual and annual reports; (3) periodic and unannounced audits; and (4) through clear policies, regulations, and protocol. In sum, we realize these accountability measures may not be well received by those in leadership positions; however, "everybody needs to be accountable to somebody."

Clear infractions of ethical behavior may result in loss of a job, forced resignation, prosecution, and civil suits. However, more subtle ethical violations inevitably will affect a leader's reputation, especially when such practices are habitual. This is particularly relevant in academic settings where one's moral character commands respect and closes/opens professional opportunities. The following are examples of how unethical behavior affects leaders' and their institutions reputations:

- *Professional Growth.* Leaders who deviate from ethical standards jeopardize their potential for career mobility, added professional responsibilities, and increased earnings. Essentially, their professional standing will be stagnant.

- *Collegiality.* Collegiality is inhibited by unethical actions. Suspicions of unethical behavior can mar social relationships and networking, and lead to increased organizational marginalization and alienation.

- *Change.* Leaders require buy-in from multiple organizational stakeholders in order to facilitate and actualize organizational change. The perception of unethical behavior will reduce the overall support needed to successfully implement sought-out changes.

- *External Relationships.* In order to be successful in their posts, leaders must be able to establish and maintain relationships with policymakers, community members, alumni, and potential donors. When the reputations of the leaders are damaged, they are rendered ineffective in these capacities.

- *Institutional Impact.* Ultimately, the institutions, students, and communities that leaders serve are the most affected by unethical behavior. Loss of political and social networks impedes the ability of the leaders to advocate for their respective institutions as well as changes needed to improve student success.

- *Institutional Reputation.* Leaders who behave unethically directly impact their institutions in multiple ways. Their actions can: (a) reduce public support for the institution, which can result in lack of support for needed institutional initiatives (e.g., bond measures); (b) hamper student, staff, and faculty recruitment efforts; and (c) result in greater scrutiny and account-ability by accreditation bodies, state/local government, and the media.

Irrespective of an organization's standard of ethics, it is important for leaders to function with an ethical leadership approach. Many organizations, including some community colleges, have an organization culture which facilitates uneth-ical behavior. For example, notable community colleges have lost their accred-itation due to unethical use of resources. In such cases, unethical behavior had become the norm within the institution. Though it is important to employ ethi-cal leadership because "it's the right thing to do" and to avoid the consequences discussed above, there are several important benefits for community college leaders, and leaders in general, who do so:

- *Improved Work Environment*—Leadership that is ethical impacts sev-eral important factors linked to an improved work environment: (a) increased levels of job satisfaction for employees (Brown, Treviño, & Harrison, 2005); (b) enhanced commitment to the organization on behalf of employees (Zun, May, & Avolio, 2004); (c) interpersonal rela-tions marked by care and equity (Brown & Treviño, 2006); and (d) higher levels of trust between leaders and employees (Brown & Treviño, 2006; Zun, May, & Avolio, 2004)
- *Enhanced Confidence in Leadership*—When leaders are perceived by employees to be ethical, employee satisfaction with leadership increases (Brown, Treviño, & Harrison, 2005). Thus, community college leaders seeking to galvanize support amongst the ranks of their faculty, staff, and administration should first examine their personal actions, to ensure that their leadership is ethical.
- *Ethical Actions from Followers*—Leaders who exude ethical behaviors model the actions that they seek in others by setting the standard of conduct for all members of their organization. Brown and Treviño (2006) examined linkages between ethical approaches to leadership and ethical actions. Their research suggests that when leaders exhibit ethical qualities, those whom they lead emulate those qualities. This is said to occur, even "when the leader is not physically present" (p. 606).
- *Ethical Actions from Community*— Ethical behavior among leaders can influence ethical behavior among constituents (e.g., community

members, students, parents). This is particularly important for leaders, especially since they are considered role models, mentors, advisor, and advocates for the students and communities that they serve. These individuals implicitly and explicitly influence the ethical climate of behavior within institutions.

Ethical Leadership

Ethical behavior can serve as a guiding framework for leaders in their quest to manage, transform, and maneuver the complexities of leading community colleges. To improve the process of decision making in the community college, leaders should consider the intersection of leadership and ethics.

Ethics—"refers to standards of behavior that tell us how human beings ought to act in the many situations in which they find themselves" (Velasquez et al., 2009, Para 2). As noted by Velasquez et al., (2009) there is a need for individuals to extend these standards of behavior to every aspect of their lives and facet of society. For community college leaders, we argue that this extends to every aspect and facet of the institutions that they serve. Another concept linked to ethics, is that of morality. These concepts, while distinct, are very interrelated and interdependent (Exley, 2003–04). While ethics deal with the "standards of behavior" needed to guide actions, Starratt (2004) notes that Morality—"is the living, the acting out of ethical beliefs and commitments" (p. 5). In essence, ethics is the establishing of standards, and morality is the acting out of those standards.

The challenge of expanding ethical behavior in community colleges can be limited by the nature of discussions taking place. Often, when the topics of ethics or morality are addressed, conversations center on issues of academic integrity/honesty, plagiarism, and cheating on behalf of students (for example, see Community College Week, 2003; Lambert, 2005; Swanger, 2002; Weiler, 2004). This myopic focus, while important, fails to adequately address: (a) the role of the organization in facilitating unethical action (Davis, 2003–04) and (b) the wide-ranging ethical dilemmas that community college leaders, faculty, staff, and students face on a daily basis.

Bearing this in mind, we advocate the usage of ethical leadership to guide both students and educational personnel alike. Brown, Treviño, & Harrison, (2005) state that: Ethical Leadership is "the demonstration of normatively appropriate conduct through personal actions and interpersonal relationships, and the promotion of such conduct to followers through two-way communication, reinforcement, and decision making" (p. 120). Key to this definition is the notion that ethical leadership is exuded through personal character as exhibited through one's actions, interpersonal communications, and decision making. Embedded here are the interlinked concepts of ethics, the "established standard," and morality, "the activity of leading ethically," therein, our preference for using this particular definition.

Ethical Decision Making

Davis (2007a) notes that identifying ethical courses of action can be difficult, especially given the numerous potential pitfalls that community college leaders face. With this in mind, Davis outlines ten primary areas in which community college presidents and board members encounter ethical challenges. We believe these ten areas have applicability to all community college leaders, and include:

1. "Truth-or-reputation dilemma." In their fervor to present themselves in the best possible light, community college presidents and trustees may not be fully forthright about the issues facing community colleges. This is attributed to high public scrutiny of the community college. An example of this pitfall occurs when boards have private meetings to discuss institutional affairs, despite public hearing laws (p. 48).

2. "Inertia can become the enemy of responsible behavior." When new leaders assume positions of power, some practices that were in place during the prior administration continue. Some leaders stumble when they allow practices to continue that are not ethical. Looking the other way, pretending to not know, or attributing behavior to previous administrations can ensnare leaders, as they are ultimately responsible for what occurs within their institutions, regardless of what others have done (p. 50).

3. "Tension between academic and real-world values." Some values within academia and the "real-world" are juxtaposed. Valuing diversity, believing in students' ability to achieve, and desiring for improved understanding of students' realities are values more likely to be affirmed in academia. In contrast, the business world is competitive, seeks the bottom-line, and at times can be cutthroat. When leaders encounter conflicting values between polar schools of thought, ethical dilemmas can emerge (p. 51).

4. "Demands of the marketplace and academic standards." Leaders can face dilemmas which are a result of conflicting demands between the marketplace and academia. Investing in facilities, sports teams, and special programs which raise the value of the institutions, can result in fewer resources for institutional needs. When this occurs too often, these actions can pose significant challenges to leaders' reputations (p. 52).

5. "Lack of ethical consensus in our pluralistic society." Varying dogmatic views, cultural beliefs, viewpoints, and values can present conflicts for educational leaders as contesting ethical viewpoints prevent progress toward stated goals. These issues can make ethical decision making an arduous and complex process (p. 53).

6. "Benefiting local vendors and making a profit for the college." Many community colleges have become more focused on leveraging the benefits of their captive student consumers. Selling food, clothing, books, and access to fitness resources among other items can result in direct competition with local vendors. This can create animosity as these vendors pay taxes, which go to publicly supported community colleges. In addition to selling products, colleges also have investments, which can create large funding reserves. Excessive reserves can open leaders to accusations of unethical behavior, especially if there are underfunded plans, programs, and services (p. 53).

7. "Tempted to bend the law." Overregulation of public colleges from state and federal government can make community college leadership very difficult. Sometimes, these excessive rules hamper colleges' efforts to seek the best interests of their students and the organization. When the law conflicts with the interests of the institution, leaders face ethical dilemmas when they bend or ignore regulations (p. 54). Unclear laws can also lead to leaders being "tempted" to be unethical. For example, vague state legislative mandates or requirements can create openings for different interpretations. This can lead to the promotion of self-interests in policies and practices.

8. "Violate the duties of loyalty, care, and obedience." Leaders should show obedience to the organization by following state, federal, and organizational regulations and demonstrate care through diligent preparation and attendance at meetings. Often, leaders fall prey to ethical questions of their loyalty, as conflicting interests muddle their reputation. For example, when leaders have the authority to approve their own travel, ethical appropriation of monies can be questioned. Leaders

who hide expenditures place their reputation and that of the organization into question (p. 54).

9. "Tension exists between candor and respect." Due to the highly political nature of leadership roles, leaders may be averse to addressing ethical dilemmas regarding other leaders, or to being questioned about their own ethical actions. Retaliatory factors may be of concern in these circumstances. This can produce an environment where ethical issues go unaddressed (p. 57).

10. "Ethics presents a challenge at the systems level." When systems and practices are unclear, absent or ineffective, ethical dilemmas can emerge. For example, when disasters occur (natural or otherwise), institutions are confronted with whether they have systems in place to address the circumstances they face. Old systems, unclear guidelines, and lack of planning pose problems to resolving issues. Another example occurs when guidelines for leadership training are not in place, which presents challenges to leaders' incorporation and effectiveness within the organization. (p. 58)

These ten areas of concern addressed by Davis (2007a, b) serve as a snapshot into a number of issues which pose ethical challenges for community college leaders. Leaders who encounter the issues described earlier, or other ethical dilemmas, can be aided in decision making by reviewing: existing codes of ethics within the profession, multiple ethical paradigms, and ethical decision-making models. Leaders can use codes of ethics and ethical paradigms as tools to examine issues. Armed with these tools, leaders can use ethical decision-making models to aid them in the decision-making process. To better contextualize ethical decision making, information is provided on: (a) *ethical tools* (e.g., professional codes, ethical paradigms); and (b) ethical decision-making models; as well as a (c) discussion on how these ethical tools and decision-making models can be used in a systematic process to engage dilemmas.

Ethical Tools

Codes of Ethics

As noted, in Brown, Treviño, & Harrison (2005) the definition of ethical leadership identifies an interrelationship between ethical leadership and decision making. With this in mind, the focus is on how leaders can engage in ethical decision making. We define *Ethical Decision Making* as the process by which established standards of behavior are used by leaders to approach, evaluate, and construct decisions. The phrase "standards of behavior" comes from Velasquez et al., (2009). For community college leaders, these behaviors are identified within previously established professional codes of ethics. Thus, educational leaders should be knowledgeable of professional codes when approaching any decision-making process, ethical or otherwise.

In 2005, the American Association of Community Colleges' (AACC) Board of Directors approved a *Recommended Code of Ethics for Chief Executive Officers of Community Colleges*. This code serves as a model for professionally recognized "standards of behavior" for all community college leaders. The preamble to the code notes the responsibility of community college CEOs to illustrate ethical behavior through their personal actions and leadership which can be modeled in their institutions. The code also calls for community college leaders to uphold, both outwardly and inwardly, four principles: (1) trust and respect for all individuals; (2) honesty in all actions; (3) just and fair treatment of all people; and (4) integrity in all actions (Para. 5). The code of ethics for the AACC outlines 33 specific ethical guidelines for leaders to 5 groups: oversight board(s); campus personnel (e.g., administration, faculty, and staff); students; institutions of education; and the greater community. Our analysis of CEOs responsibilities to these respective groups is as follows:

- *Oversight Board(s)*—CEOs have the responsibility to enable board members to have effective oversight of their organizations and honor their authority by: (a) facilitating an environment of collaboration for the best interest of the institutions that they serve; (b) providing them with accurate information and enough advice to make informed decisions; (c) implementing their charges and plans; (d) portraying their positions in an accurate manner in all communications; and (e) abstaining from real, potential, and perceived conflicts of interests.
- *Campus Personnel*—AACC guidelines highlight CEOs' responsibilities that fall in to four areas: (1) Standards—the CEOs are expected to promote excellence in access, instruction, learning, and application of knowledge as well as organizational ethics; (2) Culture—the CEOs should facilitate an environment of collaboration, understanding and respect for individual's contributions; (3) Power—CEOs must not abuse their power by exploiting their position for undue gain. In addition, they should work arduously to ensure that campus personnel do not

exploit their own authority with students (e.g., sexual relationships); (4)
Fairness—CEOs must create an environment of where equity, fairness,
and rights to employees are established, maintained, and respected.

- *Students*—The AACC code of ethics presents guidelines which seem
to indicate responsibilities to students in three areas: (1) Input—CEOs
are encouraged to seek input from students in decision-making processes; (2) Access and Opportunity—CEOs are expected to encourage
access and provide opportunities for the advancement of diversity and
equitable dealings with students; (3) Well-Being—CEOs must create
campus environments that foster the academic and personal well-being
of students through the development of safe academic settings which
are free of harassment, bigotry, and abuse; and (4) Academics—CEOs
must ensure that their institutions provide accurate information on
academic programming and facilitate programmatic success through
adequate funding.

- *Institutions of Education*—AACC guidelines for CEOs fall into two categories: (1) Partnerships—CEOs are encouraged to work in partnership
with other educational institutions. In this process, they are to maintain agreements (i.e., articulations) established with other institutions;
and (2) Communication—CEOs should create an atmosphere of internal and interorganizational dialogue that is candid about information,
changes, financial circumstances, and needs.

- *The Greater Community*—CEOs are responsible to the communities
that they serve in three primary ways: (1) Community Integrity—CEOs
must be responsive to local and regional needs and trends, and in doing
so, they must be pragmatic about expectations and forthright about
intended contributions; (2) Community Involvement—CEOs must
encourage community involvement in their institutions by seeking
stakeholders' input, opinions, recommendations on institutional policy,
and operations; and (3) Legal—CEOs should maintain their integrity
by abstaining from real, potential, and perceived conflicts of interests
and respecting established policy, rules, and law.

While some of the responsibilities identified within the AACC code are not specific to lower-, mid-, and even some senior-level administrators, the spirit of this
code is still applicable to all community college leaders. Ideally, this code should
be institutionalized within the organizational culture of the community college.
This code can be modified and used by all community college leaders, as they

are responsible to: *Supervisors*—leaders must honor the authority and facilitate oversight from those to whom they report by: supporting interorganizational collaboration, providing accurate data to their supervisor(s), implementing their given charges, portraying all communication accurately, and avoiding conflicts of interest. *Campus Colleagues*—leaders must maintain: (a) high standards regarding the promotion of excellence in access, teaching, ethics, and application of information learned; (b) a culture of collaboration and mutual respect for colleagues; (c) responsible stewardship of the authority given to them over other personnel and students; and (d) an environment where equity, fairness, and rights are extended to all. *Students*—Above all, leaders are responsible to the students that they serve. Their task is to: (a) create avenues for student input on decision making; (b) promote access and opportunity through an environment where equity and diversity are respected ideals; (c) create a safe academic environment where learning is not inhibited by harassment, discrimination, or abuse; and (d) provide students with accurate information about academic programming and support existing programs to the best of their abilities. *Institutions of Education*—Leaders are responsible for: (a) maintaining positive relationships with other educational institutions and if directed, to work in establishing and maintaining successful working partnership with them; and (b) for maintaining an environment where open and candid dialogue is encouraged and fostered. *The Greater Community*—Leaders are responsible to the communities that they serve, by: (a) being pragmatic about expectations, and seeking the best interests of the local community; (b) encouraging (when possible) local involvement in campus programming, planning, and operations; and (c) avoiding conflicts of interest and following previously established policy and law.

In addition to the AACC code, many community college associations have established guidelines or standards of ethics meant to guide members' actions (e.g., Association of Community College Trustees[2], Association of California Community College Administrations[3]). Also, many community college districts and campuses have their own code of ethics (e.g., Virginia Highlands Community College,[4] Imperial Valley College[5]).

These codes or "standards of behavior," serve to guide leadership behavior, However, three primary factors prevent this from occurring. First, many educators (at all levels) are unaware or have little knowledge of the codes of ethics

---

[2] http://www.acct.org/resources/center/ethicalguide.php
[3] See http://www.accca.org/i4a/pages/index.cfm?pageid=3338
[4] http://www.vhcc.edu/index.aspx?page=814
[5] http://imperial.edu/index.php?pid=4804

that are in place for their profession. Secondly, some scholars are critical of the overly simplistic and often bombastic nature of codes that do exist (Strike & Ternasky, 1993). Thirdly, professional codes of ethics fail to adequately address the daily operations, issues, and dilemmas facing educational leaders (Shapiro & Stefkovich, 2005). Fourth, even for leaders who are acquainted with ethical codes, it remains to be seen whether they transfer their knowledge of the code into practice. As exemplified above, there are substantial ethics of practice that are inclusive in the codes of ethics, which serve as standards of behavior. Often, widespread knowledge of ethical codes does not occur until public ethical breaches have taken place.

When reflecting on the ethical dilemmas, leaders should consider how the codes of ethics that guide the profession are relevant. With respect to the AACC code, there are five areas of consideration that must be given when addressing a dilemma:

- *Supervisors.* What data, if any, will you be responsible for relaying to your superiors? How will you provide superiors with accurate data? Is interorganizational collaboration needed to facilitate the collection and sharing of data to address this issue? What actions are needed in order to portray all communications accurately? How will you avoid any potential perceptions of conflicting interests or impropriety?
- *Campus Colleagues.* How can you bring the highest standards of excellence to a difficult dilemma? What can you do to address an issue, while still maintaining a culture of collaboration and mutual respect? How can you approach a dilemma as a responsible steward of your authority? What steps/actions will need to be taken to ensure that equity, fairness, and rights are extended to all involved when an issue arises?
- *Students.* What role or considerations, if any, do students play in a dilemma? Does a dilemma have any ramifications for creating an academic environment where learning is not inhibited by harassment, discrimination, or abuse? Are any issues regarding the support of existing programs raised in this issue?
- *Institutions of Education.* Does a dilemma affect any current, potential, or future relationships with other educational institutions? What role should you play, if any, in open and candid dialogues between institutions of higher education?
- *Greater Community.* How can you address an issue with the best interests of the local community at heart? What policy or laws, if any, should be taken into consideration?

Ethical Paradigms

While the nature of these questions may provide thought-provoking considerations, the codes that provoke these questions are merely one facet of the ethical toolkit of leaders. As a result, ethical leaders must recognize that these codes serve one primary function: establishing standards for practice. Ethical codes, in and of, themselves are not enough to govern ethical decision. When making decisions, leaders must be cognizant of the ethical paradigms from which they view the world. They must also consider other paradigms which may shed additional light on approaching ethical decision-making processes. *Ethical Paradigms*—is defined as an ethical lens or point of view that individuals use to view the world and respond to dilemmas. While there are a number of ethical paradigms in existence (e.g., utilitarianism, categorical imperative, communitarianism, altruism, virtue approach, common good approach[6]), the focus here is on ethical paradigms which have been developed specifically for educational leaders and reflect elements of the paradigms above.

Shapiro and Stefkovich (2005) espouse that there are four primary ethical paradigms that can aid educational leaders in the decision-making process, which include: "the ethics of justice, critique, care, and the profession" (p. 7). Individuals can have an inclination towards certain paradigms over others. In explicating this point, Shapiro and Stefkovich note that religious individuals may be disposed towards specific principles such as compassion or empathy; therefore, favoring the ethics of care. By learning about these paradigms, leaders can examine which ethical paradigms they lean towards, and become attuned to other paradigms, so they can use one or multiple paradigms when approaching decision making.

As noted by Shapiro & Stefkovich (2005), educational leaders who employ the *ethic of justice* view the world through, place trust in, and make decisions from the "rule of law and the more abstract concepts of fairness, equity, and justice" (p. 13). From this standpoint, while leaders follow the "rule of law," there is a belief that laws will improve over time (Delgado, 1995). Maxcy (2002) situates the ethical concept of justice within the work of John Rawls, who equated the notion of justice to that of fairness. Rawls advocates addressing dilemmas by discarding

---

[6] For discussions of these alternative paradigms see: Wallin, D. L. (2007). Ethical leadership: The role of the president. In D. M. Hellmich (ed.)., *Ethical leadership in the community college: Bridging theory and daily practice* (pp. 33–45). Bolton, MA: Anker Publishing Company. Velasquez, M., Moberg, D., Meyer, M. J., Shanks, T., McLean, M. R., DeCosse, D., André, C., & Hanson, K. O. (2009). *A framework for thinking ethically*. Santa Clara, CA: Markkula Center for Applied Ethics.

of all presuppositions. From this position (which he called the veil of ignorance), Rawls notes that decisions should be made from the lens of universal liberty, equity, and opportunity. Rawls's idea has its origins from the philosophical views of Aristotle, Rousseau, Dewey, and others who placed an emphasis on the importance of society rather than individual persons. Thus, these philosophers advocate that individuals should abide within the confines of the community order for the betterment of all (Shapiro & Gross, 2008). Due to this focus on being attuned to the needs, operations, and importance of society, "ethical issues such as due process and privacy rights are often balanced against the need for civility and the good of the majority" (Shapiro & Stefkovich, 2005, p. 13).

Leader's who view the world through the *ethic of critique* are highly critical of the ethic of justice. In general, they believe that inherent within this paradigm are social structures which subjugate individuals based upon race, class, gender, and other factors (Caldwell, Shapiro, & Gross, 2007; Shapiro & Stefkovich, 2005). The ethic of critique is rooted in critical theory. According to McLaren (2003), critical theory assumes that "men and women are essentially unfree and inhabit a world rife with contradictions and asymmetries of power and privilege" (p. 69). Thus, critical theorists examine how power is created and maintained in society. In like manner, those employing the ethic of critique examine dilemmas through an appraisal of law, policy, and structures as well as the courses of action that led to their enactment. The focus of this critique is on uncovering hidden and unspoken values that lead to inequity (Shapiro & Stefkovich, 2005).

Leaders who employ the *ethic of care* paradigm—focus on "the consequences of [their] decisions and actions" (Caldwell, Shapiro, & Gross, 2007). Concepts such as compassion, understanding, and trust undergird this ethic. When addressing dilemmas from this paradigm, leaders are concerned with supporting, affirming, and empowering the disadvantaged. The ethic of care emerges from feminism (Shapiro & Stefkovich, 2005) and is a critical assessment of the ethic of justice, which is viewed as the prevailing patriarchal paradigm (Caldwell Shapiro, & Gross, 2007). Leaders who use this paradigm are encouraged to approach decision making by empowering, hearing, and reflecting upon the needs of all groups (Shapiro & Stefkovich, 2005).

The *ethic of profession* was developed by Joan Shapiro and Jacqueline Stefkovich. The purpose of the ethic is to address ethical frames situated within a given field. They note that leaders should approach dilemmas with several concepts in mind: (a) the codes specific to their profession, as informed by their experiential knowledge in the field; (b) their personal ethical lens, based upon their own lived realities; (c) the needs and expectations of the local community;

(d) codes specific to professional organizations and association in the field; (e) the standards of those within the leaders' professional communities; and (f) placing primary focus on the needs of students. While certain aspects of this approach, such as considering professional codes, may seem to be in alignment with the ethic of justice, this approach is more complex in that many concepts are considered as well (Shapiro & Stefkovich, 2005).

These four lenses (four primary ethical paradigms) can enable leaders to analyze ethical dilemmas better. They serve to prompt four distinct ways of thinking about issues that arise. They also provide for specific lines of questioning, which can aid leaders in addressing a specific dilemma, as well as other dilemmas that they face. Below are questions associated with each paradigm:

- *The Ethic of Justice*—What regulatory guidelines (e.g., laws, codes, policies) are in place that should be considered as part of this dilemma? Is one regulatory guideline more pertinent than others? Are these guidelines just? Should they be employed? If so, how? If not, is this exception appropriate and what are the ramifications? How do all these considerations relate to the importance of community rather than the individual? (Caldwell, Shapiro, & Gross, 2007; Shapiro & Stefkovich, 2005).
- *The Ethic of Critique*—What led to the enactment of the "rule of law"? Who played a role in their development? What voices were absent or powerless during their enactment? What social structures do these laws uphold? Who gains from these structures? Who do they disadvantage or oppress? (Caldwell, Shapiro, & Gross, 2007; Shapiro & Stefkovich, 2005).
- *The Ethic of Care*—How will the decisions made affect all groups and constituencies? Who will gain from the decisions made? Who will be disadvantaged by the decisions? What are the long-term implications of the decisions? To what degree should one reciprocate support received from others? (Caldwell, Shapiro, & Gross, 2007; Shapiro & Stefkovich, 2005).
- *The Ethic of Profession*—What guidelines do professional codes have for addressing this dilemma? How would those within the profession approach this dilemma? What would the local community want? What would be a student-centered approach to this dilemma? How should personal ethical codes be taken into account? How does experiential knowledge inform this issue? Taking all these questions into account,

what is my professional conclusion? (Caldwell, Shapiro, & Gross, 2007; Shapiro & Stefkovich, 2005).

Although leaders gravitate towards certain paradigms that are attuned to their views, perspectives, and practices over others, it is critical that leaders make an effort to be inclusive of the four paradigms (e.g., ethic of justice, ethic of critique, ethic of care, ethic of profession) in leading their respective community colleges. It will enable them to approach complex issues from a comprehensive standpoint. Armed with these four paradigms, as well as the code of ethics which guides leadership in the community colleges, leaders are better poised to make thoughtful ethical decisions. The following ethical decision-making models are presented to assist community college leaders in the process of decision making. The models are enhanced by the critical questions, which are derived from codes of ethics and ethical paradigms.

Ethical Decision-Making Models

There are many approaches that can be taken to engage in decision making from an ethical standpoint. As such, we will describe three ethical decision-making models: (a) the community college president and trustee model developed by Anderson & Davies (2000); (b) a general ethical decision-making model from the Markkula Center for Applied Ethics (Markkula, 2009; Velasquez et al., 2009); and (c) a variation of the Nevarez & Wood Leadership Case Study Model, presented in the Preface. Ethical decision-making models are tools and processes that can be used to gauge and inform leaders on how to resolve ethical dilemmas.

Anderson & Davies Model

Anderson & Davies (2000) identify six steps to be taken by community college presidents and trustees to address dilemmas. They note that these steps are "nonlinear" and "multidimensional" in nature (p. 726). The following steps comprise their model:

1. "Identifying the Ethical Dilemma"—When engaging in ethical decision making, the authors suggest that leaders begin by identifying the problem or problems at hand. They note that this step is vital since ethical codes may provide little insight or direction, or may even conflict on

how to address the issues being faced (p. 718).

2. "Gathering Facts, Self-Monitoring, and Consulting"—After identifying the problem(s), leaders are to gather information pertinent to the case. Then, leaders should consider their perspective on what is the right or wrong course of action. After this, leaders should consult a colleague who is removed from this dilemma (p. 719).

3. "Asking Important Questions"—Next, Anderson and Davies state that leaders should consider questions in four areas: (a) their personal feelings about the dilemma; (b) additional information related to the potential impact of the decision on individuals, community, and legislative representatives. Also, prior actions by other leaders in similar positions should be taken into account; (c) internal and external political ramifications of the dilemma and potential decisions; and (d) guidelines provided by ethical codes (p. 720).

4. "Creating Alternative Courses of Action"—After asking important questions, leaders should consider different courses of actions that could be taken to address the dilemma (p. 722).

5. "Evaluating the Alternatives"—After considering different courses of actions, leaders should evaluate what is the best approach to resolving the conflict. This evaluation should include attention to ethics, the law, values, and motivations (p. 722).

6. "Implementing the Course of Action by Moral Follow-Through and Virtue Ethics"—The last step of ethical decision making involves leaders implementing a course of action that is grounded in one's moral compass and guided by virtuous characteristics (p. 725).

Markkula Center Model

Velasquez et al., (2009) espouses a five-stage ethical decision-making model. The authors note that ethical decisions are arrived at through "a trained sensitivity to ethical issues and a practiced method for exploring the ethical aspects of a decision and weighing the considerations that should impact our choice of a course of action" (Para. 15). Their stages are as follows:

1. "Recognize an Ethical Issue"—Leaders should consider how a decision could impact individuals or groups. Examination of alternatives as well as whether the alternatives are good or bad is needed. An assessment should be made about whether the issue is a matter of law, efficiency, or some-thing else (Markkula, 2009, p. 2).

2. "Get the Facts"—In order to decide whether information is available to make a decision, individuals must examine known facts and identify what is unknown. Identification of stakeholders, solicitation of their opinions, and analyzing who has a stake in the decision is needed (Markkula, 2009, p. 2).

3. "Evaluate Alternative Actions"—Individuals must consider multiple alternatives or courses of actions to resolving the dilemma. The following questions should be considered: (a) which alternatives afford the best outcome with the least damage? (b) how can the rights of all who are involved be honored? (c) which approach provides for the most equitable outcome? (d) is the best interest of the greater community being taken into account? and (e) what alternative mirrors my ideal values? (Markkula, 2009, p. 2).

4. "Make a Decision and Test It"—Determine which approach provides for the best possible outcome and would be considered respectable if made public (Markkula, 2009, p. 2)

5. "Act and Reflect on the Outcome"—After a decision is made, enact the decision with the concern for all interested parties. Also, evaluate the outcome and identify what was learned.

Nevarez & Wood Leadership Framework

The Nevarez & Wood Leadership Case Study Framework can be modified to serve as a framework for ethical decision making. Only slight modifications are needed. Rather than focusing on leadership/administrative models and transformation-data-driven decision making, these approaches become the conceptual underpinning of the model. With this in mind, the foundation of the six-step process remains the same.

1. Assume the role of the leader, administrator, or both.
2. Examine the dilemma and develop relevant information in accordance with:

   - Setting—provide contextual factors describing the characteristics of the location
   - Key Characters/Groups—Who are the central figures/groups involved in the dilemma? What role does each play?
   - Special Circumstances—What is/are the X factor(s)? What additional elements need to be considered in solving the dilemma?

3. Identify underlying problem(s): State the problem(s) clearly and concisely. In identifying the problem(s), refer to information collected in
steps 1, 2, and 3. This will allow you to give specific direction to resolving the dilemma.
4. Analyze problems through multiple approaches. Leaders should view
the dilemma through ethical paradigms (e.g., ethic of justice, ethic of
critique, ethic of care, ethic of profession) and identify possible resolutions to the dilemma.
5. Refer to steps 1–4 in identifying an overall resolution to the case.

The above models have several aspects in common (see Table 1). They all engage
in: (a) problem(s) identification; (b) gathering data; (c) conceptualizing and
evaluating potential courses of action(s); and (d) employing the appropriate
action(s). Armed with one or more of these decision-making models, or at least
understanding the steps they have in common, leaders possess the knowledge
necessary to evaluate ethical dilemmas.

In summary, approaching ethical dilemmas armed with codes of ethics, ethical paradigms, and ethical decision-making models identified in this chapter can
enable leaders to consider a wider array of factors, approaches, and outcomes.

Table 1 Similarities in Approaching Ethical Decision Making

Common steps	Anderson & Davies (2000)	Markkula, 2009; Velasquez et al., 2009	Nevarez & Wood Leadership case study framework
Problem(s) identification	Identify the ethical dilemma (step 1)	Recognize the issue (step 1)	Identify underlying problem(s) (step 4)
Gather data	Gathering facts, self-monitoring, and consulting (step 2)	Get the facts (step 2)	Examine the dilemma and develop relevant information (step 2)
Conceptualize and evaluate potential courses of action	Creating alternative courses of action (step 4); evaluating the alternatives (step 5)	Evaluate alternative actions (step 3)	Analyze problems through multiple approaches (step 4)
Employ the appropriate action(s)	Implementing the course of action by moral follow-through and virtue ethics (step 6)	Make a decision and test it (step 4); Act and reflect on the outcome (step 5)	Identify an overall resolution to the case (step 5)

We suggest that leaders become familiar with the codes of ethics that guide their profession. This should occur prior to assuming a leadership position; or, for those who are currently in leadership positions, this should occur immediately. As previously noted, these codes will provide a general understanding of the "standards of behavior" which guide the profession. Once confronted with ethical dilemmas, leaders should employ an ethical decision-making framework such as those identified by: Anderson & Davies, the Markkula Center, and Nevarez & Wood. At the very least, leaders can use the common steps among these models identified above (see Table 1) to approach dilemmas. When leaders reach the stage in each respective model that calls for them to *conceptualize and evaluate potential courses of action*, they should analyze the issue from multiple ethical paradigms (e.g., justice, critique, care, profession). As noted by Velasquez et al., (2009), once leaders determine a course of action, they should be reflective of the process, decision(s), and outcome(s), this will allow them to improve ethical decision making in future contexts.

Case Study

The following case study provides you with an ethical dilemma which will allow leaders to use the ethical tools provided in this chapter (e.g., codes of ethics, ethical paradigms, ethical decision-making models), to analyze and find a resolution to the case. Pay particular attention to analyzing the case study from multiple ethical paradigms (e.g., ethic of justice, critique, care, profession).

Mark G. Edelstein, President
Lakes Region Community College
Laconia, New Hampshire

The Problem Student

Background

McClain Community College (MCC) is a large suburban institution with a long-standing reputation for academic quality and high transfer rates.

Because of its reputation, it draws a diverse student body from throughout the region. In fact, many students drive by other colleges to attend MCC. The college offers its 25,000 students a broad array of technical and liberal arts programs and is especially known for its outstanding programs in science and math. The proximity of a major urban center and a large, prestigious research university has enabled the college to attract a particularly talented and well-qualified faculty. The college employs almost 300 full-time faculty and hundreds of additional part-timers.

Faculty members have a tradition of strong leadership and extensive involvement in college decision making. However, this involvement has not led to a particularly "collegial" environment. Many faculty members are suspicious of college administrators and believe that the role of administration should be extremely limited. The large faculty senate and the faculty union work very closely together to maintain the faculty's sense of empowerment.

A new president was appointed to MCC five years ago and a new academic vice president four years ago. Both have attempted to move the college, which has become very traditional in its outlook, into a more innovative mode. The introduction of new technologies, the expansion of distance education, and the development of a more flexible and varied course schedule have all raised concerns among the faculty. Talk about the need for change in higher education has threatened some of the faculty and made them feel that their current efforts are not sufficiently appreciated.

Statement of the Problem

You are the college president and have recently been informed by your academic vice president of a case in which a member of the math department has inappropriately changed the final grade she awarded to a student in the previous semester. The faculty member, Dr. Simms, is the former chair of the math department and a very highly regarded teacher. Her reason for changing the student's grade from a "C" to an "A" is that she felt harassed and intimidated by the student and believed that the only way she could get him to stop contacting her was to accede to his demands for a better grade. The academic vice president reviewed the student's quiz and test scores for the semester, and it was clear that he had not earned a grade higher than a "C."

The student, David, is a young man in his early twenties, who has come to the attention of the vice president for student services on several occasions. While some faculty members have been able to work quite well with David, others, particularly women, have complained about his odd intensity and erratic behavior. This is the second course that David has taken with Dr. Simms. Dr. Simms has spoken on a number of occasions with the vice president for student services about her discomfort with this student. David has monopolized her office hours, written, emailed, and called her frequently both in her office and at her home. While he has not physically threatened nor sexually harassed her, Dr. Simms has complained about his obsessiveness and other behaviors she considers "paranoid."

The vice president has called David into her office twice and warned him about inappropriate contacts with Dr. Simms. After each discussion, his behavior improves for a time but eventually reverts. The vice president believes that David has "psychological problems," but that he has broken no rules or regulations and can no more be excluded from a particular class than could a person with a physical disability. She believes that a large, open-access institution such as MCC will always have a certain number of people with psychological or behavioral problems and that the college needs to be as tolerant as possible. Dr. Simms, on the other hand, feels that the college has not fulfilled its responsibility to protect her from what she perceives as a threat.

The president of the Faculty Senate and the president of the Faculty Union have both dropped by your office to discuss the issue of the grade change, which has become public knowledge. They advise you that any type of disciplinary action against a respected senior faculty member would be received quite badly. The current math chair informs you that a letter is being drafted by the department in unanimous support of Dr. Simms. The academic vice president is sympathetic to Dr. Simms, but feels that he must reverse her grade change and that the college must take some formal action to point out that the change of grade was a lapse of professional ethics. He believes that the academic integrity of the institution requires that some action be taken.

References

American Association of Community Colleges (2005). Recommended code of ethics of CEOs of community colleges. Washington, DC: AACC. Retrieved August 28, 2009, from: http://www.aacc.nche.edu/About/Positions/Pages/ps11102005.aspx

Anderson, S. K., & Davies, T. G. (2000), An ethical decision-making model: A necessary tool for community college presidents and boards of trustees. *Community College Journal of Research and Practice*, 24, 711–727.

Brown, M. E., Treviño, L. K., & Harrison, D. (2005). Ethical leadership: A social learning perspective for construct development and testing. *Organizational Behavior and Human Decision Processes*, 97, 117–134.

Brown, M. E., & Treviño, L. K. (2006). Ethical leadership: A review and future directions. *The Leadership Quarterly*, 17, 595–616.

Caldwell, C., Shapiro, J. P., & Gross, S. J. (2007). Ethical leadership in higher education admission: Equality vs. equity. *Journal of College Admission*, 14–19.

Community College Week (2003). Kansas college gives first 'xf' grade to plagiarist. *Community College Week* (December 8).

Davis, G. (2003–04). Ethics: An educational imperative. *The Community College Journal* (December/January), 74(3), 6–9.

Davis, G. W. (2007a). Why presidents and trustees should care about ethics. In D. M. Hellmich (ed.). *Ethical leadership in the community college: Bridging theory and daily practice* (pp. 46–60). Bolton, MA: Anker Publishing Company.

Davis, G. W. (2007b). A guide to ethical decision-making by presidents and boards. In D. M. Hellmich (ed.). *Ethical leadership in the community college: Bridging theory and daily practice* (pp. 154–165). Bolton, MA: Anker Publishing Company.

Delgado, R. (1995). *Critical race theory: The cutting edge*. Philadelphia, PA: Temple University Press.

Exley, R. (2003–04). Morality across the curriculum. *The Community College Journal* (December/January), 74(3), 10–13.

Lambert, S. (2005). We must promote academic integrity: Now. *Community College Week* (February 28), 17(15), 4–5.

Maesschalck, J. (2004). The impact of new public management reforms on public servants' ethics: Towards a theory. *Public Administration* (June), 82(2), 465–489.

Markkula (2009). *Making an ethical decision*. Santa Clara, CA: Markkula Center for Applied Ethics.

Maxcy, S. J. (2002). *Ethical school leadership*. Lanham, MD: The Scarecrow Press.

McLaren, P. (2003). Critical pedagogy: A look at the major concepts. In A. Darder., M. Baltodano., & R. D. Torres (Eds.). *The critical pedagogy reader* (pp. 69–96). New York: Routledge.

Reynolds, J. M. (1998). Fired professor says Cal. Community college enrolls "phantom students." *The Chronicle of Higher Education*.

Shapiro, J. P., & Gross, S. J. (2008). *Ethical educational leadership in turbulent times: (Re)solving moral dilemmas*. New York: Lawrence Erlbaum Associates.

Shapiro, J. P., & Stefkovich, J. A. (2005). *Ethical leadership and decision making in education: Applying theoretical perspectives to complex dilemmas* (2nd ed.). Mahwah, NJ: Lawrence Erlbaum Associates.

Starratt, R. (2004). *Ethical leadership*. San Francisco, CA: Jossey-Bass.

Strike, K. A., & Ternasky, P. L. (1993). *Ethics for professionals in education: Perspectives for preparation and practice*. New York: Teachers College Press.

Sullivan, L. (2001). Four generations of community college leadership. *Community College Journal of Research & Practice* (September), 25(8), 559–571.

Swanger, D. (2002). Ethics: The Elephant on the Table. *Community College Week* (November 25), 15(8), 5.

Vaughan, G. (1992). *Dilemmas of leadership: Decision making and ethics in the community college.* San Francisco, CA: Jossey-Bass Publishers.

Velasquez, M., Moberg, D., Meyer, M. J., Shanks, T., McLean, M. R., DeCosse, D., André, C., & Hanson, K. O. (2009). *A framework for thinking ethically.* Santa Clara, CA: Markkula Center for Applied Ethics. Retrieved June 10, 2009, from: http://www.scu.edu/ethics/practicing/decision/framework.html

Wanat, T. (1996). College president resigns after his resume is questioned. *The Chronicle of Higher Education* (February).

Weiler, A. (2004). Using technology to take down plagiarism. *Community College Week* (March 15), 4–5.

Wills, E. (2005). Basketball scandal claims president. *The Chronicle of Higher Education* (August), 51, 48. Retrieved on June 10, 2009, from: *http://chronicle.com/weekly/v51/i48/48a02402.htm*

Wu, S. (2006). Community college's ex-chief is convicted. *The Chronicle of Higher Education* (October), 53, 10. Retrieved on June 10, 2009, from: http://chronicle.com/weekly/v53/i10/10a02903.htm

Zun, W., May, D. R., & Avolio, B. J. (2004). The impact of ethical leadership behavior on employee outcomes: The roles of psychological empowerment and authenticity. *Journal of Leadership & Organizational Studies*, 11(1), 16–26

CHAPTER SIX

FACULTY IN THE COMMUNITY COLLEGE

This chapter focuses on faculty in the community college. Specific attention is given to three areas: (a) faculty demographics (e.g., full time vs. part-time faculty, tenure status, teaching load, degree status, rank, salary, and job satisfaction); (b) faculty preparation and development programs; and (c) the current status of faculty diversity and the benefits of diversification.

When reading this chapter, consider the following questions:

- Do faculty trends affect the overall success of the community college? If so, how? What action should be taken (if any) in addressing the current status of community college faculty?
- What is the status and role of faculty preparation and development programs? Is there a need for these programs? If so, why?
- What are the benefits (if any) of faculty diversity? What role (if any) should leaders play in the faculty diversification process?

Faculty members are the pillars of community colleges, as they play multiple roles in developing, sustaining, and driving the vision of the community college. Their hard work and dedication has allowed these institutions to survive and thrive over the past century. This is indicative of the exponential institutional growth and student enrollment, which has resulted in the development of nearly 1,200 institutions serving more than 11.7 million students (AACC, 2009). As a result, the community college has become a dominant and integral force within the nation's postsecondary educational system. The critical role played by community colleges and subsequently faculty members will become even more evident over the coming decades, as nearly a million more credit students will enroll in community colleges by 2017 if current enrollment growth rates remain constant.[1]

---

[1] We derived this projection based upon growth patterns that occurred during the preceding decade (1997–2007).

Faculty have influenced this growth through firsthand contact with prospective students; serving as mentors, role models, and advisors to students; and maintaining an institutional reputation of quality. The following points serve as a snapshot of reasons why it is important for leaders to consider the status and supportive structures needed to sustain faculty in the community college:

- *Mission.* Faculty members serve to drive and realize the mission of the community college (e.g., opportunity, access, serving local community needs). Primarily, this is accomplished through the faculty's engagement in teaching and service. The role faculty play in facilitating the mission has significant importance to the values of equity, social justice, and change. These values in turn, reflect a unique focus on providing all community members with an opportunity to educate themselves. It also benefits both the individual and the public. Individuals who hold a college degree tend to earn more money, have enhanced job alternatives, tend to be happier in their careers, and become critical consumers. Society benefits from increased human capital, tax base, and greater levels of civic engagement (Davila & Mora, 2007; Futrell, 1999; Vernez & Mizell, 2001).

- *Informal Leadership.* Faculty members serve as informal leaders within the community college. Through their efforts in the faculty senate, on departmental, college, and institutional committees, leading institutional initiatives, and scholarly service, they are integral to campus leadership. The leadership capacity of community colleges has the potential of minimizing the community colleges vision. Faculty serve to fill impending leadership voids, especially considering that 84.4 percent of presidents have taught full-time or part-time in the community college prior to assuming their posts (Duree, 2007). Through these experiences, faculty members serve as a major source of prospective leaders.

- *Collegiality.* Many colleges operate through a system of shared governance. This process of consensus can lead to dissonance between faculty and campus administration since interests, viewpoints, and needs vary across groups. This dissonance, if not addressed, can lead to a disenfranchised organization where institutional needs are not being met. This statement is made in light of the influence faculty have on the overall governance structure of community colleges. For example, the Almanac

(2008–09a) reports that college presidents identified faculty as the top constituent group which poses challenges to their leadership. Faculty play the role of questioning policies and processes that ensure equitable practices are being adhered to by campus administration, alumni, legislators, community members, and so on. For the overall well-being of community college, it is critical that there is a mutual sense of respect and understanding between faculty and administrators to foster an environment of collegiality.

- *Support.* Leaders should be attuned to faculty needs, levels of satisfaction, and issues. By doing so, they will be better able to provide support for faculty members. In particular, faculty members need to be provided with instructional resources, adequate salaries, office space, technological resources, and professional development that facilitate their success in the classroom. This has significant implications for the overall academic success of students, which is the central benchmark used to gauge the institutional failure or achievement.

- *Durability.* Faculty members are the pillars of their institutions, often outlasting even the longest of administrations. As a result, faculty members serve as a repository of institutional culture and memory. This enhanced understanding of policies, personalities, governance structures, resources, and services often enables them to better aid students, junior faculty, and community members in navigating through the overall functioning of the community college. While durability has its benefits, sometimes seasoned faculty can be detrimental to organizational change within the college. This can be attributed to a reverence for old behaviors, practices, and policies that may no longer be in the best interest of students and the institution.

- *Institutional Reputation.* Faculty members are the first line of communication between the local community and their respective institutions. Institutional perceptions are shaped by faculty members' success in multiple areas (e.g., teaching, service, community engagement, scholarly contributions). These areas have important implications for the public's perception of the institution, which in turn influences community support for the institution (e.g., bond measures, alumni donations). The level of support provided by the public is one factor which determines the quality and value of the institution. This has become increasingly important as federal and state funding for community colleges continues to diminish.

In consideration of the integral role faculty play in community colleges as outlined above, it is important to understand their overall status (e.g., demographic trends, issues, contributions). By doing so, leaders will be better able to facilitate faculty retention and success in postsecondary education.

Faculty Demographics

The following faculty demographic data focuses on tenure status, teaching load, degree status, rank, and salary within community colleges. For additional detailed information on faculty demographics (e.g., race/ethnicity, gender, age), see Chapter 7 on *Demographic Trends*.

In 2007, there were 358,925 total faculty members in the community colleges, representing a 23.6 percent increase from 1997 (see Figure 1). Of these faculty members, the vast majority are part-timers (68.5 percent). Data illustrates that the percentage of full-time faculty is decreasing. For instance, in 1997, 45.6 percent of community colleges' faculties were full-timers. By 2007, only 31.4 percent of faculty members were full-time. Thus, full-time faculty representation declined by 14.2 percent in only ten years. Also on a downward trajectory are the percentages of tenured/tenure-track faculty. In 1997, 21 percent of full-time faculty were either tenured or on tenure track. By 2007, the percentage of full-time faculty who were tenured or on tenure track decreased to 18 percent, a three percent decline (Digest of Education Statistics, 1990; 2008).

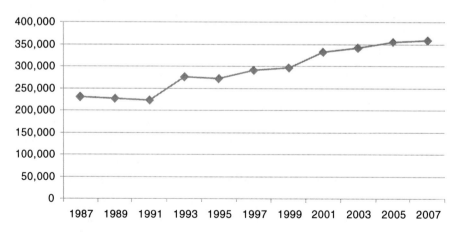

Figure 1 Total Number of Community College Faculty, 1987 to 2007
Source: Digest of Education Statistics (1990–2008). *Employees in institutions of higher education, by primary occupation, employment status, sex, and by type and control of institution.* Washington, DC: National Center for Education Statistics.

The primary activity of community college faculty is teaching. Provasnik and Planty, (2008) in an analysis of 2003 data from the National Study of Postsecondary Faculty (NSOPF), compare the main activities of faculty in community colleges, public four-year universities, and private four-year universities. In the community college, 89 percent of faculty report that their main activity is teaching; this contrasts with public and private four-year faculty who report teaching as their primary activity at 63 percent and 72 percent respectively. While 15 percent of public four-year universities and 9 percent of private four-year universities report research as an important, main activity, it is not at the community college, where less than 1 percent of the faculty report engaging in research. This shows clear differences in faculty responsibilities at two-year and four-year institutions. When teaching responsibilities are disaggregated by time status at the community college level (e.g., part-time faculty, full-time faculty), the distribution of faculty by credit hours taught reveals a heavy workload for full-time faculty. Nearly 60 percent of full-time community college faculty teach 15 credits or more as compared to only 9.5 percent of part-timers. In contrast, part-time faculty have smaller workloads, with 41.3 percent teaching less than 4 units (see Figure 2) (U.S. Department of Education, 2004).

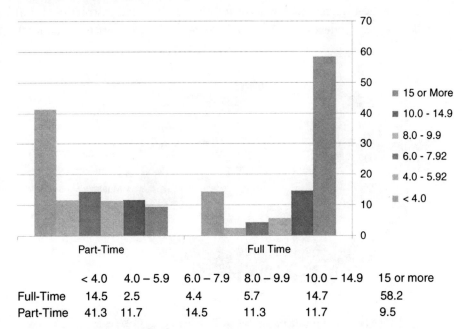

	< 4.0	4.0 – 5.9	6.0 – 7.9	8.0 – 9.9	10.0 – 14.9	15 or more
Full-Time	14.5	2.5	4.4	5.7	14.7	58.2
Part-Time	41.3	11.7	14.5	11.3	11.7	9.5

Figure 2 Distribution of Full-Time and Part-Time Faculty by Number of Credits Taught, 2003
Source: U.S. Department of Education (2004). National Center for Education Statistics, National Study of Postsecondary Faculty (NSOPF: 04). Note: Data presented in the 2008 Digest.

Leaders should be cautious in interpreting the above data for two reasons: (1) a large percentage of full-time faculty members are unsatisfied with their teaching load. According to the Chronicle of Higher Education Almanac (2008–09b), only 54% of full-time two-year college faculty report being satisfied or very satisfied with their teaching load; and (2) a high percentage of faculty teach at multiple institutions. JBL Associates (2008) notes "part-time/adjunct faculty members in public two-year colleges teach less than half of the average number of classes taught by full-time tenured and tenure-track faculty members. It is important to note that this is the teaching load for a single institution and does not take into account the fact that a part-time/adjunct faculty member may teach at multiple institutions and carry a heavier teaching load as a result" (p. 5).

The degree status of community college faculty is best understood, since the vast majority of faculty time is devoted to instruction at the general education level (Twombly & Townsend, 2008). While approximately 58 percent of public and 48 percent private four-year faculty possess doctoral degrees, the vast majority of community college faculty do not (NSOPF, 2004). Only 17.9 percent of the faculty in community colleges possess doctoral degrees. In fact, nearly the same percentage of faculty merely possess a bachelor's degree or less (17.2 percent). The highest degree held by most full-time faculty and instructional staff in public two-year colleges is the master's degree (63.3 percent) (see Figure 3).

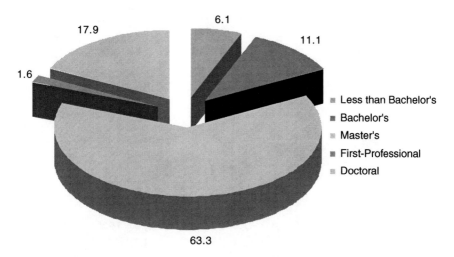

Figure 3 Full-time Faculty & Instructional Staff in Two-Year Public Colleges by Highest Degree
Source: Digest of Education Statistics (2008). *Table 252. Full-time and part-time faculty and instructional staff in degree-granting institutions, by type and control of institution and selected characteristics: Fall 1992, fall 1998, and fall 2003.* Washington, DC: National Center for Education Statistics.

This data has important implications for the leadership pipeline, since most community college presidents (88.4 percent) possess doctoral degrees (Weisman & Vaughan, 2006). In fact, the doctorate is widely viewed as a baseline requirement for the presidency. As fewer faculty members are hired for tenure-track positions, the market for community college faculty has become increasingly competitive. Thus, the percentage of faculty with master's degrees or less may decrease, except in those fields where higher degrees are not currently being awarded (heating, ventilation, and air conditioning, trades, cosmetology). Despite this possibility, Cohen & Brawer (2003) note that doctorate holders may not be the best fit for teaching in community colleges as they "have been prepared as researchers not teachers…[and] they expect fewer teaching hours and higher salaries" (p. 78)

The higher the degree status, rank, and tenure at the institution the more community college faculty members earn. This is indicative of full-professors earning the highest average salary at $71,910. Other faculty members' average earnings were as follows: associate professors ($58,708); assistant professors ($51,329); instructors ($44,174); and lecturers ($48,338). This data illustrates that assistant professors make only $2,991 more than lecturers (see Figure 4). While lecturers do not generally have service requirements, assistant professors have numerous responsibilities including advising and contributing to their departments, colleges, institution, and community in addition to their teaching loads. However, there are notable salary differences between assistant professor

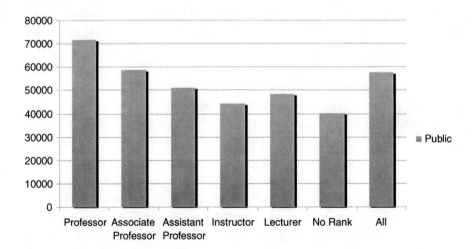

Figure 4 Average Salary for Full-Time Faculty, 2007–2008
Source: Almanac (2008–09c). *Average salaries of full-time faculty members, 2007–08*. Washington, DC: Chronicle of Higher Education.

to associate professor ($7,379) and associate professor to full-professor ($13,202) (Almanac, 2008–09c). Faculty salary data are best contextualized in comparison to administrator salaries with senior leadership receiving, in some case, triple the salary of their faculty members (e.g., chief executive of a single institution, $156,870; executive vice president, $127,721; chief academic officer, $110,151) (Almanac, 2008–09d).[2] Salary disparities become even more evident when one considers that between 1997 and 2007 the percentage of new administrators nearly doubled the growth rate of new full-time tenure-track faculty (AFT, 2009). Faculty–administrators salary differences may explain why only 50.5 percent of community college full-time faculty members report being satisfied or very satisfied with their salaries and benefits (Almanac, 2008–09b).

The data presented above illustrates a number of continuous and emerging challenges facing faculty members in the community colleges. Despite these issues and trends, 81.5 percent of full-time community college faculty report being satisfied or very satisfied with their positions. It is also important to note that 70.4 percent report being satisfied-to-very-satisfied with their social relationships with other faculty members. This is the highest rating for social relationships among all institutional types (e.g., private four-years, public four-years). One of the key benefits in faculty feeling a sense of connectedness to their colleagues is improved collegiality, retention, and commitment to organization. There are additional aspects of the job, which further illustrate faculty satisfaction. In some areas, faculty members appear to be very satisfied (e.g., autonomy and independence, professional relationships with other faculty members, opportunities to develop new ideas), while in other areas, faculty opinions are split (e.g., relationship with the administration, opportunity for scholarly pursuits, and prospects for career advancement). This illustrates the multidimensional satisfaction of faculty across various aspects of their jobs (see Table 1) (Almanac, 2008–09b).

The data presented in this section is important in that it: (a) informs leaders about faculty status in accordance with their salaries, workload, rank, and satisfaction; (b) provides administrators with the data necessary to create a system of support for faculty; (c) challenges leaders to expand the capabilities of their personnel, and the organization as a whole, to better meet the needs of their students; and (d) provides leaders with information needed to develop collegiality, solidarity, and mutual respect among campus personnel. One pathway in developing faculty capacity is through faculty preparation and development.

---

[2] Note: administrator salaries reported are for public and private two-year colleges.

Table 1

Aspects of the job	Percentage satisfied or very satisfied
Overall satisfaction	81.5%
Autonomy and independence	80.9%
Professional relationships with other faculty members	82%
Opportunities to develop new ideas	73.4%
Relationship with the administration	60.5%
Opportunity for scholarly pursuits	48.9%
Prospects for career advancement	47.9%

Source: Almanac (2008–09b). *Opinions and attitudes of full-time faculty members.* Washington, DC: The Chronicle of Higher Education.

Faculty Preparation and Development

Community colleges are experiencing tremendous change. As a result, there is a strong need to recruit and prepare community college faculty to transcend the current realities of the profession. New structures, processes, and policies must be considered in order to meet the needs of a changing student population. This need has been made clear, now more than ever, for several reasons:

- *Aging.* As noted in Chapter 7 on *Demographic Trends,* the community college professoriate is aging. In 1987, the percentage of full-time faculty/ instructional staff who were 55 years and older was 22.8 percent. This percent has risen steadily over the years, to 23.8 percent in 1992, 35.3 percent in 1998, and 37.3 percent in 2003 (Digest, 2008). Data also indicates that a large percentage of part-time faculty members (34.8 percent) are 55 years or older (Almanac, 2008–09e). These trends suggest an aging faculty, which leads to increased retirements.
- *Increased Enrollment.* As noted earlier, projections indicate that community college enrollment is on the rise. This trend is not new, nor does it show signs of slowing-down. With rising tuition and fees at four-year colleges and universities, community colleges continue to meet their mission of open access while maintaining affordability. With rising enrollment trends, there were demands to increase new faculty hires, as illustrated between 1997 and 2007 (see Figure 1).
- *Diversity.* An increasing influx of diverse students (e.g., race/ethnicity, gender, age, religious affiliations, sexual orientation), calls for faculty to

have knowledge about student learning styles, issues, and experiences. Possessing such knowledge will better enable faculty to contextualize teaching and learning activities in accordance with the realities of students that they serve. The increasing enrollment trend data indicates the majority of this growth consists of diverse students.

- *Retention.* The unique reasons why students enroll in community colleges (e.g., transfer, skills development, leisure, certification, terminal degree) informs the type of expertise needed by community faculty. In addition, community colleges tend to serve "non-traditional" student populations (e.g., older students, part-time students, veterans). These unique student interests and student groups call for faculty to have specialized expertise specific to the aspirations and needs of the students that they serve. For example, faculty members need to be attuned to the social, emotional, and psychological needs of these populations.

From the early 1900s to the 1960s, community college faculty members came primarily from the ranks of secondary school teachers (Cohen & Brawer, 2003). This trend is understandable considering that many community colleges began as extensions of high schools. For example, in the 1920s 80 percent of community college instructors had high school teaching experience (Eells, 1931). However, as these institutions matured, their ties with K-12 education and the employing of teachers from secondary schools declined. However, "as the number of newly employed instructors decline in the 1970s, the proportion of instructors with prior secondary school experience decline with it" (Cohen & Brawer, 2003, p. 77). There has been a paradigm shift, where now, prior secondary school experience is not primary qualification of new faculty hires. There are growing numbers of faculty coming from graduate programs. Since these programs do not necessarily focus on the unique realities of teaching and learning in the community college, efforts have been made to prepare students for faculty positions, they include:

- *Gradutate Programs.* There are a few graduate-level programs, which focus on preparing students to enter the professoriate at the community college. These programs give specific attention to curricular and pedagogical needs in the community college. They allow students to take graduate-level coursework in the disciplines they desire to teach (e.g., English, mathematics, psychology, communications, child development). In addition to discipline-specific coursework, students also take some classes on the community college (e.g., community college history, community college ethics). After completion of coursework students engage in a practicum/internship in which they gain teaching experience in the community college under the supervision of a faculty member. Some of these programs include: (a) the Doctor of Arts in Community College Education & Master of Arts in Interdisciplinary Studies concentration in Community College Teaching at George Mason University; (b) the Master of Arts in Teaching (MAT) in Community College Instruction at Mississippi State University; and (c) the Masters of Education program with a concentration in Community College Teaching and Learning at the University of Illinois.[3]

- *Post-master's certificate programs.* There are a number of programs (credit and noncredit) designed to train faculty who have already attained their master's degree. Post-master's certificate programs prepare faculty to teach in the community college. These programs provide students with basic information on community colleges and inform them about teaching, curricular, and pedagogical concerns specific to these institutions. Some programs offer a practicum component as well. Some of these programs include: (a) the Post-Master's Certificate in Community College Teaching at Seattle University; (b) the Community College Teaching Certificate at Iowa State University; (c) the Community College Teaching Certificate Program at Central Washington University; d) the Community College Teaching Graduate Certificate Program at the University of North Carolina; and e) the Community College Faculty Preparation Certificate Program at California State University, Sacramento.[4]

- *Internal campus/system programs.* Some campuses and systems operate their own faculty development apprenticeship and internship programs. Often, these programs are designed to increase faculty diversity and/ or faculty within specific disciplines of needs. These programs usually attract master's and doctoral degree holders who lack substantive teaching experience in the community college. These aspiring faculty members

---

[3] http://www.dacce.gmu.edu/programs.html; http://www.distance.msstate.edu/ccs/mat.html; http://education.illinois.edu/hre/online/cctl.htm

[4] http://www2.seattleu.edu/coe/adedm/default.aspx?id=5392;http://www.cclp. hs.iastate.edu/imsep/certificate.shtml;http://www.cwuce.org/cct/;http://online. northcarolina.edu/program.php?id=304;http://www.cce.csus.edu/catalog/course_group_detail. asp?group_number=133&group_version=1

are paired with campus faculty who supervise their classroom teaching. Some examples of these programs include: (a) the Faculty Diversity Internship Program in the Los Rios Community College District; (b) the Faculty Internship Program at San Joaquin Delta College; (c) the Faculty Diversity Internship Program at Hawkeye Community College; (d) the Faculty Internship program at Portland Community College; and (e) the Future Faculty Internship Program at Malcolm X Community College.[5]

Additional modalities of providing prospective and current community college faculty with the skills necessary for teaching exist. These alternative modes include system-wide courses which now serve as substitutes for community college credentialing requirements (e.g., Maricopa Community Colleges Teaching and Learning in the Community College Course); and Specialist programs on community college teaching (e.g., Arkansas State University's Specialist in Community College Teaching).[6]

The programs mentioned above serve a multiplicity of purposes. The primary purpose is to develop prospective and current community college faculty skills in the areas of teaching and learning. These programs provide prospective faculty members with an opportunity to gain valuable teaching experience through a supervised teaching practicum and develop relationships that may lead to future employment and insights to the field from the lenses of current faculty in the profession. For current faculty, the programs provide an opportunity to stay up-to-date on pedagogical teaching and learning theories, framework and philosophies, and a venue to hone their teaching skills; further, graduate-level credit translates into higher earning potential. For all faculty members, these programs serve to increase their knowledge of the diverse students that the community college serves.

Faculty Diversity

As the community college student population continues to become more diverse, there are benefits accrued when diverse faculty are well represented. Primarily,

[5] http://www.losrios.edu/hr/downloads/FDIP%202009–2010/FDIP_2009_2010_Application.pdf; http://www.deltacollege.edu/org/acadsen/facultyinternshipprogram_000.html; http://www.hawkeye.cc.ia.us/employment/facultyDiversityInternProg.aspx; http://www.pcc.edu/about/faculty/interns/; http://members.tripod.com/ffip_csu/

[6] http://www2.astate.edu/a/education/elcse/degrees/community-college-teaching.dot

the points made in the following section focus on women and racial/ethnic faculty; however, we believe that the benefits of these faculty members are relevant to other diverse faculty. In examining higher education institutions in the twenty-first century (an era adequately described as post-affirmative action), there exists a need to consistently analyze the proportional representation[7] of diverse faculty. Gauging the equity of representation affords individuals the opportunity to determine where the nation stands in actualizing national democratic ideals that espouse educational opportunity for all. This notion is directly tied to the mission of the community college in creating access and opportunity for all. Proportional representation is an imperative component of an institution's measure of diversity and inclusivity, and serves as an indicator of an institution's goal of meeting educational equity measures. It is an opportune time for institutions to take advantage of massive faculty retirements by hiring faculty who are reflective of the students that they serve. For instance, Gilroy (2008) states that: "community college faculties are undergoing a massive turnover with many institutions expecting to replace at least one-third of their faculty" as a result of retirements in the coming years (p. 24). For better or worse, new replacements will fall under the category of part-time faculty.

While many postsecondary institutions purport diversity goals that seek to increase representation of diverse faculty, the success of these efforts has been both stagnant and irregular (Carter, 1994). This is especially disconcerting considering the high enrollment growth among diverse students in community colleges (Perna, 2003). Nicholas & Oliver (1994) note that increasing the representation of diverse faculty in community colleges is "the right thing to do" (p. 39). However, it is doubtful that philosophical reasoning alone will produce diversification of the professoriate (Wood, 2008).

Challenges

Pipeline Issues

Literature on community colleges attributes diverse faculty underrepresentation to competition with other colleges and universities over applicants (Knoell, 1994; Manzo, 2000). Another primary reason cited for the dearth of diverse faculty

---

[7] Proportional representation "is a relative numerical or percentage comparison between the racial/ethnic background of students, administrators, teachers [faculty], and other school personnel nationwide" (Nevarez and Wood, 2007, p. 277)

in the community college is an inadequate supply of minority degree holders (Rifkin, 2000). This supply or pipeline argument suggests that colleges and universities around the country are not producing enough master and doctoral degree holders in order to provide a qualified pool of applicants to fill the faculty ranks (Journal of Blacks in Higher Education, 2001). This argument, however, does not take into consideration degree holder trends. Between the 1992–1993 and 2002–2003 academic years, the percentage of degrees awarded per year to minority graduates increased among all ethnic groups: Blacks (+1.9 percent); Hispanics (+1.2 percent); Asian Americans (+ 1.2 percent); and Native Americans (+ 0.1 percent) (see Table 2). Trower & Chait (2002) state that even when one takes into account the low number of diverse doctoral degree holders, the professoriate as a whole is not reflective of these increases. While enrollments for these graduates are not close to reaching proportional representation, the number of masters and doctorates conferred is sufficient to fill faculty openings. Clearly, this lack of proportional representation indicates the presence of a number of intentional and, perhaps, unintentional barriers to hiring highly qualified faculty for these positions.

As noted in Chapter 7 on *Demographic Trends*, most community college faculty do not possess doctoral degrees; however, an examination of master's degree holders in the academic pipeline illustrates a similar theme to doctoral degree recipients. Between the 1992–1993 and 2002–2003 school years, the percentage of diverse master's degree holders increased as follows: African Americans from 5.3 percent to 7.8 percent; Hispanics from 2.9 percent to 4.4 percent; Asian Americans from 3.8 percent to 4.8 percent; and American Indians from 0.4 percent to 0.5 percent. This accounted for a total increase of 5.1 percent

Table 2   Doctoral Degrees Conferred by Race, 1992–1993 to 2002–2003

	Caucasian	Black	Hispanic	Asian-American	Native American	Total
1992–93	26,816	1,350	824	1,578	107	42,132
	(63.6%)	(3.2%)	(2.0%)	(3.7%)	(0.3%)	(100%)
	25,863	2,362	1,457	2,259	185	
2002–03	(56.2%)	(5.1%)	(3.2%)	(4.9%)	(0.4%)	46,024

Source: U.S. Department of Education, National Center for Education Statistics (2005). *Postsecondary Institutions in the United States: Fall 2003 and Degrees and Other Awards Conferred: 2002–03* (NCES 2005–154). U.S. Department of Education (2006). National Center for Education Statistics, Higher Education General Information Survey (HEGIS), "Degrees and Other Formal Awards Conferred" surveys, 1976–77 and 1980–81; and 1988–89 through 2004–05 Integrated Postsecondary Education Data System, "Completions Survey" (IPEDS-C:89–99), and Fall 2000 through Fall 2005.

(U.S. Department of Education, 2005). Despite these increases, diverse faculty representation is not proportionally reflective of master degree awardees.

Hiring

In an examination of recruitment and hiring barriers of diverse faculty in two-year colleges, Opp and Smith (1994) found two primary types of barriers, attitudinal and structural. Attitudinal barriers are viewpoints that are motivated by racism or discrimination, while structural barriers deal with the lack of effort to identify potential diverse candidates. In initiating recruitment efforts, ideologies and group affinities are often significant barriers to diversifying the faculty in community college institutions. Harvey (1994) notes that faculty members serving on hiring committees often choose other individuals who have commonalities with them in terms of educational and life experiences as well as similarities in values. This tendency may result in less faculty diversification depending upon the background of individuals on the hiring committee.

Myths about faculty diversity also have affected the representation of diverse faculty. The perpetuation of these myths impedes efforts in increasing the hiring, retention, and success of diverse faculty. Examples of myths include (among others): (a) highly qualified diverse faculty are at prominent universities and corporations (Peoples & Smith, 2005); (b) diverse faculty are aggressively recruited by four-year universities, which are perceived to be more prestigious (Carter, 1994; Smith & Moreno, 2006); and (c) diverse faculty lack the qualifications necessary for hiring considerations (Nicholas & Oliver, 1994).

Campus Climate

Bower (2002) notes that disaffection and discrimination toward diverse faculty is common in the community college. For example, it is well documented that diverse faculty experience discrimination in course evaluations, especially when they teach courses that focus on issues of diversity. As a result, many diverse faculty members are affected by campus climates that are characterized as prejudicial (Carter, 1994; Harvey, 1994; Owens, Reis, & Hall, 1994; Zamani, 2000) and unsupportive (Johnsrud & Sadao, 1998; Medina & Luna, 2000; Padilla, 1994; Tierney & Bensimon, 1996) which leads to isolation, alienation, and marginalization. These factors (among other issues) create significant levels of dissatisfaction among many diverse community college faculty (Corbin, 1998).

Research suggests that diverse faculty members are less likely to fill full-time posts than their majority counterparts. Kendrick (1995) notes that diverse community college faculty are largely represented in the lower ranks in their institutions. Carter (1994) affirms this fact, noting that Native American, Hispanic, Asian American, and African American faculty are more likely to be "concentrated in lecturer and instructor positions" (p. 10). These placements restrict diverse faculty from becoming fully incorporated into the institutions that they serve. Delgado-Romero et al., (2003) state that faculty of color lie at the bottom of the faculty pyramid. Their analysis reveals that there are more diverse faculty at the rank of instructors, lecturers, and on-tenure-line faculty than tenure-track assistant, associate, or full-time professors.

Benefits

Robertson & Frier (1994) state that emphasis is needed on the distinctive and exclusive advantages that faculty diversity brings to community colleges. This is needed in order to contextualize the aforementioned challenges faced by diverse faculty (e.g., pipeline, hiring, climate issues), which can lead to greater efforts to increase, retain, and ensure the success of diverse faculty. Benefits accrued by community colleges with a well-represented pool of diverse faculty are numerous. Below is a snapshot of diverse faculty benefits.

Role Models/Mentors

Literature on the benefits of diverse faculty in the community college is replete with references to the engagement of faculty as role models and mentors to students (Cain, 1982; Opp, 2002; Opp & Smith, 1994; Owens, Reis, & Hall, 1994; Robertson & Frier 1994). Diverse faculty role models are described as creating and maintaining an affirming atmosphere for diverse students that: (a) enables their academic success (Robertson & Frier, 1994); (b) enhances the overall quality of their education (Cain, 1982); (c) creates aspirations for academic achievement (Opp & Smith, 1994); and (d) provides educational opportunities (Opp, 2002). Diverse faculty role models are critical to student success in that they may be the first and only close contact that diverse students have had with college graduates (Robertson & Frier, 1994). This is due to the high percentages of first-generation college students that many community colleges serve.

Lovell, Alexander, & Kirkpatrick (2002) note that mentoring relationships from diverse faculty members enables students to feel welcome in the college environment by providing visible examples of individuals who have succeeded academically despite barriers common to many first-time college students. Often, diverse faculty possess a unique attentiveness to cultural issues facing diverse students and can communicate, empathize, support, and express value for these students and their lived realities (Manzo, 2000; Valadez, 1994). Often these actions are attributed to their passion for student success and dedication to the mission of student equity (Manzo, 2000). These efforts can lead to high program completion rates for diverse students at the community college (Opp, 2002).

Campus Environment

One primary reason that diverse faculty can influence student achievement is due to their role in creating a hospitable campus climate (Knoell, 1994). Opp (2001) points out that diverse faculty can "contribute to the development of a campus climate that is perceived by prospective students of color as tolerant and accepting of diversity" (p. 83). This belief is echoed by other scholars who describe the environment created by diverse community college faculty as "inviting" (Robertson & Frier, 1994, p. 70); "reducing the level of alienation" (Cain, 1982, p. 23); and "welcoming" (Knoell, 1994, p. 28). Kee (1999), in a survey of 1,450 community college presidents, found that campus climates described as harmonious (essentially campuses with a lack of racial discrimination and which embrace pluralism) were comprised of 60 percent or more of diverse faculty. This study noted that as faculty diversity decreased, so did the description of institutional climate as being harmonious. Similar findings are evident from Licitra (2005) who examined Latino transfer students from the California community college system to four-year universities and noted that the presence of Latino faculty attributed to the creation of a welcoming campus climate.

Global Marketplace

Carter (1994) notes that community college leaders are attempting to "reshape their institutions to be more responsive to major societal shifts that engulf our nation and world" (p. 3). One of these shifts includes the need for community colleges to prepare students to compete in a diverse global marketplace. This environment will require workers who are culturally competent and are able to collaborate and work with diverse cultures and racial/ethnic groups (Chapman, 2001; Kirkpatrick, 2001). Workers who lack the cultural competence needed to compete in this multicultural global community will find it difficult to achieve employment. If hired, they will become liabilities to their organizations (Bucher, 2000; Nevarez & Borunda, 2004). Diverse faculty can aid students and educational institutions in addressing misconceptions, myths, and prejudices that permeate society (Harvey, 1994; Opp & Smith, 1994). By aiding students in debunking discriminatory and biased perceptions of diverse communities, faculty can better prepare students to operate in the global economy (Garcia and Moses, 2000; Umbach, 2006). As a result, increasing the presence of diverse faculty in the community college serves as an avenue to meet the demands of the global marketplace.

Case Study

The chapter began with a review of the current status of faculty demographics, a preview of faculty preparation, and development programs, and concluded with the current status of faculty diversity and benefits of faculty diversification. The specific challenges and opportunities were discussed. The case study that follows chapter content contains many of the contextual elements of this chapter. In analyzing the case study, pay particular attention to how myths, perceptions, and misnomers about faculty, in general, can hinder the practice of leadership in the community college. Also consider how factual information on the status of faculty can lead to a credible resolution.

President & Superintendent Francisco Rodriguez
Mira Costa Community College
Oceanside, California

When Language and College Policies Collide

Background

Lincoln Valley Community College (LVCC) offers a friendly, welcoming atmosphere where excellence is the standard, diversity is celebrated, and students come first. LVCC offers a vibrant intellectual environment with a multicultural student body of 20,000. The college serves a student population composed of 35 percent Hispanic/Latino, 20 percent Asian American, 15 percent African American, 2 percent Native American, 22 percent White, and 6 percent international students. The gender makeup of the campus is 60 percent female and 40 percent male. Despite its size, at LVCC commitment to providing a quality education remains a top priority. As such, students enjoy personalized attention from their professors with a faculty–student ratio of 18:1.

LVCC is launching its first associate's degree program in administration studies. The program is an interdisciplinary degree, a joint venture between the business and government departments. Students enrolled in the program can have a concentration in business/industry or in public affairs. Many entry-level employees have taken advantage of this program in order to meet new university employment requirements and to attain salary increases. The students seeking admission into the administration studies program are highly diverse in terms of race/ethnicity and gender, reflective of the campus student demographic makeup.

The program is the first generalized administration program offered in the district. Its charge is to build the next cadre of visionary leaders. As a result, it has received a great deal of press, even being featured by local television stations. If successful, other district colleges will be offered an opportunity to launch similar programs in the coming years. This program is also unique in that it is the only academic program on campus that has its own placement test. Students who desire to enter the program must take one year of general education courses and pass the test to "officially" be granted formal admittance to the program. The content of the test was informed by core curricular areas (e.g., introduction to business, introduction to government) previously taken by students, and thus serves as a culminating exam to ensure students gained the knowledge necessary to be successful in the program.

Statement of the Problem

You are a tenure-track assistant professor at the college and have been given the opportunity to coordinate the program. This is your first administrative role and you hope that it can serve as a platform to transition into higher levels of academic affairs administration. As a new coordinator, you are striving to implement the placement test, which is scheduled to be administered in one week. The elements of the test include: (a) a timed written examination (students will be given 6 hours to complete an exam designed to be completed in a 3-hour period); (b) students choose in advance whether they will write an examination essay specific to their concentration of choice (e.g., business/industry or public affairs); (c) on-site lunch break allowed (students may bring their own lunch, however lunch will be provided); discussions of examination are prohibited during the break; (d) evaluation rubric shared with students prior to the examination; (e) eight faculty (three assistants, 2 associates, and three full-time faculty) will serve on the placement examination's grading committee; each exam will be read by two faculty members; in the event that these two disagree on the outcome to be assigned, a committee consisting of you and the chairs of the business and government departments will render a final decision; and (f) possible outcomes are: (1) Pass or (2) Fail. If students fail, they must wait one full year to retake the examination.

Michelle King is an older, returning student with a vast amount of practical experience in the field of administration. She is also an English Language Learner (ELL). Currently, she works at the college full time and is well respected by her peers. She has even received the staff member of the year award for her exemplary service to the college. However, due to new requirements for her post, which necessitate (at a minimum) an associate's degree, she is concerned that she will receive a pink slip or be terminated if she does not meet this new requirement. Though she is not required to receive her degree in administration studies, her immediate supervisor has strongly recommended it.

During her first year as a student, Michelle excelled in both her introductory to government and business courses. She is viewed by the faculty as a good student with a track record of getting straight A's in her classes. Upon the completion of her first year of coursework, she has complained extensively about the fairness of the procedures relevant to the placement exam. This sentiment has intensified two weeks prior to the scheduled exam. She feels the timed element of the exam is unfair to ELL students and has been increasingly adamant about requesting that extra time be granted to ELL students. To further complicate matters, a considerable number of part-time faculty members support this demand; however, most tenured/tenure-track faculty do not.

The college has a reputation for meeting the needs of its ELL students, and for many of the students seeking enrollment in the program, this was one of the primary reasons (focus on equity) they sought enrollment in the administration studies program. However, upon you seeking clarity and guidance from the chairs of the government and business departments, and even the provost, it was apparent that existing policies on equity are ambiguous, at best. Accommodations are mandated for disability students and no reference is made to accommodations for ELL students. As the program coordinator, how would you resolve this problem?

References

AACC (2009). *About AACC*. Washington, DC: American Association of Community Colleges. Retrieved September 1, 2009, from: http://www.aacc.nche.edu/About/Pages/default.aspx

AFT (2009). *American academic: The state of the higher education workforce 1997–2007.* NY: American Federation of Teachers. Retrieved November 14, 2009, from: http://www.aftface.org/storage/face/documents/ameracad_report_97–07for_web.pdf

Almanac (2008–09a). *Profile of college presidents 2006: What constituent groups provide the greatest challenge to you?* Washington, DC: Chronicle of Higher Education.

Almanac (2008–09b). *Opinions and attitudes of full time faculty members; Aspects of job described as satisfactory or very satisfactory.* Washington, DC: Chronicle of Higher Education.

Almanac (2008–09c). *Average salaries of full-time faculty members.* Washington, DC: Chronicle of Higher Education.

Almanac (2008–09d). *Median salaries of college administrators by job category and type of institution.* Washington, DC: Chronicle of Higher Education.

Almanac (2008–09e). *Part time, non-tenured faculty trends.* Washington, DC; Chronicle of Higher Education.

Bower, B. L. (2002). Campus life for faculty of color: Still strangers after all these years? *New Directions for Community Colleges*, 118, 79–87.

Bucher, R. D. (2000). *Diversity consciousness: Opening our minds to people, cultures, and opportunities.* Upper Saddle River, NJ: Prentice-Hall.

Cain, R. A. (1982). Equal educational opportunity and the community college. *The Journal of Negro Education*, 51(1), 16–28.

Carter, D. J. (1994). The status of faculty in community colleges: What do we know? *New Directions for Community Colleges*, 87, 3–18.

Chapman, B. G. (2001). *Minority faculty recruitment in community colleges: Commitment, attitudes, beliefs, and perceptions of Chief Academic Officers.* Unpublished Doctoral Dissertation, The University of Texas at Austin.

Cohen, A. M., & Brawer, F. B. (2003). *The American community college*, (4th Ed.). San Francisco, CA: Jossey-Bass.

Corbin, S. K. T. (1998). *Role perceptions and job satisfaction of community college faculty.* Unpublished Doctoral Dissertation, the Catholic University of America.

Davila A., & Mora, M. T. (2007). *Do gender and ethnicity affect civic engagement and academic progress? working paper 53.* College Park, MD: Center for Information and Research on Civic Learning and Engagement.

Delgado-Romero, E. A., Flores, L., Gloria, A., Arredondo, P., & Castellanos, J. (2003). The majority in the minority: Developmental career challenges for Latino and Latina psychology faculty. In J. Castellanos & L. Jones (Eds.). *The majority in the minority: Retaining Latina/o faculty, administrators, and students in the 21st century* (pp. 257–283). Sterling, VA: Stylus Books.

Digest of Education Statistics (1990–2008). *Employees in institutions of higher education, by primary occupation, employment status, sex, and by type and control of institution.* Washington, DC: National Center for Education Statistics.

Digest of Education Statistics (2008). *Table 252. Full-time and part-time faculty and instructional staff in degree-granting institutions, by type and control of institution and selected characteristics: Fall 1992, fall 1998, and fall 2003.* Washington, DC: National Center for Education Statistics.

Duree, C. A. (2007). *The challenges of the community college presidency in the new millennium: Pathways, preparation, competencies, and leadership programs needed to survive.* Unpublished doctoral dissertation, Iowa State University.

Eells, W. B. (1931). *The junior college.* Boston, MA: Houghton Mifflin.

Futrell, M. (1999). The challenge of the 21st century: Developing a highly qualified cadre of teachers to teach our nation's diverse student population. *Journal of Negro Education*, 68(3), 318–334.

Garcia, M., & Moses, J. (2000). *Succeeding in an academic career: A guide for faculty of color.* Westport, CT: Greenwood Press.

Gilroy, M. (2008). The new wave of community college faculty. *The Hispanic Outlook in Higher Education*, 18(11), 24–26.

Harvey, W. B. (1994). African American faculty in community colleges: Why they aren't there. *New Directions for Community Colleges*, 87, 19–26.

JLB Associates (2008). Reversing course: The troubled state of academic staffing and a path forward. Washington, DC: JLB Associates. Retrieved September 2, 2009, from: http://www.aft.org/pubs-reports/higher_ed/ReversingCourse.pdf

Johnsrud, L. K., & Sadao, K. C. (1998). The common experience of "otherness": Ethnic and racial minority faculty. *The Review of Higher Education*, 21(4), 315–342.

Journal of Blacks in Higher Education (2001). No blacks in the pipeline: The standard explanation for low percentage of Black faculty continues to be much of a red herring, *The Journal of Blacks in Higher Education*, 33, 77–78.

Kee, A. M. (1999). *Campus climate: Perceptions, policies and programs in community colleges. AACC Research Brief.* Washington, DC: American Association of Community Colleges.

Kendrick, L. L. (1995). An analysis of the cultural diversity initiatives in Louisiana Public Community College. Unpublished Doctoral Dissertation, The Union Institute Graduate School, Cincinnati, OH.

Kirkpatrick, L. (2001). *Multicultural strategies for community colleges: Expanding faculty diversity. Eric Digest.* Los Angeles, CA: ERIC Clearinghouse for Community Colleges.

Knoell, D. M. (1994). California community college faculty from historically underrepresented racial and ethnic groups. *New Directions for Community Colleges*, 87, 27–34.

Licitra, J. C. (2005). A descriptive study of major influences that affect the transfer success of Hispanics from the community college to the 4-year university. Unpublished Doctoral Dissertation, Alliant International University, San Diego, CA.

Lovell, N. B., Alexander, M. L., & Kirkpatrick, L. A. (2002). Minority faculty at community colleges. Fastback 490. Bloomington, IN: Phi Delta Kappa Educational Foundation.

Manzo, K. K. (2000). Community college faculty. Black Issues in Higher Education, 17(13), 54–57.

Medina, C., & Luna, G. (2000). Narratives from Latina professors in higher education. Anthropology & Education Quarterly, 31(1), 47–66.

Nevarez, C., & Borunda, R. (2004). Faculty of color: Contesting the last frontier. Sacramento, CA: Serna Center.

Nevarez, C., & Wood, J. L. (2007). Developing urban school leaders: Building on solutions 15 years after the Los Angeles riots. Educational Studies, 42(3), 266–280.

Nicholas, F. W., & Oliver, A. R. (1994). Achieving diversity among community college faculty. New Directions for Community Colleges, 87, 35–42.

NSOPF (2004). U.S. Department of Education, National Center for Education Statistics, 2004 National Study of Postsecondary Faculty (NSOPF:04).

Opp, R. D. (2001). Enhancing recruitment success for two-year college students of color. Community College Journal of Research and Practice, 25, 71–86.

Opp, R.D. (2002). Enhancing program completion rates among two-year college students of color. Community College Journal of Research and Practice, 26, 147–163.

Opp, R., & Smith, A. (1994). Effective strategies for enhancing minority faculty recruitment. Community College Journal of Research and Practice, 18(2), 147–163.

Owens, J. S., Reis, F. W., & Hall, K. M. (1994). Bridging the gap: Recruitment and retention of minority faculty members. New Directions for Community Colleges, 87, 57–64.

Padilla, A. M. (1994). Ethnic minority scholars, research, and mentoring: Current and future issues. Educational Researcher, 23(4), 24–27.

Peoples, R. III, & Smith, A. B. (2005). Hiring minority faculty: Success in Texas. Washington, DC: American Association of Community Colleges.

Perna, L. W. (2003). The status of women and minorities among community college faculty. Research in Higher Education, 44(2), 205–240.

Provasnik, S., & Planty, M. (2008). Community colleges: Special supplement to the condition of education 2008: Statistical analysis report. Washington, DC: National Center for Education Statistics.

Rifkin, T. (2000). Public community college faculty. New expeditions: Charting the second century of community colleges: Issues Paper No. 4. Washington: American Association of Community Colleges.

Robertson, P., & Frier, T. (1994). Recruitment and retention of minority faculty. New Directions for Community Colleges, 22(3), 65–71.

Smith, D. G., & Moreno, J. F. (2006, September 29). Hiring the next generation of professors: Will myths remain excuses? Chronicle of Higher Education, 53(6), B22.

Tierney, W., & Bensimon, E. (1996) Promotion and tenure: Community and socialization in academe. Albany: State University of New York Press.

Trower, C. A., & Chait, R. P. (2002). Faculty Diversity: Too little for too long. Harvard Magazine, 104(4), 33–38.

Twombly, S., & Townsend, B. K. (2008). Community college faculty: What we know and need to know. Community College Review (36)1, 5–24.

Umbach, P. D. (2006). The contribution of faculty of color to undergraduate education. Research in Higher Education, 47(3), 317–345.

U.S. Department of Education, National Center for Education Statistics (2005). Postsecondary institutions in the United States: Fall 2003 and degrees and other awards conferred: 2002–03 (NCES 2005–154).

U.S. Department of Education (2006). National Center for Education Statistics, Higher Education General Information Survey (HEGIS), "Degrees and Other Formal Awards Conferred" surveys, 1976–77 and 1980–81; and 1988–89 through 2004–05 Integrated Postsecondary Education Data System, "Completions Survey" (IPEDS-C:89–99), and Fall 2000 through Fall 2005.

Valadez, J. (1994). Critical perspectives on community college education. New Directions or Community Colleges, 22(3), 81–86.

Vernez, G., & Mizell, L. (2001). GOAL: To double the rate of Hispanics earning a bachelor's degree. Santa Monica, CA: RAND.

Weisman, I. M., & Vaughan, G. B. (2006). The community college presidency 2006. Washington, DC: American Association of Community Colleges.

Wood, J. L. (2008). Ethical dilemmas in African American faculty representation. eJournal of Education Policy. Retrieved July 2, 2009, from: https://www4.nau.edu/cee/jep/journals.aspx?id=162

Zamani, E. M. (2000). Sources and information regarding effective retention strategies for students of color. New Directions for Community Colleges, 112, 95–104.

CHAPTER SEVEN

DEMOGRAPHIC TRENDS

This chapter introduces select demographic information on community colleges that focuses on: (a) institutional characteristics; (b) students' characteristics; (c) faculty characteristics; and (d) administrators' characteristics. Demographic trends are contextualized as an opportunity to further meet the changing needs of an increasingly diverse student population.

When reading this chapter, consider the following questions:

- How do the demographic trends within your institution correspond to the national demographic landscape of community colleges? What are the implications of these trends for the future of the community college?
- What social, political, and economic factors contribute to these trends? What are the implications of these factors for community colleges?
- How can demographic data be used to inform leadership practices?

The landscape of the community college is evolving at an unprecedented rate (e.g., enrollment trends, mission, accountability measures, and funding sources). Depending upon the leader, this can serve as an opportunity to further meet the changing needs of an increasingly diverse student population or serve as a deterrent to the well-being of the community college. For example, one leader may see the increasing racial/ethnic diversity of students, faculty, and staff, and use it as an opportunity to create programs and policies that meet the needs of these groups. Another leader may see these changes as a threat to campus stability. Understanding and examining the breadth and depth of these trends, and how leaders are experiencing these trends can serve as a diagnostic tool in assessing the institution's responsiveness to the needs of its constituency. For leaders who understand and meet the challenges posed by demographic changes, several opportunities will arise, which allow them to:

- Engage in strategic planning that takes into account current demographic trends and future changes. Thus, leaders can be proactive rather than reactive in developing and sustaining an environment of success.
- Serve as agents of change in facilitating understanding, affirmation, and action towards addressing the needs of a changing populous.
- Identify individuals within the organization who are attuned to and reflective of the demographic characteristics (e.g., race, class, gender) of the institution. Leaders can draw upon their talents to integrate and acculturate constituents (e.g., students, community members) in the overall campus life experience.
- Assess and evaluate whether the universal community college mission of opportunity is being met in light of demographic trends (e.g., racial/ethnic, gender, and socioeconomic representation).
- Understand the demographic context in which policies were developed, implemented, and enacted. By doing so, leaders will be better equipped to assess whether the objectives of policies are outdated and are in need of revision or elimination or whether new policies are warranted to meet the needs of the current demographic context.

Demographic Trends

This chapter presents select demographic information on community colleges which focuses on: (a) institutional characteristics including the number, type, and regional placement of community colleges; (b) students characteristics by age, race/ethnicity, and gender; (c) faculty characteristics by age, race/ethnicity, gender, and rank; and (d) administrators' characteristics by race/ethnicity, gender, and rank. What follows is an examination of demographic trends in the community college.

Institutional Characteristics

We use the term *Institutional characteristics* to refer to attributes of community colleges including the number, overall enrollment, size, locale, type, and control of institutions.

Since the founding of Joliet Junior College in 1901, the community college has experienced exponential growth. As illustrated in Figure 1, in slightly more than 100 years, the community college has grown from one institution to 1,117. This number of colleges is not inclusive of branch campuses, which if included, would increase to 1,600 total campuses (American Association of Community Colleges, 2009). The greatest growth period experienced by community colleges occurred between 1960 and 1970 with a 45 percent growth rate in only a 10-year period. It is particularly important to note that during this time the baby boomers reached college age, thereby, increasing enrollment and subsequently the demand to increase the number of new community colleges.

Leaders should be attentive to the increasing number of community colleges in that greater accessibility to postsecondary education is created by an increasing number of institutions. This better enables the community college to meet its mission of serving local community needs. Also, more community colleges allows institutions to better focus on the unique needs of smaller geographic regions as opposed to larger regions. Thus, policies, practices, and structures can be enacted which aid these institutions in better meeting the needs of the communities in which they serve.

In 1963, there was a total enrollment of 850,361 students in the community colleges. By the late 1970s, community college enrollments had exploded reaching 4,042,942 by 1977, an increase of more than fourfold in only 14 years (see Figure 2). The "enrollment increase resulted from three factors: Baby boomers continued to come of age, more parents desired a postsecondary education for their children,

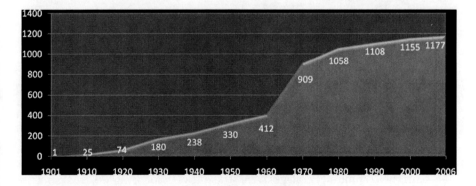

Figure 1 Number of Community College Institutions, 1900–1910
Source: Phillippe, K. A. & Sullivan, L. G. (2005). *National Profile of Community Colleges: Trends & Statistics*. Washington, DC: American Association of Community Colleges. American Association of Community Colleges (2009). *Fast Facts*. Washington, DC: AACC.

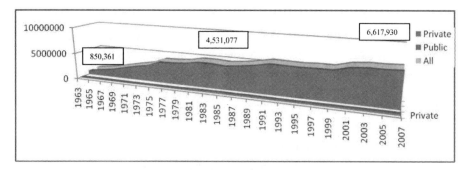

Figure 2 Total Enrollment for Two-Year Colleges, 1963–2007
Source: Digest of Education Statistics. (2009). Table 189. Total fall enrollment in degree-granting institutions, by control and type of institution: 1963 through 2007. Washington, DC: National Center for Education Statistics.

and students sought draft deferment during the Vietnam War" (Kasper, 2002–03, pp. 15–16). By 2007, more than 6.6 million students attended two-year colleges; this indicates a continued upward enrollment trend influenced by:

- Affordability—Increased tuition in private, public, and for-profit colleges and universities has been a determining factor in students' decisions to attend community colleges. Millions of students enroll in these institutions as an affordable avenue for completing their academic goals (e.g., general education, skill development, certificate completion, leisure activities, and terminal degree).
- Population Growth—The population of the United States has risen. This has translated into enrollment increases for community colleges. Population increases coupled with heightened expectations for acquiring at least some college training have resulted in an increase of college attendees.
- Student Diversity—An increasing number of students, who have not traditionally had access to college, are now able to enroll via the open-door admissions policy of the community college system. This includes students of color,[1] part-time students, retirees, and even those who were formerly incarcerated. For example, in 1976 only 19.5 percent of students in the community colleges were students of color. By 2006, this percentage had risen to 37.1 percent (Almanac, 1996–97; 2008–09).

---

[1] Students of color include all nonwhite students. It should be noted that an increasing number of students are marking "mixed" or "other."

- Increased Admissions Standards—Raised admission standards at four-year institutions have resulted in increased student enrollment at community colleges. A notable number of students enter the community college with the intent to transfer via articulation and guaranteed transfer agreements between community colleges and their four-year counterparts.
- Geographic Proximity—Due to the increased number of community college institutions, which are evenly distributed across the country, access to these institutions has improved. Thus, many students attend community colleges due to their close geographic proximity, which allows students to keep family ties, work while attending college, and live at home while attending college.
- Economic Trends—Student enrollment is influenced by the national economy. In challenging economic times, enrollments increase as new students seek skills that will make them more marketable in an increasingly competitive workforce.

The vast majority of two-year students are enrolled in the public community colleges. In 2007, only 293,811 students were enrolled in private colleges, in comparison to 6,324,119 in public institutions. In fact, students in public institutions account for 95.5 percent of all two-year college students (Digest of Education Statistics, 2009). The large percentage of enrollment in public community colleges has not always been the case. The first two-year colleges were private colleges; however, by 1921, Koos (1924) reports that private colleges accounted for only 47.6 percent of two-year college enrollment. Public two-year college enrollments have continued to be more prevalent compared to private colleges. This trend has shown an upward trajectory since the early 1900s. The implications of this trend illustrate greater college access for millions of students who traditionally did not have an opportunity to attend higher education institutions.

Community colleges vary in size, with a tendency to be smaller institutions in comparison to four-year universities. In 2006, 57 percent of community colleges in the nation served less than 5,000 students. Because of their small size, these institutions offer students a personable campus environment attuned to meeting their academic and social needs. Students often attest to the benefits of attending smaller institutions where relationships can be more easily established with faculty, staff, and other students (see Figure 3).

A revealing trend among community colleges in the nation is that they are evenly distributed across geographic regions (e.g., urban, rural, suburban). Even in rural locales, community colleges have a significant presence in the local

Percentage distribution of public community colleges by size

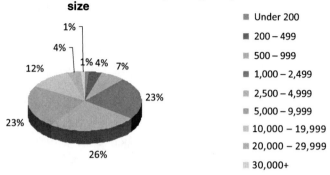

Figure 3 Percentage Distribution of Public Community Colleges by Size, 2006
Source: U.S. Department of Education, (2007). National Center for Education Statistics, 2006–07 Integrated Postsecondary Education Data System (IPEDS), Enrollment component.

community. For example, in 2006, 29.05 percent of community colleges were located in rural areas. This distribution once again reifies the important role that community colleges play in educating communities traditionally not served by four-year universities (see Table 1).

Student Characteristics

Student characteristics—refers to the race/ethnicity, gender, age, choice of academic plan, and other demographic descriptors of students. The demographic characteristics of students in the community college are continually evolving; thus, the importance of tracking student characteristics can serve as a platform to facilitate their success.

The vast majority of students in the community college are Caucasian. In line with national demographic trends, the percentage of Caucasian students in the community college is on a downward trajectory. For instance, in 1986, 77 percent of community college students were Caucasian; however, by 2006,

Table 1 Percentage Distribution of Public Community Colleges by Community Type, 2006

	City	Suburban	Town	Rural	All
Number	304	186	250	303	1043
Percent	29.14%	17.83%	23.96%	29.05%	

Source: U.S. Department of Education (2007). National Center for Education Statistics, 2006–07 Integrated Postsecondary Education Data System (IPEDS), Spring, Enrollment component.

only 59 percent of students were Caucasian. This represents a decrease of nearly 20 percent in a 20-year time-frame. In contrast, the percentage of students of color is on the rise. This is due to a multiplicity of factors, including increased: (a) national population representation for communities of color; (b) access rates for communities of color; (c) social, economic, and cultural capital for students of color; (d) affordability of community college institutions; (e) opportunity for students to reside in their home communities while attending the local community college; and (f) awareness of the smaller, close-knit, and welcoming campus communities. In 1986, the representation of students of color attending community colleges was as follows: African American (10 percent); Hispanic (7 percent); Native American (1 percent); and Asian American (4 percent) (See Figure 4). By 2006, all groups (except for Native Americans) had experienced increases in student population percentage. For example, African American representation rose by 3 percent; Hispanics by 8 percent; and Asian Americans by 3 percent. With the increasing population of students of color in the community college, it is imperative that leaders use this demographic information to prepare their institutions to address the needs of these groups. For example, leaders who see this trajectory could plan efforts to diversify campus staff, faculty, and administration in order to ensure the racial/ethnic composition of students

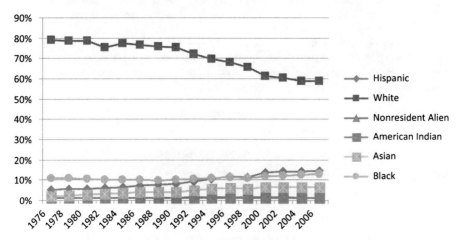

Figure 4 Percentage Enrollment in Two-Year Colleges by Race/Ethnicity, 1976–2006
Source: Almanac. (2008–09). *College Enrollment by Racial and Ethnic Group, Selected Years.* Washington, DC: Chronicle of Higher Education. Digest of Education Statistics. (1990). *Table 190—Total enrollment in institutions of higher education, by type and control of institution and race/ethnicity of student: Fall 1976 to fall 1988.* Washington, DC: National Center for Education Statistics. Almanac. (1996–97). *College Enrollment by Racial and Ethnic Group, Selected Years.* Washington, DC: Chronicle of Higher Education. Almanac. (1999–00). *College Enrollment by Racial and Ethnic Group, Selected Years.* Washington, DC: Chronicle of Higher Education.

is reflected among community college personnel (Almanac, 1996–97, 1999–00, 2008–09; Digest, 1990).

The gender balance has shifted; now the majority of students are female. In 1970, women represented only 37.2 percent of community college students. In 2005, the percentage had risen to 55 percent. This represents a total increase of almost 18 percent (see Figure 5, Table 2). The gender shift is more apparent when data is disaggregated by gender specific to race/ethnicity. When viewed, this data illustrates that African American and Hispanic males are falling behind in terms of gender representation. The following factors have influenced this shift: (a) the stereotypical portrayals of minority males in the media as criminals, athletes, and entertainers downplays the importance of education; (b) the cultural expectation for males to work full-time and/or raise a family; and (c) lack of college-related

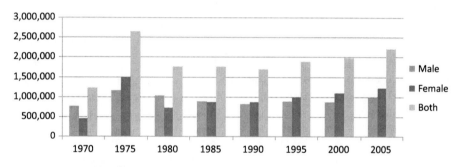

Figure 5 Gender of Public and Private Two-Year Colleges by Five-Year Increments
Source: Digest of Education Statistics. (2008a). Table 196. Total fall enrollment in degree-granting institutions, by attendance status, sex of student, and type and control of institution: Selected years, 1970 through 2006. Washington, DC: National Center for Education Statistics.

Table 2 Percent Enrollment by Age in Two-Year Colleges, 1987–2007

	Under18	18–19	20–21	22–24	25–29	30–34	35–39	40–49	50–64	65 and Over
1987	1.90%	19.60%	13.70%	12.90%	15.30%	11.80%	8.50%	9.30%	3.90%	1.70%
1991	1.80%	16.20%	14.30%	11.20%	12.90%	10.50%	8.20%	8.90%	2.80%	0.80%
1995	3.00%	18.70%	14.80%	13.40%	14.40%	10.70%	8.70%	10.60%	3.60%	1.10%
1999	4.30%	21.00%	15.80%	12.90%	13.00%	8.60%	7.60%	10.00%	4.20%	1.10%
2003	5.10%	20.60%	16.40%	13.80%	12.80%	8.80%	6.50%	9.80%	4.40%	0.90%
2007	6.70%	22.20%	16.70%	13.60%	13.00%	7.70%	6.00%	8.30%	4.50%	0.90%

Note: age unknown not included. Source: Digest of Education Statistics. (1990–2008a). Total fall enrollment in degree-granting institutions, by control and type of institution, age, and attendance status of student. Washington, DC: National Center for Education Statistics.

information, which has a direct impact on issues of access, retention, and completion (Digest of Education Statistics, 2008a).

Information on the gender distribution can be used to initiate efforts to narrow the gender participation gap. This can be done through various outreach efforts that include: (a) the creation of pipeline programs which mentor students as early as preschool; (b) the implementation of marketing campaigns which specifically target male populations; and (c) grassroots initiatives where college leaders are visible in communities where high concentrations of males reside (e.g., athletic programs, juvenile retention centers, articulation agreements).

The percentage of student enrollment by age in two-year colleges reveals an upward trend among students in the age groups of 22–24 and under, with 18- to 19-year-olds making up the largest percentage of students of any age (22.2 percent). There is a perception that the age of the traditional community college student is no longer the 18-year-old entering college from high school. However, data illustrates this is not the case. By examining trends, which show a decline of middle-age to older students, with the exception of 40 and above, it appears 18-year-old students continue to make up the majority of students attending community colleges. Consequently, the perpetual advocacy for students to attend college has led to greater numbers of younger students of color making up a larger percentage of these students. This is due to enhanced access, financial aid, support services, and so on. A notable decline exists among the middle-age student population (25 through 49) with older students showing modest gains (50–64) (Digest of Education Statistics, 1990–2008a).

Factors influencing the decline of middle-aged students are often a direct result of family, community, and societal influences, which socialize students to certain career paths and lifestyles. Students not enrolled in college directly from high school confront challenges with enrolling in subsequent years. They face family and work responsibilities and difficulties acculturating into a "nonacademic" lifestyle, and they lack confidence to do well academically. Many of these students do not want to postpone the economic and social gratification that comes from full-time employment. The desire to immediately accrue respectful earnings becomes a priority as students enter the workforce and military. At times, this can be counterproductive to their academic success, as students who have been absent from an academic environment for years return to school. Ironically, a large percentage of this student age-group is pressured within their respective professions to attain the appropriate academic credentials necessary for skill development, promotion, and salary increases. As a result, the community college does serve a large percentage of students who fall above the traditional 18 to

24 age range. These students account for 40.4 percent of college attendees. This information illustrates the role of community colleges in providing access to a wide range of students by age. There are multiple factors in place that contribute to increased access for students across age-groups. These include the following:

- G.I Bill—The GI Bill and its subsequent revisions have provided veterans with financial support to attend college, including cost-of-living expenses. This has resulted in increased access, retention, and overall academic support for veteran students.
- Open Access–The open–access mission of community colleges has afforded greater opportunities for a wide range of students by age, independent of previous academic preparation. For example, most community colleges do not require a high school diploma or general education diploma (GED) as a requirement for college entrance.
- Alternative Formats and Offerings—Community colleges have expanded greater opportunities for students across multiple age-groups, this is evident by alternative course formats (e.g., online, hybrid, evening, weekend, television) and multiple course offerings (e.g., vocational education, job skill enhancement, leisure classes, academic transfer classes, remediation classes, terminal degree).
- Social Support Services. Expanded efforts to provide a structure of academic, social, and economic support has resulted in increased opportunities for students across multiple age-groups. A sample of support services include: (a) veterans support programs; (b) Equal Opportunity Programs and Services (EOPS); (c) welfare support services; and (d) federal/state aid and tuition fee waivers.

The aforementioned data serves to inform leadership efforts in the following ways: (1) each age group has their own unique needs; as a result, there is a need to continue and expand age-appropriate support programs and retention activities in relation to academic and student affairs services; (2) financial aid should be appropriated in accordance with students' age-group needs. For example, older students often have financial commitments (e.g., housing, family) that can become hurdles to their academic success. Leaders can institutionalize financial incentives to facilitate their success; (3) alignment of appropriate curriculum, instruction, and pedagogy/andragogy, which meets the age-specific learning needs of students; and (d) outreach efforts that target specific age-groups in light of enrollment patterns and trends.

The reasons for enrolling in community colleges are widely distributed among varied interests as noted above, with only 43 percent of students indicating their intention is to complete a 2-year degree and 36 percent indicating their intention is to transfer to a 4-year university (see Figure 6). The wide-ranging intentions for enrolling in community college provides further context for leaders. People are enrolling in community colleges for reasons beyond the typical explanations used to explain student enrollment, which fall under two reasons, to transfer or graduate with a 2-year degree. This data presents a more complex picture, one where a great number of students are taking classes for personal interests, to complete a certificate, and transfer to another college. A significant percentage, 42 percent, of students enrolled in community colleges to develop their job skills. A downturn in the economy tends to drive students to enroll in community colleges in greater numbers in view of the need to gain job skills, which can translate to better opportunities for employment, career change, and promotions (Provasnik & Planty, 2008).

The variety of reasons why students enroll in community colleges has implications for community college leaders in that they can use this information to: (a) create conditions necessary to facilitate student success linked to the purpose behind why students enroll in community colleges; (b) help break the misconception about why students do not graduate or transfer at greater numbers, since many times this is not their intention; (c) promote the diverse purpose and value that the community colleges have in meeting multiple needs and interests of community members; (d) promote the important role community colleges are playing in developing job skills among workers to meet current economic demands; and (e) contribute to the

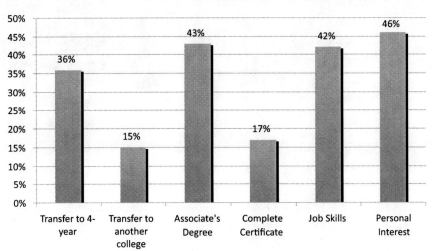

Figure 6 Enrollment intentions by percentage of community college students, 2003–04
Note: Participants could choose more than one category. Source: Provasnik, S. & Planty, M. (2008). Community colleges: Special supplement to the condition of education 2008—statistical analysis report. Washington, DC: National Center for Education Statistics.

overall emotional, psychological, and physical well-being of community members through comprehensive course offerings.

Faculty Characteristics—refers to the age, race/ethnicity, gender, rank, and other demographic descriptors of faculty. The demographic characteristics of faculty in the community college illustrate incremental growth and diversification. Faculty trends for full-time faculty and instructional staff in public two-year colleges reveal stark differences in faculty representation by age. In 1987, faculty data by age illustrated a normal distribution. By 2003, trends revealed a negatively skewed distribution indicating a heavy concentration of older faculty residing in these positions (see Figure 7). Age groups from 50–54 through 60 and over have increased while age groups under 30 through 45–49 have decreased. This indicates an aging college faculty. The evolving trends during this time period have been influenced by: (1) the aging of faculty who entered the profession during the 1960s and 1970s that are now at retirement age; (2) a dearth of faculty being prepared to enter community colleges, in large part because of a perceived lack of prestige with many faculty members entering with the community college doing as a result of the heightened competition for jobs in four-year universities; and (3) the retiring ranks of full-time faculty often being replaced with part-time,

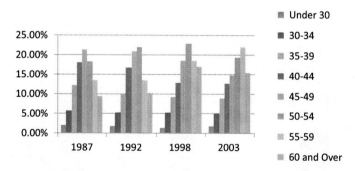

Year	Under 30	30–34	35–39	40–44	45–49	50–54	55–59	60 and Over
1987	1.90%	5.60%	12.20%	18.10%	21.20%	18.20%	13.50%	9.30%
1992	1.70%	5.30%	9.80%	16.80%	20.80%	21.90%	13.50%	10.30%
1998	1.40%	5.20%	9.10%	12.80%	18.40%	22.80%	18.40%	16.90%
2003	1.80%	5.10%	9.00%	12.70%	14.70%	19.30%	21.90%	15.40%

Figure 7   Percentage Distribution of Full-Time Faculty and Instructional Staff in Public Two-Year Colleges by Age and Selected Years, 1987, 1992, 1998, 2003
Source: Digest of Education Statistics (2008b). Full-time and part-time faculty and instructional staff in degree-granting institutions, by type and control of institution and selected characteristics. Washington, DC: National Center for Education Statistics.

adjunct, and lecturers. Largely, this explains the negatively skewed distribution of faculty by age (Digest of Education, 2008b).

The percentage distribution of full-time and instructional staff in public two-year colleges by gender indicates one primary trend. In 1987, male faculty accounted for 62.1 percent of total faculty, while female faculty accounted for 37.9 percent. By 2003, male faculty represented 50.5 percent of total faculty, while female faculty had increased to 49.5 percent, a total rise of 11.6 percent. These faculty demographics indicate near equal representation among the two groups (Digest of Education Statistics, 2008c). The following factors serve to explain the trends in increased female representation among full-time faculty and instructional staff: (1) females attend college at higher rates than males, leading to an increased pool of potential faculty candidates; (2) the community colleges mission and its alignment with the civil rights movement has created a culture of access, leading to increased parity within the faculty ranks; (3) successive waves of the feminist movement further led to greater parity for women in society; and (4) many of the programs offered at the community college prepare individuals for jobs in the workforce traditionally prescribed for women (e.g., education, nursing, paraprofessional roles). Also, some of the data presented may be misleading if taken at face value, for example the data reported here lumps together full-time faculty and instructional staff. It does not reflect the overrepresentation of full-time women in nontenure-track positions; moreover, the data does not take into account the lack of representation of female faculty in specific fields, such as the Science, Technology, Engineering and Mathematics (STEM) fields.

Over 20 years (1987–2003), the percentage distribution of full-time faculty and instructional staff in public two-year colleges by race/ethnicity indicates notable trends. First and foremost, there was a 10 percent decrease in the representation of white faculty (from 91 to 80.9) (see Figure 8). In contrast, the percentage of faculty of color (e.g., African American, Latino, Native American, Asian American) increased by nearly 10 percent (from 9 to 19.1). Although data is only being presented up to 2003, there is an overall upward trend among all faculty of color. However, there remains a lack of proportional representation [2] among communities of color (Digest of Education Statistics, 2008d) (see Figure 9).

Considering that communities of color account for approximately one-third of the overall national population but only 19.1 percent of faculty; clearly this presents a lack of proportional representation where faculty members do

---

[2] *Proportional Representation* "is a relative numerical or percentage comparison between the racial/ ethnic background of students, administrators, teachers, and other school personnel nationwide" (Nevarez & Wood, 2007, p. 277).

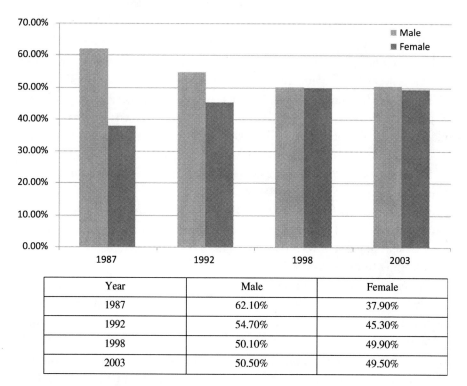

Year	Male	Female
1987	62.10%	37.90%
1992	54.70%	45.30%
1998	50.10%	49.90%
2003	50.50%	49.50%

Figure 8 Percentage Distribution of Full-Time Faculty and Instructional Staff in Public Two-Year Colleges by Gender and Selected Years, 1987, 1992, 1998, 2003

not necessarily reflect the racial/ethnic makeup of the national population. Subsequently, they also are not reflective of the student of color population, who represent about one-third of all community college students. Chapter 6 on Faculty in the *Community College* delved more into the details pertinent to the benefits accrued when diverse faculty are represented, including: (a) preparing students for a diverse global marketplace; (b) creating quality role models, mentors, and advisors; (c) encouraging effective curriculum and critical pedagogy that accounts for racial/ethnic and cultural diversity; (d) improving student recruitment efforts; (e) improving the academic achievement of students; (f) creating a welcoming campus environment; (g) serving as agents of change; and (h) enhancing the financial prosperity of state and national economies. The aforementioned points present a clear rationale for leaders to advocate for the hiring, retaining, and promoting of diverse faculty who are representative of the students that they serve.

The majority of faculties in the community colleges are part-timers. In 1987, part-time faculty represented 54.3 percent of faculty, while full-time faculty

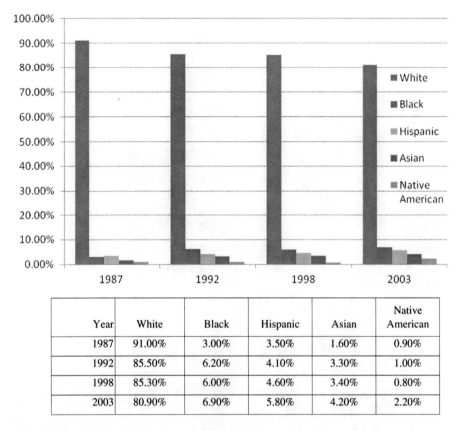

Year	White	Black	Hispanic	Asian	Native American
1987	91.00%	3.00%	3.50%	1.60%	0.90%
1992	85.50%	6.20%	4.10%	3.30%	1.00%
1998	85.30%	6.00%	4.60%	3.40%	0.80%
2003	80.90%	6.90%	5.80%	4.20%	2.20%

Figure 9 Percentage Distribution of Full-Time Faculty and Instructional Staff in Public Two-Year Colleges by Race/Ethnicity and Selected Years, 1987, 1992, 1998, 2003
Source: Digest of Education Statistics (2008d). Full-time and part-time faculty and instructional staff in degree-granting institutions, by type and control of institution, and selected characteristics. Washington, DC: National Center for Education Statistics.

represented 45.6 percent. By 2007, the percentage of part-time faculty representation had increased to 68.5 percent, a total rise of 14.2 percent, while full-time faculty decreased to 31.5 percent (see Figure 10). When full-time faculty data is disaggregated by tenured/tenure-track and nontenure-track, the percentage distribution of faculty reveals a decreasing number of tenured/tenure-track faculties. For example, in 1997, 21 percent of full-time community college faculty was tenured/tenure-track faculty, as opposed to 13 percent not on tenure-track. By 2007, the number of tenured/tenure-track faculty decreased to 18 percent, with 14 percent of faculty being nontenured track (see Figure 11). The data clearly illustrates erosion among tenured/tenure-track faculty positions. There are several potential pros, cons, and

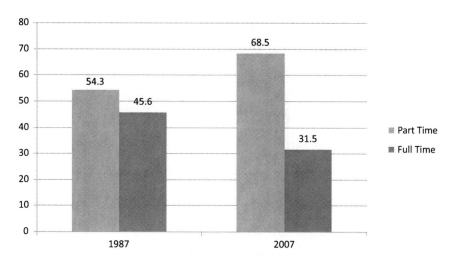

Figure 10 Percentage Distribution of Full-Time and Part-Time Faculty in Two-Year Public Colleges, 1987 and 2007
Source: Digest of Education Statistics (1987/2007). Employees in institutions of higher education by primary occupation, employment status, sex, and by type and control of institution. Washington, DC: National Center for Education Statistics.

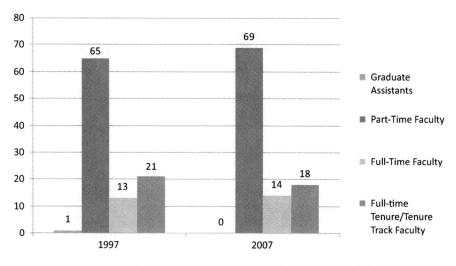

Figure 11 Percentage Distribution of Community College Instructional Staff, by Select Years
Source: U.S. Department of Education (1997/2007). National Center for Education Statistics, Integrated Postsecondary Education Data System, Fall Staff Survey Data File, Various Years.

implications of decreasing representation among full-time and tenured/tenure-track faculty (Digest of Education Statistics, 1987/2007) (see Table 3).

Table 3 Pros and Cons of Decreasing Full-Time and Tenured/Tenure-Track Faculty

Pros	Cons
Part-time faculty tends to be practitioner-oriented and grounded in the realities of the field.	Poses challenges for continuity across the curriculum considering that their faculty positions are typically not their primary jobs.
Part-time and nontenured/tenure-track faculties are more cost effective for the institution.	Poses challenges to organizational commitment due to low compensation and benefits.
Part-time and nontenured/tenure-track faculty can service as facilitators in linking the local community with the college.	Poses challenges to their incorporation and service to the institution. This can add to the workload of full-time faculty.
From the institutions perspective, the academic freedom of part-time and nontenured/tenure-track faculty is limited. Thus poor faculty can be more easily terminated.	Poses challenges for up-to-date pedagogical practices and scholarship.
From the institutions perspective, part-time and nontenured/tenure-track faculty performance can be evaluated and lead into full-time and tenured/tenure-track positions for high-quality faculty.	Poses challenges to student mentoring and advising due to their part-time status.
Part-time and nontenured/tenure-track faculty can service as facilitators in linking local/regional industries with the college.	Part-time faculty tends to be more vulnerable to renewed contracts and teaching responsibilities.

Administrator Characteristics—Refers to the age, race/ethnicity, and gender of administrators as well as other demographic descriptors. As illustrated below (see Figure 12), in 2004, less than 10 percent of community college presidents were under 50 years of age. The vast majority of presidents are seasoned people; as 68.7 percent of community college presidents are 55 and older. The average age of these presidents has increased over time. For example in 1996, the average age of a president in the community college was 54. However, in 2001, the average age had risen to 56. By 2006, the average age of a community college president had increased to 58 (Weisman & Vaughan, 2006). The aging presidency in the community college has been influenced by several trends: (1) the percentage of administrators who entered the profession during the 1960s and 1970s (usually as faculty members) are now at retirement age; (2) the increased skill-sets, knowledge, and demands of community college presidents has likely lengthened the preparation period of prospective presidents and deterred likely candidates; and (3) the lack of leaders

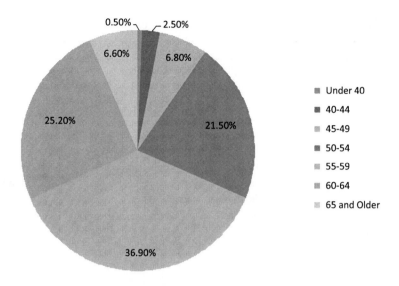

Figure 12 Age Distribution of Community College Presidents, 2004
Source: American Association of Community Colleges (2004). *AACC Membership Database (Data File)*.
Washington, DC: Author. Cited in Phillippe, K. A. & Sullivan, L. G. (2005). *National profile of community colleges: Trends and statistics*. Washington, DC: American Association of Community Colleges.

being prepared for high-level administrative roles in the community college (see Chapter 11, on *Leadership Development in the Community College*).

The percentage distribution of full-time executive, managerial, and administrative employees in public two-year colleges by gender illustrates increased administrative diversification. For example in 1987, 68.9 percent of community college administrators were male while only 31 percent were female. Ten years later, the percentage of males had decreased to 54.9 percent with females accounting for 45 percent of all administrators. By 2007, the overrepresentation of male administrators that existed in the 1980s and 1990s had subsided. This year, males accounted for only 46.2 percent of administrators. Thus, the representation of female administrators had risen from 31 percent in 1987 to 53.7 percent in 2007, an increase of 22.7 percent in 20 years (Weisman & Vaughan, 2006). While factors affecting the increase in female faculty diversification certainly played a role in this increase (e.g., higher college-attendance rate for females, community college mission of access and opportunity, impact of the feminist movement, total representation of women in community colleges due to socially feminized vocational fields), much can be attributed to the development, influence, and success of female leadership development programs (e.g., Asilomar Leadership

Skills Seminar, National Institute for Leadership Development). For example, the Asilomar Leadership Skills Seminar touts training more than 2,050 women since the mid-1980s, while the National Institute for Leadership Development (NILD) in its 28th year of operation boasts an international network of more than 6,000 women leaders. While these numbers indicate a growing number of women in

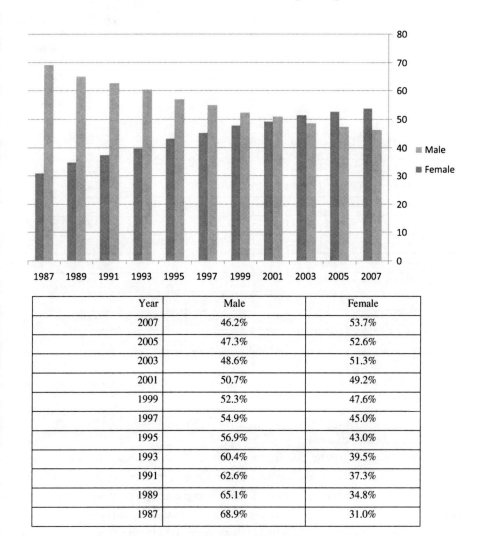

Year	Male	Female
2007	46.2%	53.7%
2005	47.3%	52.6%
2003	48.6%	51.3%
2001	50.7%	49.2%
1999	52.3%	47.6%
1997	54.9%	45.0%
1995	56.9%	43.0%
1993	60.4%	39.5%
1991	62.6%	37.3%
1989	65.1%	34.8%
1987	68.9%	31.0%

Figure 13 Full-Time Executive, Managerial, and Administrative Employees in Public Two-Year Colleges by Gender, 1987– 2007

Source: Digest of Education Statistics (1990–2008b). *Employees in degree-granting institutions, by employment status, sex, control and type of institution, and primary occupation.* Washington, DC: National Center for Education Statistics.

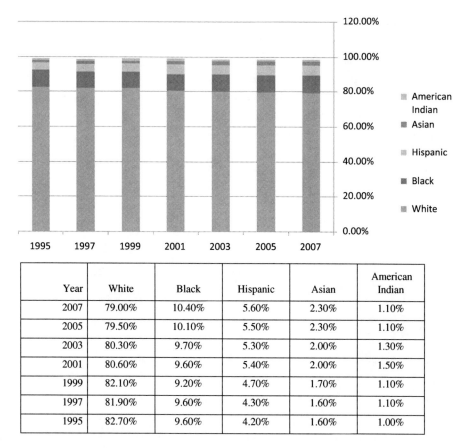

Year	White	Black	Hispanic	Asian	American Indian
2007	79.00%	10.40%	5.60%	2.30%	1.10%
2005	79.50%	10.10%	5.50%	2.30%	1.10%
2003	80.30%	9.70%	5.30%	2.00%	1.30%
2001	80.60%	9.60%	5.40%	2.00%	1.50%
1999	82.10%	9.20%	4.70%	1.70%	1.10%
1997	81.90%	9.60%	4.30%	1.60%	1.10%
1995	82.70%	9.60%	4.20%	1.60%	1.00%

Figure 14 Executive, Administrative, and Managerial Employees in Public Two-Year Colleges by Race/Ethnicity, 1995–2007
Source: Digest of Education Statistics (1990–2008c). *Employees in degree-granting institutions, by race/ethnicity, sex, employment status, control and type of institution, and primary occupation*. Washington, DC: National Center for Education Statistics.

leadership positions in the community college, this data must be approached cautiously. While women leaders accounted for 53.7 percent of all administrators in 2007, they are concentrated in the low and mid-ranks of administration. Additionally, data on female administrators in all institutional types reveals that of the 52.9 percent of women administrators, only 20 percent are women of color (Digest of Education Statistics (1990–2008b)) (see Figure 13).

Despite an upward growth trend in the general population and other statistical fronts among people of color (e.g., student enrollment, birth rates) there are few executive, administrative, and managerial employees of color. In 1995, administrators of color accounted for 16.4 percent of all community college administrators. By 2007, this percentage had risen to 19.4 percent. Though these numbers indicate an increase in administrative diversity, progress has been slow-moving. Clearly, more work needs to be done to achieve proportional representation of diversity in the community college. For example, Hispanics account for only 5.6 percent of administrators in the community college but represent 15.1 percent of the nation's population (Digest of Education Statistics, 1990–2008c). This reveals a lack of proportional representation, where the Hispanic administrator population needs to triple in order to reach proportionality. This data is even more disconcerting when one considers that by the year 2050, Hispanics will account for 30.2 percent of the national population (U.S. Census Bureau, 2008) (see Figure 14). If current growth rates among Hispanic administrators remain the same, they will only account for 10.6 percent of administrators by 2050. As noted by Valverde (2003), "although progress for the better has taken place, it has been a one step forward, two steps back occurrence; and if this forward/back trend continues, the overall status will worsen" (p. 19).

Case Study

Social, political, and economic factors contribute to the national demographic context within all social institutions; this is inclusive of community colleges. To truly understand, examine, and apply the data presented in this chapter to institutional problems, leaders must be knowledgeable and skilled in understanding how these factors influence demographic trends. A case study is presented which is designed to aid you in a critical examination of these national trends and their influence on the local level. When identifying resolution(s) be attentive to the interplay between institutional, student, faculty, and administrator characteristics in examining the following scenario.

President Cynthia Azari
Fresno City College
Fresno, California

College Influences

Background

Valley Community College (VCC) is among the oldest community colleges in the nation. Established in 1910, its open-door policy has allowed it to enjoy an enrollment of more than 25,000 students and 1,500 full-time and part-time faculty members. The local community has a high percentage of Latino students. This has translated into strong campus diversity, with nearly 38 percent of campus students describing themselves as Latino. The second largest racial/ethnic group at VCC are the whites, followed by Asian Americans, African Americans, and Native Americans. Student enrollment is at full capacity and there are waiting lists for nearly every class on campus. In trying to meet the needs of the local community, the campus has been setting up temporary classroom buildings in large mobile trailers. This step has been taken since the campus cannot afford to build new buildings or expand existing buildings. As a new community college president you have many issues to address on a daily basis. Prior to this position, you served as a vice president for student affairs at another local community college. Although, these institutions were much smaller than your VCC, they were comparable in that they: (a) are both growing campuses which are serving a wide range of students; and (b) are both experiencing financial pressures due to the economic downturn. However, this current campus differs from your previous institution in that a greater percentage of faculty and administrators are retiring. These lost positions are not being replaced by full-timers; rather, part-time faculty are being hired to save money. Thus, workload for full-time faculty and administrators has increased drastically. This has impacted the campus climate, where morale is at an all-time low and participation among faculty in various college committees has dwindled. This decline in morale has also been experienced by your senior-level staff. They have been bombarded with more and more duties as the college struggles with these retirements. An added challenge confronting existing administrators has to do with accreditation pressures. As a result of a recent accreditation site visit, the achievement outcomes of students have been questioned. This has resulted in more measures for accountability.

Statement of the Problem

Determining priorities and effective delegation are critical skills that every leader needs to develop. You have returned from a meeting with city and county officials regarding the college's involvement in a new initiative designed to attract new industries to the area, and you are trying to decide to whom the new initiative will be delegated. Upon your arrival on campus you are confronted with an array of issues related to current institutional trends which are impacting the college. The issues involved are dynamic, influential, and require your guidance. How will you address the following issues?

- People waiting in your reception area: (a) Children from the Child Development Center and their teacher to invite you to an event; (b) Vice President of instruction for scheduled weekly meeting; and (c) A local businessperson who is willing to help the college address capacity issues by building an eco-friendly building, nearly at cost.
- Telephone messages your secretary hands you: (a) Call from a board member wanting to know who from your college will submit proposals for an upcoming conference she is helping to coordinate; (b) Call from a newspaper reporter asking for a quote on the impact the budget decrease will have on enrollment; (c) Call from a parent complaining about a faculty member; (d) Call from a local legislator wanting to set up a meeting to discuss proposed legislation that will provide incentive funds for campuses with high graduation rates for underserved students.
- E-mails: (a) Financial aid director informing you of his suspicion of financial aid fraud; (b) Athletic director informing you that the basketball coach has been accused of recruitment violations; (c) Vocational dean inviting you to join the local consortium at their monthly luncheon today; (d) Signature folder; (e) Survey from a graduate student asking that you reply within two days; and (f) An email from the faculty union president, who wants to state her concern about an increasing overrepresentation of part-time faculty and a possible faculty strike if the practice continues.

References

Almanac. (2008–09). *College enrollment by racial and ethnic group, selected years.* Washington, DC: Chronicle of Higher Education.

Almanac. (1996–97). *College enrollment by racial and ethnic group, selected years.* Washington, DC: Chronicle of Higher Education.

Almanac. (1999–00). *College enrollment by racial and ethnic group, selected years.* Washington, DC: Chronicle of Higher Education.

American Association of Community Colleges (2004). *AACC membership database (data file).* Washington, DC: Author.

American Association of Community Colleges (2009). *About AACC.* Washington, DC: Author. Retrieved August 28, 2009, from: http://www.aacc.nche.edu/About/Pages/default.asx

American Association of Community Colleges (2009). *Fast Facts.* Washington, DC: Author.

Digest of Education Statistics (1987/2007). *Employees in institutions of higher education by primary occupation, employment status, sex, and by type and control of institution.* Washington, DC: National Center for Education Statistics.

Digest of Education Statistics. (1990). *Table 190: Total enrollment in institutions of higher education, by type and control of institution and race/ethnicity of student: Fall 1976 to fall 1988.* Washington, DC: National Center for Education Statistics.

Digest of Education Statistics. (1990–2008a). *Total fall enrollment in degree-granting institutions, by control and type of institution, age, and attendance status of student.* Washington, DC: National Center for Education Statistics.

Digest of Education Statistics (1990–2008b). *Employees in degree-granting institutions, by employment status, sex, control and type of institution, and primary occupation.* Washington, DC: National Center for Education Statistics.

Digest of Education Statistics (1990–2008c). *Employees in degree-granting institutions, by race/ethnicity, sex, employment status, control and type of institution, and primary occupation.* Washington, DC: National Center for Education Statistics.

Digest of Education Statistics. (2008a). *Table 196. Total fall enrollment in degree-granting institutions, by attendance status, sex of student, and type and control of institution: Selected years, 1970 through 2006.* Washington, DC: National Center for Education Statistics.

Digest of Education Statistics (2008b). *Full-time and part-time faculty and instructional staff in degree-granting institutions, by type and control of institution and selected characteristics.* Washington, DC: National Center for Education Statistics.

Digest of Education Statistics (2008c). *Full-time and part-time faculty and instructional staff in degree-granting institutions, by type and control of institution and selected characteristics.* Washington, DC: National Center for Education Statistics.

Digest of Education Statistics (2008d). *Full-time and part-time faculty and instructional staff in degree-granting institutions, by type and control of institution and selected characteristics.* Washington, DC: National Center for Education Statistics.

Digest of Education Statistics. (2009). *Table 189. Total fall enrollment in degree-granting institutions, by control and type of institution: 1963 through 2007.* Washington, DC: National Center for Education Statistics.

Kasper, H. T. (2002–03). The changing role of community college. *Occupational Outlook Quarterly,* 14–21.

Koos, L. V. (1924). *The junior college.* Minneapolis, MN: University of Minnesota.

Nevarez, C., & Wood, J. L. (2007). Developing urban school leaders: Building on solutions 15 years after the Los Angeles riots. *Educational Studies*, 42(3), 266–280.

Phillippe, K. A., & Sullivan, L. G. (2005). *National Profile of Community Colleges: Trends & Statistics*. Washington, DC: American Association of Community Colleges.

Provasnik, S., & Planty, M. (2008). *Community colleges: Special supplement to the condition of education 2008-statistical analysis report*. Washington, DC: National Center for Education Statistics.

U.S. Census Bureau (2008). Percent of the projected population by race and hispanic origin for the United States: 2008 to 2050. Washington, DC: Author. Retrieved August 20, 2008,from: http://www.census.gov/population/www/projections/tablesandcharts.html

U.S. Department of Education (2006–07). National Center for Education Statistics, Integrated Postsecondary Education Data System (IPEDS), Spring 2007, Enrollment component.

U.S. Department of Education (1997/2007). National Center for Education Statistics, Integrated Postsecondary Education Data System, Fall Staff Survey Data File, Various Years.

Valverde, L. A. (2003). *Leaders of color in higher education: Unrecognized triumphs in harsh institutions*. Walnut Creek, CA: Alta Mira.

Weisman, I. M., & Vaughan, G. B. (2006). *The community college presidency: 2006*. Washington, DC: American Association of Community Colleges.

CHAPTER EIGHT

LEADERSHIP IN STUDENT AFFAIRS

This chapter focuses on student affairs leadership in the community college. Specific attention will be given to four areas: (1) the disconnect between academic affairs and student affairs and its implications on student learning and personal development; (2) foundational and guiding student affairs documents (e.g., the Student Learning Initiative, Principles of Good Practice, Student Personnel Point of View); (3) the core functions of student affairs in relation to effective leadership practices; and (4) student development theory, with a primary focus on psychosocial theories.

When reading this chapter, consider the following questions:

- Why is there dissonance between the divisions of academic and student affairs? How does this effect student and institutional success? How can student affairs and academic affairs programming/services work cohesively to enhance student learning and personal development? What are the benefits of establishing a cohesive collaboration between these divisions?
- How do foundational/guiding student affairs documents (e.g., the Student Learning Initiative, Principles of Good Practice, and Student Personnel Point of View) address the role, function, and purpose of student affairs leaders? Do earlier documents address the current realities of community college students? If so, how? If not, what new guiding principles are needed?
- What are the core functions of student affairs? How do student affairs programming and services advance student learning and personal development?
- What are the primary student development theories? What are the differences between these theories? How do they benefit the practice of student affairs leadership?

Noticeably missing in the extensive literature on community colleges are studies that address the nature, roles, functions, and importance of student affairs[1] in relation to student success. Even fewer studies exist which examine leadership in student affairs. This dearth of research is indicative of the lack of reverence that student affairs leaders and personnel are given in many two- and four-year institutions (Hirt, Esteban, & McGuire, 2003; Mattox & Creamer, 1998). Their leadership is affected historically and contemporarily by limited funding, institutional support, and concern for the quality of student affairs services needed to enhance student learning and personal development. This is due to the perceived focus on social as opposed to academic development (Bloland, Stamatakos, & Rogers, 1996). Thus, a lack of: (a) research on these professionals; (b) internal respect for their operations; (c) funding for their programs and services; and (d) concern for the quality of their programming inevitably jeopardizes the success of students.

The status of student affairs leaders in the community college is not a new phenomenon. It has been formed by a legacy of underappreciation shaped by its origins. Early student affairs programming and services were designed to serve in a supportive or supplemental fashion to academic affairs (Burley & Butner, 2000). Creamer (1994) notes that in the 1930s community colleges lacked a substantive historical foundation from which to guide their student service programming. However, even by this time, career counseling, campus life activities, and orientation were core functions of student services. Although the operations of student services had been defined, their impact on student development was questioned. Additionally, these operations were not systematically instituted as core functions of the college. Rather, functions pertinent to academic affairs were the primary focus. Today, student affairs (or student services) refers to the conglomerate of campus operations that focus on the technical aspects of students' attendance (e.g., outreach, orientation, registration, enrollment, financial aid, assessment, counseling, judicial affairs); campus life operations of colleges that encourage students social integration into the campus community (e.g., student government, student clubs and organizations, intramural and sanctioned athletics programs, housing); and practices that reside in the margins of academic and student affairs (e.g., service learning, retention programs, academic advising).

---

[1] This chapter will use the terms *student affairs* and *student services* interchangeably.

Student Affairs Operations

Student affairs encompasses a wide variety of operations: (1) the technical operations (e.g., registration, counseling), which allow for students to attend college; (2) the campus life operations (e.g., student government, clubs/organizations), which provide for an affirmative campus environment; and (3) the nexus operations (e.g., academic advising, retention programs), which reside in the margins of academic and student affairs. These three core functions of student affairs are intertwined. Below we explicate *some* core functions in these areas:

Outreach. Generally, outreach officers serve as the first official communication between community colleges and the students. Often, outreach officers are supported in this operation by retention program officials (e.g., Extended Opportunities Programs and Services—EOP&S, Mathematics Engineering and Science Achievement—MESA) and faculty in vocational–technical programs (Cohen & Brawer, 2003). Outreach officials aid students with information on college matriculation (e.g., college programs, application, assessment tests) through presentations and one-on-one advising to community groups; parents; prison-release programs; and junior high/high school students, teachers, and counselors. Outreach efforts facilitate the matriculation of students through the college. This is accomplished through deliberate programs and services that are designed to demystify and uncomplicate the proc ess by which a student enrolls and begins taking classes. These officials connect students to the institution and provide them with direct support and the necessary tools to begin coursework. This function is of critical importance to the survival of the institution, especially considering that: (a) enrollment, in most funding structures, generates monies for the institution; (b) it creates educational opportunities for students who may lack the cultural capital or "know-how" to apply to college; and (c) it directly relates to the community college mission of "open access," by making the process of attending college more accessible.

Orientation/Registration. The purpose of orientation is to prepare students for academic and campus life. Orientation programming throughout the nation is offered in different ways; some colleges provide online orientations, some conduct in-person orientations, and others provide both options for students. Orientation programming is usually the result of collaborations between various student affairs offices (e.g., retention programs, counseling, outreach), and academic affairs (e.g., faculty). Orientation programs typically encompass a variety of services, such as: (a) allowing students to register for classes; (b) connect with other students; (c) learn about activities; (d) explore campus academic support services; (e) meet with faculty members; (f) tour and learn the history, mission, and vision of the campus; and (g) aid students in establishing a connection to the campus. Research indicates that community college students who attend orientation are more likely to have higher persistence, degree completion, and grade point averages than students who do not (Derby & Smith, 2004; Glass & Garrett, 1995). As noted, orientation programs play a critical role in students' transition from high school (or the community) to college. In light of financial constraints facing many colleges in this current era, the benefits of orientation programming, namely increased student success, should convince educational leaders that this is an important operation of the institution that cannot be eliminated or partially defunded. Many orientation programs are not mandatory. We believe that orientation programming should be, and must be tied to the unique needs of specific student groups. This is due to the realization that varied groups (e.g., disabled, nontraditional students, racial/ethnic students), have needs that are unique to their group.

Financial Aid. Financial aid officers facilitate students in completing the Free Application for Federal Student Aid (FAFSA). They also process students information to provide them with monies (e.g., loan, grants) to aid them in paying for school. There are many types of financial aid programs: loans, tuition discounts, work-study, private/public scholarships, and grants. These funds are designed to offset the financial cost of attending community college. Cohen & Brawer (2003) note that financial aid monies are particularly important to student access, as they are directly related to students' decision to enroll and continue in higher education. These monies are also important, as student finances are directly linked to their persistence (Hampton, 2002; Shulock & Moore, 2007; St. John et al., 2000). This is particularly important for leaders who desire to increase institutional support for students that may aid them in achieving academic success. Financial aid provides students with: (a) money allowing them to register for classes; (b) funds to supplement living expenses; (c) the fiscal stability (e.g., housing, healthcare, childcare) needed to focus on school; and (d) the resources needed to engage in coursework (e.g., books, supplies) (Shulock & Moore, 2007). Student affairs leaders should be promoting financial aid policies that: (1) facilitate student-friendly financial aid processes; and (2) ensure that various funding sources (e.g., grants, scholarships, loans, and work-study) are available to students.

Counseling. Counseling officers focus on addressing the psychosocial needs of the students. This is accomplished through a variety of services, including: (a) career counseling (e.g., personality indicators, career enhancement skills, communication skills, job placement); (b) academic advising (e.g., operate retention programs, academic planning); and (c) personal counseling (e.g., alcohol awareness, wellness information). Many community college counselors are faculty members; this adds credibility to their work. Unfortunately, this credibility is not enjoyed by all student affairs personnel. Community college counseling divisions are at the forefront of meeting the psychosocial needs of students by: (1) making students aware of campus services; (2) conducting need assessments of the students; (3) implementing strategies to address student needs; and (4) following up with students to determine the effectiveness of the intervention. Student affairs leaders must recognize that counselors serve to provide a platform for students' psychosocial stability by playing an integral role in creating a sense of community for all students (Barr, Desler, & Associates, 2000; Hamrick, Evans, & Schuh, 2002).

Student Activities. Student activities include a wide variety of operations under the jurisdiction of student affairs. These include: student government, student clubs and organizations, and athletics, among others. Student government provides a platform to engage in the decision-making process of institutional governance. Many campuses provide students with voting/nonvoting membership and input on campus committees, initiatives, faculty senate representations, and special task force committees. While student participation is more symbolic, students gain invaluable leadership experiences, which prepare them for professional employment. Thus, these experiences serve as the "training ground" for students focused on going into an array of professional settings, such as business and government. Student clubs and organizations provide a venue for student learning and personal development through a multiplicity of clubs and organizations related to varied student interests (e.g., racial ethnic affiliation, religious affiliation, political orientation, and sexual orientation). Most importantly, these organizations influence a sense of belonging among its members. This leads to students feeling as though they are integral members of the institution. In turn, it facilitates student academic success. Furthermore, it enhances interpersonal relations and organizational and leadership skills.

Athletics has played an important role in providing a sense of motivation, discipline, and aiding student social integration into the overall campus environment. Involvement with collegiate sports can enhance academic performance in the following ways. It: (a) provides students with added motivation to excel academically in class in order to meet eligibility requirements; (b) provides students with an increase of self-worth that can translate into higher academic performance; (c) benefits student athletes by providing tailored counseling, advising, instruction, and tutoring focused on their academic success. Tinto (1993) asserts the importance of student integration into the campus setting by stating that students who are engaged are more likely to succeed and graduate. The role of student activities underscores Tinto's assertions by engaging students into the campus environment. Thus, student affairs leaders should be attuned to the importance and vitality that student activities serve in impacting academic success.

Retention Programs—Retention programs provide students with services (e.g., tutoring, remediation, mentoring, computer labs, career counseling, job-skills training, childcare) that are designed to support their continuation and success in school (Cohen & Brawer, 2003). Typically, retention programs target specialized populations (e.g., adults, mothers, low-income groups, students of color, veterans) who may experience lower persistence and success rates than other campus students. Retention programs are designed to address factors that contribute to these rates. Funding for retention programs can come from a variety of places. Some retention programs are funded by the federal government through TRIO;[2] others are funded at the local campus level through institutional funds; and some are financed by private donors. As a result, retention programs vary greatly in size, scope, and resources. Retention programs operate on the margins of academic and student affairs; and depending on the campus, can be housed under either division, though usually they are within student affairs. Retention programs are unique, in that they address both the social and academic integration of students into an institution, which according to Tinto (1993) is imperative to student success. Unfortunately, many retention programs and efforts are not provided with the resources needed to enable their success (Tinto, 2006–2007). Additionally, many retention efforts are isolated to small population-specific programs that address the realities of a limited student population. Thus, it is imperative that these efforts be supported and expanded by community college leaders in order to enhance the persistence and success rates of all students. Leaders should recognize that retention programs are vital to the success of community colleges in meeting their mission of "open access" and "student success."

A multiplicity of benefits can be gained for leaders who understand the benefits of student affairs, support their efforts, and advocate for their equal status in the decision-making process.

---

[2] Every leader in higher education must become familiar with the TRIO programs. Title IV under the Higher Education Act of 1965 provides funds for the federal TRIO programs (Council for Opportunity in Education, 2009). Originally, there were three programs, hence the name TRIO, now TRIO includes six "outreach and support programs targeted to serve and assist low-income, first-generation college students, and students with disabilities to progress through the academic pipeline from middle school to postbaccalaureate programs" (http://www.ed.gov/about/offices/list/ope/trio/index.html).

- *Retention.* Student affairs professionals serve to facilitate the transition and retention of community college students through the use of an array of programs and practices (e.g., counseling, housing assistance, student activities). These practices are of critical importance in that they serve to socially integrate students into the overall campus environment. Lack of social integration has been cited as a primary reason why students do not complete their studies (Tinto, 1993).
- *Quality Graduates.* While academic affairs focuses on developing the cognitive abilities of students; student affairs programs and services address students' learning by primarily aiding in their psychosocial development. Both aspects of student development and learning are needed for well-balanced graduates who excel both academically and socially. We believe that this accrued dual knowledge base leads to individuals being more adaptable in multiple settings (e.g., professional, social) (American College Personnel Association, 1994).
- *Public Image.* Retention efforts, career advising, and articulation are core student affairs operations. Evidence of successful student affairs programming and services corresponds with high attainment, career placement, and transfer rates. This can lead to a positive public image for institutions as their reputation for successfully educating the "whole" student is seen by industry, other colleges/universities, and the local community.
- *Linkage to Community.* Student affairs services are the primary campus entity in linking the college community to the local community. This is done through a variety of operations, such as: outreach efforts, articulation agreements, establishing relationships with industry, relationship building with community partners, developing internship opportunities for students, community services, and service-learning.
- *Forges Partnerships for Students.* Understanding the importance of coordinating with student and academic affairs will allow leaders to be better poised in educating the "whole" student. In addition, student affairs professionals also work with various entities (e.g., families, communities, churches, nonprofit organizations, government, employers) to eliminate external barriers to learning. This is done through programs and services that are dedicated to primarily providing stability in the affective disposition and lived realities of students.

As noted above, student affairs programming and services leads to improved retention efforts, the development of quality graduates, a respected public image, and linkage to the local community. Student affairs operations are directly linked to three core aspects of the community college mission: (1) serving "local community needs," (2) providing "comprehensive educational programming," and (3) student success (i.e., aiding students in achieving their academic and career goals).

The vast majority of students enrolled in community colleges today will not graduate. For example, only 35.7 percent of all public two-year college students will attain a degree (e.g., certificate, associate) within seven years of their enrollment. When data is disaggregated by racial/ethnic affiliation, wide disparities are seen. Seven-year attainment rates for students by race/ethnicity are as follows: Asian American, 38.9 percent; White, 38.1 percent; Black, 26 percent; and Hispanic, 29.5 percent (Hoachlander et al., 2003). Academic affairs, in and of itself, cannot facilitate their success. The diversity of students in these institutions require a merging of academic and student affairs, in order to address their heterogeneous (e.g., psychological, social, academic) development needs. In fact, the poor persistence, graduation, transfer, and attainment rates of community college students can be attributed to, at least in part, the relegation of student affairs offices to the periphery of two-year institutions.

It is important for community college leaders to have a comprehensive knowledge base focused on academic affairs (i.e., cognitive development)[3] and student affairs (i.e., affective development)[4] (Bloland, Stamatakos, & Rogers, 1996). The unfortunate dichotomy that exists between academic and student affairs polarizes these two philosophies (i.e., affective, cognitive) of student development and learning. The American College Personnel Association (1994) developed *the Student Learning Imperative (SLI)*, which recommends that student affairs personnel simultaneously address both student learning and student development. This document states "learning, personal development, and student development are all inextricably intertwined and inseparable" (p. 2). Furthermore, the document emphasizes a seamless approach to student success, which will allow leaders to cater to the overall developmental needs of the "whole" student. This document presents a critical introspection by questioning the role of student affairs in meeting the needs of the students. It critically challenges student affairs leaders to consider whether they are succeeding in establishing discourse, developing programming and services, and implementing preventions and interventions to

---

[3] Cognitive development—"accounts for the ways an individual develops critical thinking and reasoning processes" (Barr et al., 2000, p. 236).

[4] Affective development—involves the temperamental, emotional, self-esteem, and self-concept development of individuals.

facilitate student learning and personal development. The notions raised by this consideration have been informed by core hallmarks of student affairs and higher education. These hallmarks are:

- *Distinguishing Factors of Educated Individuals.* The report outlines five distinguishing skills and abilities that a college-educated person should posses, they are: (1) the ability to engage in critical thinking, analysis, and reflection; (2) the ability to transfer academic knowledge bases (e.g., theory, models, research) into practice to address issues which arise in professional and social settings; (3) knowledge, appreciation, and inclusiveness with regards to diversity; (4) the ability to confront issues and resolve conflicts; and (e) a well-developed self-efficacy, locus of control,[5] moral compass, and overall identity.

- *Developing Affective and Cognitive Individuals.* The report notes that the role of student affairs is to enhance student learning and personal development, which leads to the affective and cognitive development of students. While a dichotomy between these two concepts exists in academe, in the "real" world, they are intricately connected. Valued employees are well-developed on both ends (cognitive and affective) rather than being limited to one. Problem solving, decision making, and conflict resolution are areas where both abilities are required to adequately address issues that arise.

- *Learning in Multiple Contexts.* Student affairs practitioners recognize that learning is not limited to the classroom. Experiences outside of the institution, inside the institution, and in class, work collaboratively to shape student learning and development. When collaborations, connections, and engagements are made with individuals internal to the institution (e.g., faculty, staff, and student-to-student) and external to the institution (e.g., industry, community), learning is enhanced. Student development activities which occur in concert with academic experiences allow for the development of the "whole" student.

- *Purposeful Activities.* Students' affairs leaders are responsible for planning, implementing, and promoting purposeful activities centered on the major philosophies of student affairs (affective development) and

---

[5] Locus of control—refers to an individual's belief of what controls their future. In general, an internal locus of control suggests that individuals control their own future; while, an external locus of control suggests that outside forces will determine their future.

academic affairs (cognitive development). Once this process has been actualized, effective and efficient learning enhances students' academic and personal development. For example, operationalizing purposeful student affairs planning and activities such as tutoring, mentoring, counseling, and advising has a direct positive impact on student success.

- *Assessment and Evaluation.* In order for student affairs professionals to ensure that they and their institutions are successful in developing the "whole" student, regular assessment and evaluation efforts must be undertaken. The core elements which drive this assessment should be centered on the status of student learning and personal development. Assessments can focus on a variety of areas, including, but not limited to: student satisfaction, identity development, affective disposition, social integration, and campus climate. Regular assessment and evaluation should drive policies, processes, programs, and services.

- *Relationship Building.* The collaboration between student affairs and academic affairs, as spearheaded by student affairs, is to enhance student learning and personal development through varied activities. Relationship building is needed across and within divisions in order to work collectively toward the holistic education of students.

Guiding Leadership Practices for Student Affairs

The National Association for Student Personnel Administrators (NASPA) is the prominent national body for student affairs administrators and officials for all colleges and universities. All student affairs leaders should be affiliated with this organization, in consideration of the organization's advocacy in holistic education. This provides student affairs administrators with practical training, examples, research, and guidance for tailoring programs and services conducive to promoting the cognitive and affective development of students. NASPA has established *Principles of Good Practice*[6] for student affairs practitioners, which guide the profession. These principles state that an effective student affairs leader:

> Engages students in active learning; helps students develop coherent values and ethical standards; sets and communicates high expectations for student learning; uses systematic inquiry to improve institutional performance; uses resources effectively

---

[6] This document was first drafted in 1987 and revised in 1996.

to achieve institutional missions and goals; forges educational partnerships that advance student learning; and builds supportive and inclusive communities (NASPA, 1996, Para. 1).

These seven principles represent the contemporary professional values of student affairs professionals. They are anchored in foundational values established by the American Council of Education (ACE) nearly eight decades ago. In 1937, *the Student Personnel Point of View* was released by ACE. This foundational document provided the philosophical underpinning for the profession of student affairs. It espoused professional roles, which encouraged practitioners "to consider the student as a whole" in programming and services (p. 2). In order to illustrate the role of student professionals from the *Student Personnel Point of View* to the *Seven Principles of Good Practice*, we have linked concepts articulated within both documents (see Table 1). The overlap seen within these documents illustrates core values of the profession that continue to be emphasized, with particular attention to further explicating the concept of educating the "whole" student.

These documents illustrate core values that have stayed constant among student affairs leaders since the 1930s. This can be seen as both a benefit and a drawback. It is a benefit in the sense that there is consistency in: (a) the operations, services, and support student affairs professionals provide to students; (b) promoting core values across generations of student affairs leaders with regard to core principles of the profession which enables common understanding and values that drive the discipline toward a unified vision focused on enhancing student learning and personal development; and (c) operations that have led to the creation of student developmental theories (e.g., psychosocial, typologies, structural-cognitive), which now serve to inform the philosophical underpinnings of the discipline.

Notwithstanding these benefits, drawbacks exist in several areas: (1) The students of 1937 are not the students of today. Today's community college students are very diverse. Shaw (1999) contended that student service professionals in the community college often take a myopic approach to the affective development of students. For example, Shaw notes that institutions approach students' identity development without recognition of vast differences that exist between students of varying backgrounds. (2) The aforementioned values inform practices and services which have changed little since the 1930s. When these efforts are not aligned with the *current* realities of the changing student demographics, the impact is adverse, none, or minimal. Outcomes are reflective of benchmarks (e.g., graduation, transfer, attainment rates) used to assess the effectiveness of

Table 1 Guiding Leadership Practices for Student Affairs

Principles of good practice (NASPA, 1996)	Student personnel point of view (ACE, 1937)
Engages students in active learning	Assisting the student to clarify his occupational aims and his educational plans in relation to them
Helps students develop coherent values and ethical standards	Supervising, evaluating, and developing the religious life and interests of students.
Sets and communicates high expectations for student learning	Assisting the student to reach his maximum effectiveness through clarification of his purposes, improvement of study methods, speech habits, personal appearance, manners, etc.
Uses systematic inquiry to improve institutional performance	Carrying on studies designed to evaluate and improve these functions and services
Uses resources effectively to achieve institutional missions and goals	Interpreting institutional objectives and opportunities to prospective students and their parents and to workers in secondary education
Forges educational partnerships that advance student learning;	Articulates college and vocational experience
Builds supportive and inclusive communities	Maintaining student group morale by evaluating, understanding, and developing student mores...Supervising, evaluating, and developing the extracurricular activities of students...Supervising, evaluating, and developing the social life and interests of students.

Source: NASPA (1996); ACE (1937). Direct quotes are used in this table.

institutions in meeting the academic, social, and psychological needs of students. (3) The emphasis of the 1937 document is on "enhancing" student learning and personal development. Student affairs programming is an integral facet of the educational process that directly affects both the cognitive and affective development of students (Blimling, 2002; Pascarella & Terenzini, 1991; Tinto, 1993). This is not reflected adequately in current language regarding the role of student affairs, which still states that its role is to "enhance," "encourage," "support," and "affirm" the cognitive and affective development of students. Such statements truly undermine the importance of student affairs, which co-educates, co-socializes, and co-prepares students in tandem with (not supplemental to) academic affairs operations.

In large part, the inability of student affairs to illustrate its importance in higher education indicates a lack of success on the part of student affairs leaders and officials in articulating the their contribution to student academic success. In reality, they should not have to articulate their benefits, as their benefits are both logical and compelling. In actuality, many academic affairs officers do not fully comprehend their contributions. Student affairs officers must communicate their importance, as their lack of equal footing with academic affairs has implications for their ability to positively affect students. In this current era, where external forces (e.g., budget constraints, shifting demographics, accountability) are producing radical changes in the structure of the community college, there is an increased need for community college leaders (including those in student affairs) to justify all elements of their operations. To do so, student affairs leaders must do two things: (1) they must provide a cogent rationale for their role in co-educating, co-socializing, and co-preparing students; and (2) they must present research, which substantiates their worth and success in these operations. This being said, it is not only incumbent upon student affairs to work collaboratively and equally with academic affairs, but for academic affairs leaders to do the same. Once equal footing is in place, student affairs leaders will benefit from increased funding allocations in institutional operations as well as becoming integral entities in the core functions of the institution.

Student Development Theories

While student affairs efforts are guided by retention/persistence theory (e.g., Spady, Bean, & Metzner, Tinto, Astin, Hagedorn) and by student development theory, Gansemer-Topf, Ross, & Johnson (2006) note that *student development theories* refer to "research and theory associated with the development of college students" (p. 19). They note that this domain of theory is rooted in sociological and psychological research. King and Howard-Hamilton (2000) identify three primary areas of student development theory; they are: (1) typological theories; (2) cognitive-structural theories; and (3) psychosocial theories. While typological theories and cognitive-structural theories are integral to successful student affairs operations, we believe that psychosocial theories best articulate the functions of student affairs leaders. We will briefly describe typologies theories and cognitive-structural theories before explicating several psychosocial theories.

Typological Theories. Typology theories focus on personal preferences, approaches and differences, "typically describing ways in which students approach the world (including, of course, how they approach their learning environments)" (King & Howard-Hamilton, 2000, p. 32). These personal differences are grounded in the backgrounds, traditions, values, customs, and life experiences of students. Differences also are evident based upon racial/ethnic affiliation, gender, religious upbringing, sexual preferences, and so on. These factors shape their personalities (e.g., views, assumptions, beliefs, attitudes) as well as their styles of learning (e.g., audio, visual, kinesthetic). Once typologies are formed among individuals, they remain relatively stable throughout one's life trajectory. A variety of instruments, indicators, descriptors, and general evaluation tools focused on evaluating individual's typology through questionnaires that allow for character classification within specific typologies are available. In utilizing these tools, leaders should recognize that in order to gain a comprehensive view of one's typology, multiple assessment efforts are warranted. Primary typologies theories include: Myers-Briggs Type Indicator (Myers, 1987); Holland's Theory of Vocational Choice (1966), and Kolb's Theory of Learning Development (1976).

Cognitive-Structural Theories. Cognitive-Structural theories focus on how individuals view and elicit meaning from experiences in their lives as well as how they develop critical thinking skills. This domain of theories includes: students' perceptions of future occupations as well as theory related to their intellectual and moral development (King & Howard-Hamilton, 2000). The focus of these theories is on "how" people think, as opposed to "what" they think. Cognitive dissonance (e.g., intellectual ambiguity and conflict, turmoil among cognitive constructs) allows for cognitive growth. Cognitive-structural theories depict individuals' development on stage scales, ranging from very simplistic understandings of the world, to more complex understandings which are dynamic and multifaceted in nature. One's advancement through successive stages is influenced by life experiences as well as encounters with varying viewpoints, perspectives, and ideas. Stage succession occurs as these experiences and new ideas are examined, reflected upon, and ultimately resolved by the individual. There are several primary areas of cognitive-structural theories, including: moral development, faith development, ego development, interpersonal awareness, and maturation theory (Hamrick, Evans, & Schuh, 2002).

Pyschosocial theories. Psychosocial theories focus on the developmental process of students by which students "come to know themselves and learn to relate effectively with those around them" (Hamrick, Evans, & Schuh, 2002, p. 141). Erikson (1959, 1968) serves as a foundational theorist for understanding life span development. He addresses eight total stages of development, which are associated with five periods of life (Hamrick, Evans, & Schuh, 2002). Hamrick, Evans,

& Schuh, (2002) associate these stages as follows: (1) preschool period (e.g., basic trust vs. basic mistrust, autonomy vs. shame and doubt, initiative vs. guilt), (2) childhood (e.g., industry vs. inferiority), (3) early adulthood (e.g., identity vs. identity diffusion, intimacy and distantiation vs. self-absorption), (4) middle adulthood (e.g., generativity vs. stagnation), and (e) late adulthood (e.g., integrity vs. despair and disgust). While every student who enters the community college does so at different stages of development, Erickson's identity versus identity diffusion stage, intimacy and distantiation versus self-absorption, and generativity versus stagnation stages may provide the best understanding to these students.[7] Erickson (1980) describes these stages as follows:

- *Identity versus Identity Diffusion.* Identity versus identity diffusion is a stage associated with puberty. In this stage, youth are concerned with the opinions of others. In this process, individuals struggle with their identity, trying to reconcile whether to be themselves, or not. In large part, this process is shaped by peer influences. This identity development process can be complicated by identity diffusion. Identity diffusion occurs when youth affected by the pressures of this process (along with its stereotypes, expectations), coupled with occupational uncertainty loses their identity. Erickson notes that adolescents help each other in this process by associations (e.g., cliques).
- *Intimacy and Distantiation versus Self-Absorption.* In the Intimacy and distantiation versus self-absorption stage, one's identity is developed through intimate relationships with others. The type of relationships (positive or negative) experienced at a young age, informs identity development. Individuals go through a process of identity ambivalence where, through reflection and intimate interaction, their development is shaped. For those who have developed a positive self-identity and healthy relationships with others (e.g., building friendships, intimate interactions), healthier and easier relationships are formed. For those who do not establish positive intimacy with others (beyond sexual relations), they are vulnerable to volatile intimate relationships. This occurs as relationships are seen as a challenge to one's being. Individuals who are self-absorbed are not cognizant of the feelings, thoughts, and perceptions of others. They are attuned merely to their own ends.

---

[7] Other stages may apply as well. Leaders would be served to understand prior stages not explicated in this chapter.

- *Generativity versus Stagnation.* In the generativity versus stagnation stage, individuals come to a place where they are concerned with addressing the needs and development of others, especially their children. Generativity is a marker of healthy development; whereas those who do not embrace or reach generativity are susceptible to negative interpersonal relations, referred to as stagnation. Individuals in stagnation are self-indulged, egocentric, and exhibit poor interpersonal relations as their primary concerns are for themselves, and not others (e.g., children). Those in stagnation generally have poor conceptions of personal, family, and community relations.

Expanding on Erickson's eight stages, Marcia (1966) developed four stages focused on the identity development of young adults. These stages assess the type of experiences encountered by these individuals in response to crisis and commitment, "Crisis refers to the adolescent's period of engagement in choosing among meaningful alternatives; commitment refers to the degree of personal investment the individual exhibits" (p. 551). The four stages explicated by Marcia are: (1) identity achievement—individuals who do not possess a clear sense of being with respect to their values, personal goals, and future aspirations; (2) moratorium—an anxious time in young adulthood, where individuals are uncertain about their aspirations and engage in self-introspection in which they battle within, as an attempt to solidify their future commitments; (3) foreclosure—when individuals lack retrospection in learning from past experiences and instead, allow others to define their identity; and (4) identity diffusion—when individuals do not conceptualize, plan, or actively engage in their future commitments but have a tendency to change occupational directions and dedications at a whim.

Chickering (1969) also extrapolated his own identity development theory of college students based on Erikson's (1959, 1968) model of eight developmental crises. This theory provides a framework for understanding the establishment of identity development during the college years. His work centered on examining the comprehensive manner in which identity among college age students is developed, and the internal and external developmental factors that either: (1) hinder; (2) stagnate development; or (3) facilitate the progression of identify development. Chickering identified seven processes that surround identify development (psychosocial and cognitive) among college students by delineating the issues that surround each task. These seven processes became known as vectors. This term was used to identify the dynamic fluidity involved with the seven stages, with particular attention to pinpointing the overlapping commonalities across vectors, and a step-by-step progression of identify development (Hamrick, Evans, & Schuh, 2002).

Although the seven vectors of identity development were first developed to address the stages of identity development during adolescence and early adulthood, they have been readily applied to college-age students. The broad applicability across multiple age groups and its expansive conceptual nature provides student affairs leaders with guiding principles, while making allowance for contextual interpretation (Chickering & Reisser, 1993). Chickering and Reisser's revised vectors of 1993 account for environmental factors that influence a college student's identity development (e.g., curriculum and instruction, faculty–advisee relationship, campus diversity, student affairs support services). These environmental factors account for elements of a student's life that influence identity development. The outlook on environmental factors coupled with individual factors provide a systematic manner in which to view identity development and subsequently understanding self and others. The seven vectors are synthesized below.

- *Developing competence (Vector 1).* Developing confidence serves as a foundation to a strong sense of identity. Three types of competence include: intellectual competence, physical and manual skills, and interpersonal competence. The understanding of one's abilities, skills, and intellectual capacity is of critical importance since it serves as a platform for one to elicit meaning of past, current, and future experiences. Physical and manual competence can serve as point of identity growth, in that it allows an individual to express his or herself creatively through physical and personal discipline. Interpersonal skills involve the development of communication skills (e.g., listening, working cohesively within a group context). Individuals with interpersonal skills are cognizant of context(s) in which they operate; they behave, and communicate in accordance with normative behaviors and unspoken subtleties.
- *Managing Emotions (Vector 2).* Allowing, controlling, and using emotions to drive identity development is the cornerstone of this stage. Fear, happiness, isolation, anger, as well as other emotions are natural feelings of college students. When individuals are aware of these emotions and are able to temper them, their educational process is positively impacted. However, when individuals are overcome by their emotions, this distress can negatively affect their education, as well as their personal relationships with others.

- *Moving through Autonomy toward Interdependence (Vector 3).* Increasing social, psychological, and intellectual x development allows for the transition from dependence to independence. As students break from established bonds (e.g., parents, teachers, mentors), they begin to develop self-sufficiency, self-efficacy, and an increased internal locus of control; these are hallmarks of independence. As they engage in this process, maturation takes place, allowing them to stand on their own leaving behind a dependence upon reassurance from others.
- *Developing Mature Interpersonal Relationships (Vector 4).* Building relationships requires openness, understanding, and willingness to reduce stereotypes and biases. This serves as the basis for developing and sustaining healthy relationships based upon respect, honesty, and consideration for others. The efforts to develop mature relationships grounded on these values allows for commitment toward full and enduring relationships.
- *Establishing Identity (Vector 5).* Establishing identity refers to the condition in which people know who they are, both internally (e.g., needs, wants, desires, attitudes), and externally (e.g., authentic display of genuine self, being comfortable in an array of social, historical, and cultural contexts). Identity establishment is dependent upon prior identity formation stages (Vectors 1–4). Previous experiences and relationships are reflected upon and used to guide identity development.
- *Developing Purpose (Vector 6).* The breadth and depth of developing one's purpose determines the overall commitment to achieving this purpose. Purposes that lack clarity, guidance, and commitment are typically short lived and will succumb to premature departure. Developing and reaching one's purpose includes: establishing a plan of action driven by efforts of perseverance, work ethic, mentorship, structural support, faith, and peer support.
- *Developing Integrity (Vector 7).* Developing integrity is the process in which one operates in a reliable, honest, and forthright manner. Integrity involves both: (a) the establishment of and steadfast dedication to one's personal convictions (e.g., perceptions, values, principles); and (b) the willingness to reevaluate those convictions through openness, consideration, and respect for the viewpoints of others.

Erickson's, Marcia's, and Chickering's theories address realities common to individuals in general. They serve as a foundation for other psychosocial development theories. However, they are inadequate in describing realities specific to identity development with specific racial/ethnic groups. Now, identity development theories exist that focus on many groups, including Blacks (e.g., Baldwin & Bell, 1982, 1985; Cross, 1991); Whites (e.g., Helms, 1990, 1993); Asian Americans (e.g., Ibrahim, Ohnishi, & Sandhu, 1997, Kim 1981), and Hispanics (e.g., Casas & Pytluk, 1995). There are also models that focus on sexual identity development (e.g., Cass, 1979; D'Augelli, 1994) and intercultural sensitivity (Bennett, 1993). To provide an example of how these models address identity development, we will explicate Helms's (1990) Racial Identity Development Theory (RIDT) and Bennett's (1993) Development Model of Intercultural Sensitivity (DMIS).

First, Helms's (1990) RIDT describes six stages of identity development (e.g., contact, reintegration, disintegration, pseudo-independence, immersion–emersion, and autonomy), which individuals encounter in relationship to their racial/ethnic affiliation. These stages are conceptualized on a continuum from negative to positive viewpoints of racial/ethnic affiliation.

Contact. In this stage, individuals exhibit large voids of understanding as it relates to race, racism, and racialization. Generally, few interactions have taken place with people other than those of the same racial/ethnic affiliation. As a result, these individuals are insensible and unconscious to racism, often purporting to be color-blind.

Reintegration. In the reintegration stage, individuals exhibit signs of racial, social, and cultural supremacy. They give credence to the realities of the racial/ethnic group in which they identify. Cultural variance is discredited.

Disintegration. In this stage, encounters and interactions with individuals from different racial/ethnic groups create internal conflict. The individual becomes unsettled over views on race, racism, and racialization. Issues regarding race and morality, which drive polarized perspectives, are the root of internal discontent.

Pseudo-independence. In the pseudo-independence stage, rudimentary understanding of multiple racial/ethnic, social, and cultural groups begins. Marginal involvement with these groups occurs, and to some extent is sought out. These experiences shape the individual perceptions of others groups, leading to positive identity development occurring in the next two stages.

Immersion–Emersion. Immersion–Emersion is the first positive stage of identity development. Interactions with individuals of different racial/ethnic affiliation have led to an altering of one's previous views on race, racism, and racialization. Dominant group status is questioned and meaning about race and ethnicity is elicited. Development of a positive racial/ethnic identity occurs as one engages in addressing racism/ethnocentrism, bigotry, stereotypes, and bias.

Autonomy. Autonomy is the final stage of racial/identity development. In this stage, an individual has become aware of their racial/ethnic affiliation, culture, and values, as well as the meaning behind these areas of awareness. The individual's role in advancing racism is acknowledged and addressed. Privilege also is acknowledged and addressed. Racial/ethnic, social, and cultural diversity is affirmed, and apprehension toward discourse in these areas is reduced.

Bennett's (1993) DMIS identifies a six-stage process explaining intercultural sensitivity. His model exists on a continuum ranging from ethnocentrism to ethnorelativism. Ethnocentrism is exhibited when individuals' perceptions of the world are guided through a myopic cultural lens. Ethnorelativism occurs when multiple world views are recognized, appreciated, and used to examine the world. The six steps comprising Bennett's model are: (1) denial, (2) defense, (3) minimization, (4) acceptance, (5) adaptation, and (6) integration. The first three stages of the model (denial, defense, and minimization) are linked with the ethnocentric side of his continuum; whereas, the second three stages (acceptance, adaptation, and integration) progress toward ethnorelativism.

Denial. In the denial stage, individuals are inattentive, unconcerned, and oblivious to cultural differences. This occurs even when they personally experience and interact with those of dissimilar cultures.

Defense. In this stage, individuals who encounter cultural differences respond by being defensive. They treat cultural variance as a threat to their own being, culture, values, and beliefs. Unlike the previous stage, cultural variance is both noted and defended against.

Minimization. Minimization refers to the process by which individuals encounter cultural variance and respond by minimizing the differences that exist. This is accomplished through actions and dialogues, which emphasize parallels and similarities in diverse cultures.

Acceptance. The acceptance stage is characterized by the viewpoint that cultural variance is both recognized and valued. This stage represents the transition between an ethnocentric and ethnorelative worldview.

Adaptation. In this stage, individuals have developed an understanding and respect for cultural differences that exist among groups. However, their culture is still the frame of reference for understanding other cultures.

Integration. Integration is the last stage of Bennett's model. In this stage, various cultural differences are respected, appreciated, and affirmed. One can isolate their individual cultural lens and view the world through an ethnorelative standpoint.

The aforementioned models and theories of psychosocial development can serve to provide leaders with a general overview of human/identity development. These models can serve to aid student affairs leaders in examining the standpoint and status of their students. Hence, our focus heretofore has been to explicate developmental theory for the purposes of better understanding students. However, we would be remiss, if we did not end this chapter by extending this theory to apply directly to educational leaders.

Informed by Helms's (1990) RIDT as well as Bennett's (1993) DMIS, we hypothesized a new model to understand leadership in diverse secondary schools—referred to as the Leadership in Diversity Continuum Model (LDCM) (see Nevarez & Wood, 2007). While this model was developed and tested on K-12 educational leaders (Nevarez & Wood, 2008a, 2008b, 2009), it has direct applicability to community college leaders. The purpose of the LDCM was to address how the identity development of leaders (based upon RIDT and DMIS) correlates with specific leadership actions, approaches, and styles. The model employs seven stages (e.g., prohibiting, segregation, color-blind, pretext, recognition, value, and affirmation), which relate to Helms's & Bennett's models (see Table 2).

Similar to Bennett's model, the seven stages of LDCM are conceptualized on a continuum. This continuum represents four stages of cross-cultural rejection (prohibiting, segregation, color-blind, and pretext), and three stages of cross-cultural congruency (recognition, values, and affirmation). The stages of this model are depicted in Figure 1.

Table 2 Leadership in Diversity Continuum Model versus Helms's Theory and Bennett's Model

LDCM	Helms's theory	Bennett's model
	Contact	≠
Prohibiting	Disintegration	Denial
Segregation	Reintegration	Defense
Color-blind	≠	Minimization
Pretext	Pseudo-independence	≠
Recognition	Immersion–emersion	Acceptance
Value	Autonomy	Adaptation
Affirmation	≠	Integration

Note: (≠) represents incongruence.

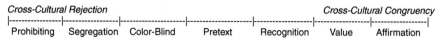

Figure 1.1 Seven modes of leadership employed by educational leaders in response to diversity.

Figure 1 *Leadership in Diversity Continuum Model (LDCM)*

The first stage identified in the model is *prohibiting*. Prohibiting leadership occurs when leaders reduce and reject diversity through exclusionary practices (e.g., firing diverse personnel, ensuring diverse personnel are not hired).

The *segregation* stage of this model occurs when leaders, rather than prohibiting diversity, systematically (both consciously and unconsciously) segregate diversity. In community colleges, this occurs when diverse personnel are concentrated in specific areas of the institution (e.g., ethnic studies departments, outreach, and retention programs). When this occurs, these personnel are not integrated within the core functions of the institution; rather they reside on its periphery. In general, when segregation occurs, diverse personnel are usually concentrated within programs that serve racial/ethnic groups.

In the *color-blind* stage, individuals reduce the importance of racial/ethnic and cultural differences by stating that they "do not see color." Colorblind leadership is rooted in assimilationist practices.

The next stage, *pretext* leadership is arguably the most common in the community college. Pretext leaders profess their dedication to diversity, speak of the need to affirm differences but fail to enact policies and practices that will promote the success of diverse individuals. For these leaders, diversity is limited to certain college operations and not institutionalized within the campus culture, policies, practices, and mission. It is a "fancier way of marginalizing" students, faculty, staff, and community members of color (Murrell, 2002, p. 41). The final three stages of the model represent individuals who exhibit cross-cultural congruency.

In the *recognition stage*, leaders begin to imbue values, issues, and importance to cultural diversity. Often, they lack in their ability to enact change, due to limited foundational knowledge on diverse racial/ethnic groups. These understandings are gained by those in the *value* stage. Value-stage leaders understand and embrace racial/ethnic and cultural diversity. Leaders in this stage become concerned with issues of educational equity, as well as social justice values.

The final stage in our model is that of *affirmation*. In this stage, leaders challenge normative practices. Values of educational equity, diversity, and social justice are central to their being.

Case Study

Student affairs leaders must be introspective and reflective about their personal identity development and intercultural sensitivity in relation to their actions as leaders. In doing so, student affairs professional must deliberately align student development models with services and support structures focused on educating the whole student (Hamrick, Evans, & Schuh, 2002). Grounding services in accordance with the development needs of students provides for purposeful efforts in preparing the students for academic and professional success. Thus, executive community college leaders need to support and require student affairs professionals to know, use, and evaluate how student development models drive their practice. An array of benefits is accrued when student development models are used as a framework to drive practices. They are useful in developing programs and policies directly aligned to addressing student needs; it allows student affairs professionals to be proactive in anticipating and addressing student issues; and student development models can be used as an evaluation tool and subsequently guide intervention efforts (Hamrick, Evans, & Schuh, 2002). Below, we present a case study which requires leaders to illustrate a foundational knowledge of student development theories and to apply this understanding in addressing a leadership dilemma.

Jim Riggs
Former President, Columbia College
Sonora, California

Facilitating Student Behavior

Background

The case takes place at Clover College, a small comprehensive community college located in the rural foothills of the Rocky Mountains. The economic base of the area is a mix of agriculture, mining, and tourism, which provides an abundance of livable-wage jobs resulting in a large stable middle class. Nearly all the students attending the college live within a 30-mile radius of the campus. The ethnic demographics of the college reflect the region, which is 75 percent white, 5 percent Native American, 10 percent Hispanic, with the remaining 10 percent split between Asian, African American, and other groups. The college has an active disabled student program (DSPS), which serves nearly 400 of the college's 3,500 students each semester. The DSPS program at Clover College serves students with several types of disabilities ranging from mobility problems, hearing and sight impairment, learning disabilities, and other disabilities including students with psychological disabilities. For many students with psychological disabilities, attending the community college is a very important part of the recovery process as they move toward an independent and productive life.

Statement of the Problem

In his role as the dean of special programs, Tim has been the administrator for the DSPS program for nearly 20 years. He has a background in rehabilitation counseling and for the past 12 years has also served as the counselor for all the disabled students at the college. Tim has developed a strong working relationship with the faculty and is frequently asked to assist them with students in their classes who have disabilities. When the only other dean in the student services division left two years ago, the vice president for student services appointed Tim, on top of all his other duties, as the student judicial and discipline officer.

One afternoon Tim received a call from a well-respected English instructor, who told him about a student in her class named Richard who, over the past month, had been "acting strange" and at times been very disruptive and confrontational. She said that she spoke with the student about a week ago regarding his behavior and the problems it was causing in the class. The instructor said that Richard seemed quite embarrassed and agreed to monitor his behavior. The instructor indicated that the essay Richard turned in three days ago dealt with his experience of being diagnosed with paranoid schizophrenia three years ago and how sometimes he has had problems with the medication. He also wrote in the essay that it was very important for him to pass the English class in order to transfer to the university in the fall.

The instructor paused for a minute and then with some urgency in her voice told Tim that if she was going to have more students like Richard in her classes, she needed training on how to deal with people with these kinds of disabilities. The following week after class the instructor asked Richard to see her in her office. Richard had been particularly disruptive that day and the instructor wanted to discuss some options with him and provide him with some referrals to services that may be helpful. During the meeting, Richard was very agitated and accused the instructor of picking on him. He told her that he knew she was going to flunk him because she was afraid of having "a mental case" in her class. The instructor tried to reassure Richard that she had no plans to flunk him and she was glad that he was in her class. He then swore at her and ran out of her office. The instructor immediately called Tim again and told him that she was concerned for her own safety as well as Richard's well-being.

After speaking with the instructor, Tim immediately left his office to look for the student. After about 30 minutes he found Richard in the cafeteria and told him that his English instructor called and was very concerned. He asked Richard to come to his office to discuss the matter. As they were walking up to the dean's office, Tim remembered the student from nearly a year ago. At that time Richard exhibited similar behavior in another class. As the discipline officer, Tim had placed Richard on disciplinary probation because of some threats he had made to another instructor and for being disruptive in class. At that time, Richard was told that he may be suspended from the college if his behavioral problems continued. Tim also remembered that Richard had quit taking his medicine at that time and had begun developing a strong fear about how the instructor disliked him and was plotting against him. Some of the conditions of Richard's disciplinary probation included him staying on his medicine while attending the college and behaving in a civil manner toward his instructors. Richard was also required to meet with the college's mental health counselor on a monthly basis.

Once they reached Tim's office he asked Richard what happened in the instructor's office that day. Richard told Tim that the instructor had been picking on him all semester so he decided to tell her that he had a mental illness. He then stated that once she found that out, she "became even meaner and was trying to flunk" him. He told Tim that after he left the instructor's office, he went immediately to the registration office and dropped her course. When asked why he dropped the class, Richard replied that the instructor would no longer have control over him.

At that point Tim reminded Richard that he had had a problem about 10 months earlier with another instructor and at that time he told Tim that he had quit taking his medication. Tim then asked Richard if he was still taking his medicine. Richard indicated that he was but he had been cutting back on the amount this past month because he was afraid he would run out before he could get a new prescription. Richard also told Tim that when he cuts back on the medication, he feels much more like himself instead of a drowsy "fat slob." He told Tim that he had cut back from four pills per day to one pill per day. Tim quickly realized that this kind of drop in medication could trigger the return of some of Richard's earlier symptoms. Tim then asked Richard if he had been meeting with the college's mental health counselor each month as required by his probation. Richard hesitated and then told Tim that he had met with her a few times, but he had been too busy with his homework and missed his last four appointments. Tim strongly advised Richard to meet with his doctor as soon as possible regarding the medication and not to adjust his medicine on his own. He also told Richard that it was critical that Richard meet on a regular basis with the mental health counselor as he had been directed earlier.

Tim offered to facilitate a meeting between Richard and the English instructor, reassuring Richard that there must have been some kind misunderstanding. Tim also told Richard that he would ask the registrar to reenroll him in the English course. Richard suddenly became agitated and told Tim that he would never go back to the English class. Richard said that since the instructor knew that he suffers from a mental illness, she was going flunk him no matter how hard he worked. As Richard stormed out of Tim's office, he shouted that he was going to sue the college for discrimination unless the college punished the English instructor for what she has done to him. Tim's responsibility is to enforce the student code of conduct in a fair and equitable manner by ensuring students who have been placed on disciplinary probation adhere to the corrective action conditions of their probation. Tim must decide what to do about this case.

References

American Council of Education (1937). *The student personnel point of view, 1937.* Washington, DC: ACE. Retrieved September 4, 2009, from: http://www.bgsu.edu/colleges/library/cac/sahp/word/THE%20STUDENT%20PERSONNEL.pdf

American College Personnel Association. (1994). *The student learning imperative: Implications for student affairs.* Alexandria, VA: Author.

Baldwin, J. A., & Bell, Y. R. (1982). *The African self-consciousness scale manual.* Tallahassee, FL: Florida A & M Psychology Department.

Baldwin, J. A., & Bell, Y. R. (1985). The African self-consciousness scale: An africentric personality questionnaire. *Western Journal of Black Studies*, 9(2), 61–68.

Barr, M. J., Desler, M. K. & Associates (eds.), 2000. *The handbook of student affairs administration.* San Francisco, CA: Jossey-Bass.

Bennett, M. J. (1993). Towards ethnorelativism: A developmental model of intercultural sensitivity. In M. Paige (Ed.). *Education for the intercultural experience* (pp. 21–72). Yarmouth, ME: Intercultural Press.

Blimling, G. S. (2002). Reflections on career development among student affairs leaders. *New Directions for Student Services*, 98, 27–36.

Bloland, P. A., Stamatakos, L. C., & Rogers, R. R. (1996). Redirecting the role of student affairs to focus on student learning. *Journal of College Student Development*, 37(2), 217–226.

Burley, H. E., & Butner, B. K. (2000). Should student affairs offer remedial education? *Community College Journal of Research and Practice*, 24, 193–205.

Casas, J. M., & Pytluk, S. D. (1995). Hispanic identity development: Implications for research and practice. In J. G. Ponterotto, J. M. Casas, L. A. Suzuki, C. M. Alexander (eds.). *Handbook of multicultural counseling* (pp. 155–180). Thousand Oaks, CA: Sage.

Cass, V. C. (1979). Homosexuality identity formation. *Journal of Homosexuality*, 4(3), 219–235.

Chickering, A. W. (1969). *Education and identity.* San Francisco, CA: Jossey-Bass.

Chickering, A. W., & Reisser, L. (1993). *Education and Identity* (2nd ed.). San Francisco, CA: Jossey-Bass.

Cohen, A. M., & Brawer, F. B. (2003). *The American community college,* (4th Ed.). San Francisco, CA: Jossey-Bass.

Council for Opportunity in Education (2009). *What is TRIO?* Washington, DC: Council for Opportunity in Education. Retrieved September 4, 2009, from: http://www.coenet.us/ecm/AM/Template.cfm?Section=What_is_TRIO&Template=/CM/HTMLDisplay.cfm&ContentID=2862

Creamer, D. G. (1994). Synthesis of literature related to historical and current functions of student services. In G. A. Baker III, J. Dudziak., & P. Tyler (eds.). *A handbook on the community college in America* (pp. 439–453). Westport, CT: Greenwood Press.

Cross, W. E., Jr. (1991). *Shades of black: Diversity in African-American identity.* Philadelphia, PA: Temple University Press.

D'Augelli, A. R. (1994). Identity development and sexual orientation: Toward a model of lesbian, gay, and bisexual development. In E. J. Trickett, R. J. Watts, & D. Birman (eds.). *Human diversity: Perspectives on people in context* (pp. 312–333). San Francisco: Jossey-Bass.

Derby, D. C., & Smith. T. (2004). An orientation course and community college retention. *Community College Journal of Research and Practice*, 28, 763–773.

Erikson, E. (1959/1980). Identity and the life cycle. *Psychological Issues*, 1, 18–164.

Erikson, E. (1968). Life cycle. In D. L. Sills & R. K. Merton (eds.). *International encyclopedia of the social sciences* (pp. 286–292). New York: MacMillan and the Free Press.

Gansemer-Topf, A. M., Ross, L. E., & Johnson, R. M. (2006). Graduate and professional student development and student affairs. *New Directions for Student Services*, 115, 19–30.

Glass, J. C., & Garrett, M. S. (1995). Student participation in a college orientation course, retention, and grade point average. *Community College Journal of Research and Practice*, 19(2), 117–132.

Hampton, P. (2002). *Academic success for African-American male community college students.* Unpublished doctoral dissertation, University of Southern California.

Hamrick, F. A., Evans, N. J., & Schuh, J. H. (2002). *Foundations of student affairs practice: How philosophy, theory, and research strengthen educational outcomes.* San Francisco, CA: Jossey-Bass.

Helms, J. E. (ed.) (1990). *Black and white racial identity: Theory, research and practice.* Westport, CT: Greenwood Press.

Helms, J. E. (1993). An overview of Black ethnic racial identity. In J. E. Helms (ed.) *Black and White racial identity: Theory, research and practice* (pp. 9–32). Westport, CT: Praeger.

Hirt, J. B., Esteban, R., & McGuire, L. (2003). Editor's choice: The worklife of student service professionals at rural community colleges. *Community College Review*, 31(1), 33–55.

Hoachlander, G., Sikora, A. C., Horn, L., & Carroll, C. D. (2003). *Community college students: Goals, academic preparation, and outcomes.* Washington, DC: National Center for Education Statistics.

Holland, J. L.(1966). *The psychology of vocational choice.* New York: Blaisdell.

Ibrahim, F. A., Ohnishi, H., & Sandhu, D. S. (1997). Asian American identity development: A culture specific model for South Asian Americans. *Journal of Multicultural Counseling and Development,*25, 34–50.

Kim, J. (1981). *Processes of Asian American identity development: A study of Japanese American women's perceptions of their struggle to achieve positive identities.* Unpublished doctoral dissertation, University of Massachusetts, Amherst.

King, P. M., & Howard-Hamilton, M. F. (2000). Using student development theory to inform institutional research. *New Directions for Institutional Research*, 108, 19–36.

Kolb, D. A. (1976). *The learning style inventory: Technical manual*, Boston, MA: McBer.

Marcia, J. E. (1966). Development and validation of ego-identity status. *Journal of Personality and School Psychology*, 3(5), 551–558.

Mattox, R. E., & Creamer, D. G. (1998). Perceptions of the scope and quality of student services functions in two-year colleges. *Community College Review*, 25(4), 3–20.

Murrell, P. (2002). *African-centered pedagogy: Developing schools of achievement for African American children.* New York: State University of New York Press.

Myers, I. B. (1987) *Introduction to type: A description of the theory and applications of the Myers-Briggs Type Indicator.* Palo Alto, CA: Consulting Psychologists Press.

NASPA (1996). *Principles of good practice for student affairs.* Washington, DC: National Association of Student Personnel Administrators. Retrieved September 4, 2009, from: http://www.naspa.org/career/goodprac.cfm

Nevarez, C., & Wood, J. L. (2007). Developing urban school leaders: Building on solutions 15 years after the Los Angeles riots. *Educational Studies*, 42(3), 266–280.

Nevarez, C., & Wood, J. L. (2008a). *Examining the perceptions of Latino urban school leaders regarding educational hurdles and the benefits of Latino teachers.* Miami, FL: The American Association of Hispanics in Higher Education.

Nevarez, C., & Wood, J. L. (2008b). *Implications and solutions for school leaders post Los Angeles riots: Experiences of urban principals.* New York: Annual Meeting of the American Educational Research Association.

Nevarez, C., & Wood, J. L. (2009). *Benefits of teachers of color: Architects in closing the achievement gap.* San Diego, CA: Annual Meeting of the American Educational Research Association.

Pascarella, E., & Terenzini, P. (1991). *How college affects students: Findings and insights from twenty years of research.* San Francisco, CA: Jossey-Bass

Shaw, K. M. (1999). Defining the self: Constructions of identity in community college students. In K. M. Shaw, J. R. Valadez, & R. A. Rhoads (eds.). *Cultural tests: Qualitative explorations of organization and student culture* (pp. 153–172). Albany: State University of New York Press.

Shulock, N., & Moore, C. (2007). *Rules of the game: How state policy creates barriers to degree completion and impedes student success in the California Community Colleges.* Sacramento: Institute for Higher Education Leadership & Policy, California State University, Sacramento.

St. John, E., Cabrera, A., Nora, A., & Asker, E. (2000). Economic influences on persistence reconsidered: How can finance research inform the reconceptualization of persistence models? In J. Braxton (Ed.). *Reworking the student departure puzzle* (pp. 29–47). Nashville, TN: Vanderbilt University Press.

Tinto, V. (1993). *Leaving college: Rethinking the causes and cures of student attrition* (2nd Ed.). Chicago, IL: University of Chicago Press.

Tinto, V. (2006–07). Research and practice of student retention: What next? *Journal of College Student Retention,* 8(1), 1–19.

CHAPTER NINE

COMMUNITY COLLEGE FINANCE

This chapter examines finance in the community college and includes: (a) an overview of revenue streams for public two-year colleges; (b) an examination of community college expenditures; and (c) funding of college for students. Particular attention is placed on assessing whether the overall picture of community college finance is in line with the mission of these institutions.

When reading this chapter, consider the following questions:

- What are the primary revenue streams for community colleges? How have these streams changed over time? What are the implications of these revenue streams on the mission of the community college?
- What are the primary expenditures for community colleges? Do these expenditure lines support the mission of the community college system?
- What role do financial aid allocations and employment play in supporting/hindering community college students' academic success? What additional factors such as non-tuition/fee costs and employment impact student success?

This chapter presents an overview of finances in the community college. For the purpose of this chapter, finance refers to revenue streams, expenditures, and student financial aid. In 2006, the *Chronicle of Higher Education* reported on what areas first-time college presidents felt that they lacked knowledge or experience for Four out of the top five areas focused on finance and budget (e.g., fundraising, capital improvement, budget, entrepreneurial ventures). Combined, they accounted for 67.4 percent of insufficiency concerns (Almanac, 2008–09). This data reveals the critical importance for prospective and current leaders to have conceptual and technical finance skills which will enable them to improve their confidence, effectiveness, efficiency, and credibility. Leaders who are deficient in the area of finance and budgeting should consider professional development in this area a must. They also can align themselves with members of their institution's leadership team that have strengths in these areas. The purpose of this alignment is to gain experiential skills from those more seasoned in this area.

It is important for leaders to examine the data presented in this chapter to assess whether the overall picture of community college finance is in line with the mission of these institutions. As leaders review information on community college revenue streams, they should consider how revenue streams sustain values of the college. For example, leaders will learn that local support for community colleges has declined markedly over time. When revenue streams decline, community colleges are forced to identify alternative revenue sources to sustain their existence while being responsive to regional workforce concerns. It is important to consider what implications this trend has for institutions to meet the needs of their local communities and to pay attention to the alignment of institutional values and these areas of expenditures.

Revenue Streams

Community colleges are challenged to provide programs and services that meet students' needs, while minimizing costs. Leaders are called upon to increase graduation and transfer rates, provide exemplary services and academic programs, meet the expansive needs of the local community, and provide greater access to postsecondary education. These tasks are particularly difficult when revenue lines to community colleges are unstable. Several examples illustrate this point: (a) states' revenue lines are often affected by reliance upon state sales tax versus property taxes. These lines are greatly impacted during economic downturns (Phillippe & Sullivan, 2005); (b) some states use lottery moneys to provide revenue to community colleges; however, these monies rise and fall based upon ticket purchases (Wattenbarger, 1994); and (c) some community colleges have benefited from bond measures, which can be based upon local property taxes. When property values decline in poor real estate markets, revenues from property taxes do as well. Given the unstable nature of funding, community college leaders must imbed assessment measures within institutional operations; this can aid them when justifying the continuation and sustenance of funding levels.

Figure 1 depicts revenue sources for public two-year colleges. We have categorized revenue streams into six sources: federal, state, local, campus, tuition/fees, and other. These sources are comprised of individual substreams of funding. Across sources, the largest revenue lines are student tuition/fees (16.64 percent),

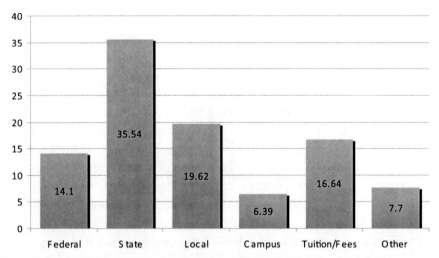

Figure 1 Categorized Revenue Streams by Origin of Funds, 2005–06

Source: Digest of Education Statistics (2008a). U.S. Department of Education, National Center for Education Statistics, 2003–04 through 2005–06 Integrated Postsecondary Education Data System, Spring 2004 through Spring 2007. Washington, DC: National Center for Education Statistics.

federal grants/contracts (10.88 percent), state appropriations (30.07 percent), and other nonoperating revenue (18.13 percent). Together, these revenue streams account for more than three-quarters of the total revenue for community colleges (Digest of Education Statistics, 2008a) (see Figure 1). Below, we describe the individual funding lines for each of the six sources (e.g., federal, state, local, campus, tuition/fees, and other). In examining this data, leaders should be mindful that the revenue streams described represent the national context for two-year public colleges, rather than specific institutions. Every community college will have differences in revenue streams, which can change from year to year.

Federal Funding

Federal support for community colleges has increased in the last ten years. For example, Cohen & Brawer (2003) indicate that only 5 percent of revenues for community colleges were derived from the federal government in the 1980s and 1990s. However, in 2005, federal support for community colleges accounted for 14.1 percent of its revenue. Federal funding streams are composed of federal grants and contracts (10.88 percent), federal appropriations (0.32 percent), and federal nonoperating grants [1] (2.90 percent) (Digest of Education Statistics, 2008a).

---

[1] Nonoperating grants—refers to funding that comes from federal, state, local government which is not generated from operations (e.g., selling of goods, providing of services) (IPEDS, 2009).

Beginning in the 1940s with the Servicemen's Readjustment Act, the federal government has provided substantial aid to support students in attending college. Cohen (2001) notes that community colleges also benefited from Vocational Act Funds from 1963, 1984, and 1985, which provided community colleges with funding for occupational programs. He notes that some community colleges have also received Title III monies, designed to support developing institutions. In 2006, the Carl D. Perkins Vocational and Technical Education Act was revised. This resulted in greater funding to community colleges. In fact, in 2007, nearly $1.1 billion in Perkins funds were distributed to community colleges (U.S. Government Accountability Office, 2008). Other federal funding opportunities to two-year colleges include some of the following: the Adult Education and Family Literary Act; Adult Basic Education, Adult Secondary Education, and English Language Acquisition funds; the Adult Basic Education to Community College Transition Projects funds; and Tech Prep Education Program funds (American Association of Community Colleges, 2008–09).

State Funding

Very little state funding was allocated to community colleges during the first third of the century (Cohen & Brawer, 2003). Around the 1940s funding structures for the community colleges began to change as states began to allocate considerable monies to these institutions. The increased state involvement in funding community colleges was likely influenced by high unemployment rates during this time. Kasper (2002–03) notes that many "began to provide job training programs as a way to ease widespread unemployment" (p. 15). State funding allocations to community colleges peaked in the 1980s at 60 percent, declined to 48 percent in 1990, and 44 percent in 1997 (Cohen & Brawer, 2003). In 2005, the largest funding source for community colleges was state funds (35.54 percent). This funding source represents state grants and contracts (4.18 percent), state appropriations (30.07 percent), and state nonoperating grants (1.29 percent) (Digest of Education Statistics, 2008a). State funds are usually acquired through intergovernmental revenue and taxes (e.g., sales, licenses, individuals, corporations) (U.S. Census, 2009).

The allocation process for state funds has changed over time. Mullin and Honeyman (2007) note that when state governments began funding community colleges, monies received were derived from individual institutional requests. They contend that the increasing number of institutions and students served prompted states to establish funding formulas to determine funding allocations. Now, three primary funding formula typologies exist; (1) no funding formula; (2) responsive funding formulas; and (3) functional component funding formulas. Mullin and Honeyman (2007)[2] explicate the differences in these funding typologies:

- *No funding* formulas were found in eight states (e.g., Alaska, Idaho, and Vermont). Typically, no funding formulas were evident in states where community colleges were appendages of state university systems, or where the number and size of institutions were not great enough to warrant individual funding formulas.
- *Responsive funding* formulas were used in 20 states (e.g., Alabama, North Dakota, and Texas). These formulas calculated expenses to determine funding levels. They also put specific formula components in place to address funding inequities among institutions. There were three primary types of responsive funding formulas: (1) *cost of education* formulas, which used student enrollment numbers to determine base funding levels; (2) *equalized funding* formulas, where funding was based upon equity markers (e.g., property values, local tax revenue); and (3) *option funding* formulas, which "allowed either state leaders or economic conditions to determine which formula will be utilized" (p. 119).
- *Functional component* funding is used in 22 states (e.g., Colorado, Washington, North Carolina). This funding formula is evident in state governments where funding distributions are rationalized based upon aspects of operational costs. This formula is evident in two primary modes: (1) generalized funding, which occurs when states use a primary calculation for one area of operation (e.g., instruction) to determine funding for that educational component; and (2) tiered funding, which is used in states where funding formulas provide monies at tiered levels for each operational component.

We believe that the specific funding typologies undertaken by individual states are influenced by: (a) the political climate of each individual state; (b) the reputation of community colleges in the state; (c) community colleges contribution to the economic vitality of each state; and (d) the fiscal stability of the state.

---

[2] Louisiana and South Dakota were not included in this study.

Local Funding

Since many of the early community colleges were appendages of high schools, local funding for these institutions was directed from local taxes. As these colleges have grown in number, size, and scope, they have been forced to compete for funds with other district- and county-level services (Wattenbarger, 1994). Cohen & Brawer (2003) illustrate the rapid decline in local funding for community colleges. In 1918, almost all (94 percent) of funding for community colleges came from local funds. In the 1950s, this had declined to 49 percent. In 2005, local sources accounted for only 19.62 percent of community college revenue. This percentage includes local grant and contract monies (1.33 percent), local appropriations (18.13 percent), and local nonoperating grants (0.16 percent) (Digest of Education Statistics, 2008a). Clearly, most local funding comes from local appropriations. Local appropriations refer to funds allocated to community colleges from local government entities (e.g., county or city governments, IPEDS, 2009). Generally, local appropriations monies come from sales, property, and income taxes. Local funding can be increased through bond measures, which increase or reallocate funds to specific entities, including community colleges.

Campus Funding

Campus funding provides 6.39 percent of the total revenue for community colleges. Campus funding contains sales and services monies (4.22 percent), gifts (0.60 percent), campus investments (1.53 percent), and endowment additions (0.04 percent) (Digest of Education Statistics, 2008a). Sales and services include revenue generated from university operations (e.g., bookstore, food services). Of particular interest to leaders, especially those seeking executive-level leadership are gifts that include bequests, pledges, income from trusts, and monetary donations (IPEDS, 2009). According to the *Chronicle of Higher Education*, 22.8 percent of first-time college presidents report that they felt insufficiently prepared for fundraising. This was the top area of insufficiency reported by all presidents (Almanac, 2008–09).

Miller (1994) reports that many community colleges are engaged in fundraising (also known as institutional advancement or institutional development). He identifies four primary forms of fundraising activities: (1) capital campaigns—which are large-scale fundraising drives that are designed to raise money for building projects and operations; (2) annual funds—which are yearly fundraising drives, hence the term annual, that raise funds for operational expenditures and usually do not have spending restrictions; (3) corporate or business support drives that seek financial support and resources (e.g., computers) from industry; and (4) deferred or planned giving, where donors pledge monies to be given at a specified time, this includes bequests. In reality, community colleges are at a disadvantage in fundraising. Jackson & Glass (2000) state that community colleges face competition in fundraising from "hospitals, public schools, and other public entities" (p. 734). Most notably, four-year universities pose significant competition for community colleges, as they can dedicate more resources, have greater prestige, and are more experienced in fundraising.

Tuition/Fees

Tuition and fees include required expenses for attending college during an academic year (IPEDS, 2009). Cohen & Brawer (2003) illustrate historical increases in the proportion of community college revenue derived from student tuition and fees. In 1918, only 6 percent of community college revenue was derived from tuition and fees. In 1950, this percentage had increased to 9 percent. In 2005, student tuition and fees accounted for 16.64 percent of total revenue for community colleges (Digest of Education Statistics, 2008a).[3] The proportion of revenue generated from student tuition and fees is directly linked to national economic conditions. In times of fiscal crises, fees increase as more revenue is needed to supplement funding lost from other sources.

As noted earlier, these percentages represent the national context; however, variation exists among states. Kenton et al., (2005) examined state government funding in eleven Midwestern states. They note that the proportion of revenue derived from student tuition and fees varies. For example, in 2000, 15.4 percent of revenue was derived from tuition and fees in Nebraska, as opposed to 36.5 percent in Ohio. Their data also indicates that tuition increased from 1990 to 2000 in eight of the eleven states examined. Tollefson (2009) states that national stabilization patterns indicate that student fees and tuition will hover around 20 percent of total community college operating revenue.

---

[3] Cohen & Brawer's data was derived from Medsker and Tillery (1971), the National Center for Education Statistics (2001), and Starrak and Hughes (1954). Funding patterns have not been linear.

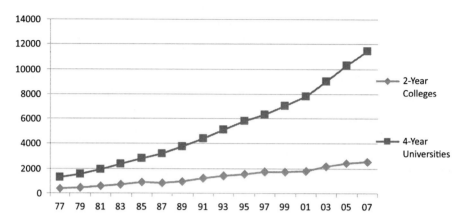

Figure 2 Student Tuition and Fees by Public Institution Type in Constant Dollars, 1977–2007
Source: Digest of Education Statistics (2008c). U.S. Department of Education, National Center for Education Statistics, Higher Education General Information Survey (HEGIS), "Institutional Characteristics of Colleges and Universities" surveys, 1965–66 through 1985–86; "Fall Enrollment in Institutions of Higher Education" surveys, 1965 through 1985; and 1986–87 through 2007–08 Integrated Postsecondary Education Data System, "Fall Enrollment Survey" (IPEDS-EF:86–99), "Institutional Characteristics Survey" (IPEDS-C:86–99), Spring 2001 through Spring 2006, and Fall 2000 through Fall 2007.

As state and local fiscal resource allocations have dwindled, the cost of attending college has increased. This trend is evident among all institution types (e.g., two-year public, two-year private, four-year public, four-year private) (see Figure 2). In 1977, the cost of tuition and fees for public two-year colleges was $378.[4] By 1987 this cost increased to $809, rising to $1,695 in 1997, and to $2,535 in 2007. Despite this fact, community colleges are by far the most affordable option for an inexpensive college education. For instance, while the average cost of attending a community college is $2,535, the average cost for tuition and fees at public four-year universities is $11,459 (Digest of Education Statistics, 2008b) (see Figure 2). When one takes into account the room, board, and book costs as well as other expenses, community college students who live at home can save $28,100 in a two-year time frame in comparison to four-year college students (Connell, 2008).

Other Funding

Other funding is comprised of a multiplicity of individual line streams. In total, it accounts for 7.7 percent of total revenue. Other funding is comprised

---

[4] Data reported in current dollars.

of other operating revenues (1.67 percent), other nonoperating revenues (0.86 percent), capital appropriations (3.99 percent), capital grants and gifts (0.73 percent), and other (0.45 percent) (Digest of Education Statistics, 2008a). The greatest proportion of other funding comes from capital appropriations. Capital appropriations are monies that come from government entities. These monies must be used for capital outlay, including building projects, the acquisition of land, or the purchasing of equipment (IPEDS, 2009). Capital appropriations are of particular importance when other monies (federal, state, local) come with guidelines that restrict their usage to operational and instructional purposes.

In sum, the proportion of revenue for community colleges from local government has decreased significantly over time. State government funding has shown a downward trend since the 1980s. In order to compensate for the loss of revenues in these areas, the federal government, campus revenue, and tuition and fees streams have increased. These trends have resulted in an added burden on individual campuses as well as the students that they serve. The implications are numerous in that they have resulted in a paradigm shift in how institutions are managed. The focus centers on instituting strategies focused on gaining revenue as a means to sustain the operations of the college. This in turn, can alter institutional priorities. For example, some presidents have been questioned for instituting a business model approach to administering their respective colleges, where the top institutional priority is fundraising and resource development as opposed to an academic model where the primary force guiding institutional leadership efforts is teaching and learning. However, it is important to note that community college leadership does not necessitate an either-or approach; rather, a simultaneous approach can be undertaken. This two fold focus supports instruction while focusing on gaining revenue for the community college.

Expenditures

There is an old adage that says "show me where you spend your money, and I'll show you where your priorities are." If one truly wants to understand the priorities of an institution, a major indicator is where expenditures lie. Leaders must constantly assess whether their priorities (as indicated by expenditures) are aligned with the mission of community colleges. There are constraints to various revenue sources. Many revenue streams come with expenditure parameters

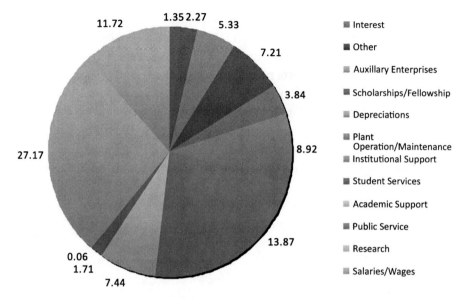

Figure 3 *Expenditures of public two-year colleges, 2005–06*
Source: Digest of Education Statistics (2008c).

which dictate where the funding can be used. In fact, few discretionary monies are available to leaders to enact desired changes. As such, budget limitations can stifle the creativity and ingenuity needed to increase student success levels. This affirms the importance of leaders having strong financial and budgeting skills in order to move their institutions toward better actualizing the mission of community colleges. Once leaders are informed about the allocation of college funds, it provides them with a sense of consciousness to design, implement, assess, and revise budgets, thereby, empowering them with the freedom to transform their institutions as needed.

As illustrated by the figure above, community colleges have 13 primary expenditures lines. Based upon the notion that the largest expenditures serve as a marker of institutional priorities, we will discuss the five largest community college expenditures (e.g., salaries/wages, institutional support, instruction, plant operation/maintenance, student services). Together, these five areas account for the vast majority (70.89 percent) of total public two-year college expenditures (see Figure 3).

- *Salaries/Wages*—Salaries and wages represent more than a quarter (27.17 percent) of all community college expenses. This aspect of two-year college budgets includes monies rendered to full-time and part-time faculty, staff, and student workers. This line also accounts for service compensations (e.g., bonuses, overtime, and leave) (IPEDS, 2009). According to the *Chronicle of Higher Education*, only 50.5 percent of full-time public two-year college faculty state that they are satisfied to very satisfied with their salaries and fringe benefits (Almanac, 2008–09). Possibly, this indicates a need to increase the salaries and wages proportion of community college budgets.

- *Institutional Support*—Institutional support refers to an array of factors related to sustaining and promoting the infrastructure of the institution. This includes costs for administrative services, activities, planning, and operations. It also pertains to technological expenses, which support campus administration (IPEDS, 2009). In essence, institutional support refers to administrative funds, which are used to support institutional operations. In 2005, institutional support accounted for 13.8 percent of total community college expenditures.

- *Instruction*—Instruction generally includes expenses to support academic functions of community colleges; this does not include salaries or fringe benefits. This expenditure line covers direct instruction (e.g., academic, occupational, and vocational) for both credit and noncredit courses, which is given in preparatory, remedial, general education, traditional, and special sessions (IPEDS, 2009). Instruction accounted for 11.72 percent of total community college expenditures in the 2005–06 academic year.

- *Student Services*—Student services refers to funding expenditures for enrollment (e.g., registrar, admissions) and programs for the psychosocial development of students (e.g., student government, campus clubs/organizations, campus life activities) (IPEDS, 2009). It is important to note that student services expenditures encompass student affairs programming. In all, student services accounts for 9.21 percent of community college expenses.

- *Plant Operations and Maintenance*—Plant operations and maintenance refer to funding that provides for the operation and maintenance of the physical buildings, lands, and equipment which the community colleges use (IPEDS, 2009). This funding line also represents costs for other operational expenses (e.g., water and electricity services). These expenditures account for 8.92 percent of total college expenses.

In accordance with institutional expenditures, institutional priorities fall under the five aforementioned categories. Two primary points can be taken from the allocation of these expenditures. First, it is important to note that operating expenses account for 97.9 percent of total expenditures. Of these operating expenditures, salaries and wages account for 27.7 percent. Occasionally, leaders refer to salaries/ wages and operating expenses as being synonymous. This complicates perceptions of salary expenditures, as it creates a skewed perception of how much revenue is actually spent on salary/wages. Second, student services accounts for 9.21 percent of total expenditures. These services include both the technical aspects of enrolling students as well as campus life programming. In consideration of the proportion of this expenditure: What are the implications (if any) to student academic success?

In all, community college expenditures are not as clear cut as one might hope. Leaders must understand the intricacies of each expense area; this task is challenged by budgets that are multifaceted, diverse, and convoluted in nature. However, by understanding the budget process, leaders will be better equipped to: (1) provide effective leadership in tumultuous financial times; (2) understand and explain the challenges of their budgets to faculty, staff, students, and community members; (3) advocate for loosened funding provisions so that monies can be used where they are most needed; and (4) be better accountable to tax-payers who provide substantial support for institutional operations. Of critical importance, is to ensure that lines of expenditures are congruent with facilitating the purposes of the community college.

Financing College for Students

College is a financial investment for students. As individuals' level of educational attainment increases, so too does their earning potential. The mean annual earnings for individuals with some high school is $21,251. However, for high school graduates, it increases to $31,286. Individuals who receive associate's degrees can expect to earn, on an average, $39,746 per year (U.S. Census Bureau, 2007). Though mean earnings differ by race/ethnicity and gender (see Figure 4) in a 30-year career span, holding all constant, the average associate degree holder will earn $253,800 more than an individual with a high school diploma. Considering the cost of tuition and fees at public two-year colleges, education is a worthy investment for those who earn a degree.

In order to finance college, many students work and/or receive financial aid. Among full-time students,[5] data indicates that a large percentage of public two-year-college students were employed (54 percent) as compared to 45 percent of

---

[5] 16 to 24 years of age.

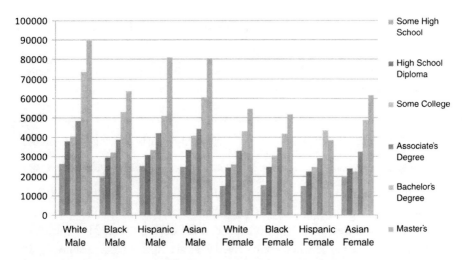

Figure 4 *Mean income for people 18 and older by race/ethnicity and gender, 2007*
Source: U.S. Census Bureau (2007). Table PINC-04. Educational Attainment: People 18 Years Old and Over, by Total Money Earnings in 2007, Work Experience in 2007, Age, Race, Hispanic Origin, and Sex. Washington, DC: Author.

public four-year-college students. Of private four-year-college students, 39 percent were employed; however, only 35 percent of private two-year-college students were employed. Part-time students, among all institutional types, are more likely to be employed. In fact, 83.4 percent of part-time students in public community colleges are employed.

The number of hours worked by students can inform the extent of their employment commitments. Table 1 illustrates that part-time students are more likely to work 20–34 and 35 hours or more per week, while full-time students are more likely to work 20 hours or less per week (Planty et al., 2009). Leaders should consider how work commitments affect student academic success, especially for those who work more than 20 hours per week and carry a full class load.

The percentage of students receiving financial aid in two-year colleges has increased since 2000. In the 2000–01 school year, 56.5 percent of students were receiving some form of financial aid. Through multiple aid offerings 35.2 percent received federal grants, 28.8 percent state/local grants, 12.1 percent institutional grants, and 15.3 percent student loans. By the 2005–06 school year, 61.5 percent of students were receiving aid, an increase of 5 percent. The percentage of students enrolled in aid programs increased in most areas. Federal grants rose to 38 percent, state/local grants to 31.9 percent, and student loans to 19.0 percent. The exception to this percentage increase occurred in institutional grants, which declined slightly to 11.3 percent (Digest of Education Statistics, 2008d).

Table 1 *Hours Worked per week by full-Time and Part-Time Public Two-Year-College Students, 2007*

Students	Percent employed	Less than 20 hours	20–34 hours	35 hours or More
Full-Time	54.0%	15.2%	28.7%	9.6%
Part-Time	83.4%	7.1%	33.7%	40.9%

Source: Planty, M., Hussar, W., Snyder, T., Kena, G., KewalRamani, A., Kemp, J., Bianco, K., Dinkes, R. (2009). *The Condition of Education 2009* (NCES 2009–081). National Center for Education Statistics, Institute of Education Sciences, U.S. Department of Education. Washington, DC.

Of the students receiving aid in public two-year colleges, differences in aid amounts are apparent by enrollment status. A large percentage of full-time students (62.3 percent) received some form of financial aid during the 2003–04 academic year. Of these students, 48.9 percent received federal aid, 18.7 percent state aid, 14.2 percent institutional aid, and 14.9 percent aid from other sources.[6] Variance in the percentage of full-time students receiving aid by institution type was apparent (e.g, four-year doctoral institution, other four-year, two-year, less than two-year institutions), as a smaller percentage of public two-year students receive aid (again 62.3 percent) as compared to 71.1 percent in all public institutions, 75.5 percent in four-year doctoral institutions, 77.0 percent in other four-year institutions, and 66.7 percent in less than two-year institutions. Primarily, this difference is seen in the percentage of students who received aid classified as other. Likely, this speaks to the tuition/fee costs for community colleges being lower than four-year institutions. Part-time students are less likely to receive aid than full-time students (43.6%). For these students, the largest percentage received federal aid (28 percent) and a smaller percentage of students received funding from state aid (9.7 percent), institutional aid (6.1 percent), and other (14.0 percent) (Digest of Education Statistics, 2008e).

Federal Aid Funding Distribution

Of the 36 percent of full-time public two-year-college students receiving federal aid in the 1992–1993 academic year, 29.9 percent of students received grants, 11.7 percent loans, 3.0 percent work study, and 1.3 percent other. By the 2003–04 school year, the percentage of students taking advantage of federal aid increased to 48.9 percent. Of these students, 34.5 percent received federal grants, 25.1 percent loans, 1.1 percent work study, and 2.8 percent other. Similar trends were seen for part-time students. In the 1992–93 academic year, only 16.5 percent of part-time public two-year-college students received federal aid. This aid was

[6] Students who received aid but did not report its source.

distributed as follows: 13.7 percent grants, 5.3 percent loans, 0.6 percent work study, and 5.5 percent other. By the 2003–04 school year, 28 percent of these student received aid, an increase of 11.5 percent in only ten years.

Most of these increases were seen in grant aid, which rose to 20 percent (an increase of 7.3 percent from 1992–93 academic year), and loan monies that increased to 10 percent (a rise of 4.7 percent). While work study rose marginally to 1 percent, other decreased to 3.1 percent. Both full-time and part-time students received the lion's share of grant monies from Pell and loan monies from Stafford (Digest of Education Statistics, 2008f, 2008g). The aforementioned numbers indicate several themes: (1) federal financial aid packages are composed of an assortment of funds, primarily from grants and loans; (2) there is an increasing percentage of students utilizing federal financial resources, both part-time and full-time students; and (3) lower percentages of part-time students use federal funds.

Despite the increases in financial aid, corresponding increases are seen in the cost of tuition, fees, supplies, and living expenses. For example, Zumeta & Frankle (2007) state:

> Non-fee attendance costs facing community college students have grown much more rapidly than the state's general cost of living in recent years. For example, rental housing costs comprise the largest share of student budgets and grew nearly 25% from 2000–2005 in California, compared with an overall inflation rate of 16% in the state. Textbook and supply costs increased by 31% during the same period. Costs for medical care and child care also outpaced general inflation by a large margin, yet they are not adequately taken into account in financial aid calculations (p. iv).

Case Study

This chapter provided a general examination of public community college revenue, expenditures, and funding for students. Leaders should be well versed in the financial matters of community colleges; this will improve their confidence, effectiveness, efficiency, and credibility. As made evident with this chapter, financial trends are multifaceted, diverse, and convoluted in nature. This presents challenges for community college leaders. When examining this case study, be mindful of the overall fiscal context in which community colleges exist and its implications for the mission of the community college.

President Gayle Hytrek
Moraine Park Technical College
Fond du Lac, Wisconsin

Pressures of Fund Raising

Background

Oakfield Community College is a multicampus community college located in the Midwest. Oakfield is one of 12 community colleges located in the state. The college is located in a rural area of the state with the three campuses located in the three largest communities in the district. In addition, evening classes, both credit and noncredit and personal enrichment classes are offered at area high schools. Like many community colleges, the median age of the students is 28, with many of the students being working adults. The student body is composed of 90 percent white/Caucasian and 10 percent minority students with Hispanic students being the largest minority group at 3.6 percent. Fifty-one percent of the 16,000-member student body is female and 49 percent are male. A large number of the students (about 40 percent) are low-income, first-generation students, meaning they are the first in their families to enter a degree program. Their parents may have taken some classes from the college but neither completed a degree.

The college budget is $70 million with 51 percent of the funds coming from local property taxes, 14 percent from state aid and state grants, 11 percent from auxiliary operations (bookstore, food service, and vending contract profits), and 24 percent from tuition and fees. For the past 10 years, state-allocated funding, based on a formula and funding through grants for specific programs, has been frozen or cut. In fact last year, all state grant funds received a midyear cut of 1 percent, which was carried over into the current funding year. Thus, in the past 10 years, the college has had to rely on increases in property taxes to close the gap. Although the taxpayers have not yet mounted a serious "taxpayer revolt," rising taxes are getting a lot of attention and it is expected that the college will have to curtail its reliance on increasing the district's mill levy to fund budget shortfalls. State law sets the maximum operational levy a community college may assess district taxpayers at 1.5 mills, or $1.50 per $1,000 of property value. Oakfield's current levy is 1.01—well below the maximum. Tuition is set by the state board with the local community college board responsible for approving the college budget, and oversight of the college and all of its operations. Historically, annual increases in tuition have been about 5 percent a year, but the state board is now concerned that some students will not be able to attend college if the annual tuition rate increase remains at that level.

Statement of the Problem

You are the new vice president for strategic advancement. Institutional research, the college foundation, and the resource development offices report directly to you. The president has informed you that she and the board believe Oakfield must look to being more competitive in state grants and looking at new sources of external funding via federal grants or federal earmarks to fund future initiatives. Especially since the federal government is now looking more favorably on funding community colleges initiatives. In this conversation she also mentioned that one of the reasons you were hired was due to your past experience as a grants officer at a neighboring community college. Your task is to determine how to best position the campus to receive federal funding. To do so, you must consider: (a) what resources you have; (b) the role institutional affiliates can play in facilitating goal attainment; (c) your personnel's expertise; (d) what changes are needed (e.g., organizational, personnel), if any; and (e) what steps you should take in attaining federal funds.

Your career goal is to become a community college president, and you believe success in securing external funding for programs through grants and/or gifts to the foundation will not only impress your current president but will also help you build the vita you need for that next step up. As the new vice president, you decide to visit with each department and meet with each of your direct reports to learn about their current efforts to secure external funding.

Molly Rand is the director for the resource development office. Molly believes she is a very competent grant writer, but since she only has one administrative assistant and a part-time staff member, she spends most of her time working on writing and overseeing the state grants, which have also decreased in number over the past three years. The part-time person spends her time proofing the grants and making sure the project directors meet the deadlines set by the state. The college has never applied for a federal grant. Molly feels she could do more if the project directors, who are the academic deans and/or faculty, would just do their job of overseeing their own grant projects. After all, the grants are funding their academic programs. As far as Molly knows, the college has never sought a federal earmark even though the U.S. representative for your area of the state lives in your district and he serves on the appropriations committee. Several private colleges in his district have received earmarks to fund new programs, especially in the health care field.

The foundation office is really only a one-person office, with the director, Judy Mirelez, spending most of her time managing the current endowment funds, working with the director of student services in reviewing and awarding scholarship applications, and promoting the foundation to employees. Less than 15 percent of the employees donate to the college foundation. All foundation funds are designated for student scholarships. Judy does have a part-time administrative assistant.

Jerry Jones is quick to tell you that the college has a robust information system and his very competent staff (a data analyst, a research specialist, and a full-time administrative assistant) can provide you with any data you need. His office does all of the state reports and the IPEDS report, and provides the data for all accreditation teams. His office has also supported the grants office by providing the data needed for the state grants.

References

Almanac (2008–09). *Profile of college presidents, 2006; What areas did you feel insufficiently prepared for in your first presidency?* Washington, DC: American Association of Community Colleges.

American Association of Community Colleges (2008–09). *Federal funding to two-year colleges.* Washington, DC: American Association of Community Colleges.

Cohen, A. M. (2001). Governmental policies affecting community colleges: A historical perspective. In B. K. Townsend & S. B. Twombly (Eds.). *Community colleges: Policy in the future context* (pp. 3–22). Westport, CT: Ablex Publishing.

Cohen, A. M., & Brawer, F. B. (2003). *The American community college* (4th ed.). San Fransciso, CA: Jossey Bass.

Connell, K. (2008). Community colleges: A great return on investment. *Christian Science Monitor* (August). Retrieved July 7, 2009, from: http://www.csmonitor.com/2008/0804/p16s01-wmgn.html

Digest of Education Statistics (2008a). *U.S. Department of Education, National Center for Education Statistics, 2003–04 through 2005–06 Integrated Postsecondary Education Data System, Spring 2004 through Spring 2007.* Washington, DC: National Center for Education Statistics.

Digest of Education Statistics (2008b). *U.S. Department of Education, National Center for Education Statistics, 2003–04 through 2005–06 Integrated Postsecondary Education Data System (IPEDS), Spring 2004 through Spring 2007.* Washington, DC: National Center for Education Statistics.

Digest of Education Statistics (2008c). *U.S. Department of Education, National Center for Education Statistics, Higher Education General Information Survey (HEGIS), "Institutional Characteristics of Colleges and Universities" surveys, 1965–66 through 1985–86; "Fall Enrollment in Institutions of Higher Education" surveys, 1965 through 1985; and 1986–87 through 2007–08 Integrated Postsecondary Education Data System, "Fall Enrollment Survey" (IPEDS-EF:86–99), "Institutional Characteristics Survey" (IPEDS-C:86–99), Spring 2001 through Spring 2006, and Fall 2000 through Fall 2007.* Washington, DC: National Center for Education Statistics.

Digest of Education Statistics (2008d). *U.S. Department of Education, National Center for Education Statistics, 2000–01 through 2005–06 Integrated Postsecondary Education Data System (IPEDS), Spring 2002 through Spring 2007.* Washington, DC: National Center for Education Statistics.

Digest of Education Statistics (2008e). *U.S. Department of Education, National Center for Education Statistics, 2003–04 National Postsecondary Student Aid Study (NPSAS:04).* Washington, DC: National Center for Education Statistics.

Digest of Education Statistics (2008f). *U.S. Department of Education, National Center for Education Statistics, 1992–93, 1995–96, 1999–2000, and 2003–04 National Postsecondary Student Aid Studies (NPSAS:93, NPSAS:96, NPSAS:2000, and NPSAS:04).* Washington, DC: National Center for Education Statistics.

Digest of Education Statistics (2008g). *U.S. Department of Education, National Center for Education Statistics, 1992–93, 1995–96, 1999–2000, and 2003–04 National Postsecondary Student Aid Studies (NPSAS:93, NPSAS:96, NPSAS:2000, and NPSAS:04).* Washington, DC: National Center for Education Statistics.

IPEDS (2009). *Glossary: Integrated postsecondary education data system.* Washington, DC: National Center for Education Statistics.

Jackson, K. L., & Glass, J. C. (2000). Emerging trends and critical issues affecting private fund-raising among community colleges. *Community College Journal of Research and Practice, 24,* 729–744.

Kasper, H. T. (2002–03). The changing role of community college. *Occupational Outlook Quarterly,* 14–21.

Kenton, C. P., Huba, M. E., Schuh, J. H., & Shelly, M. C. (2005). Financing community colleges: A longitudinal study of 11 states. *Community College Journal of Research and Practice, 29,* 109–122.

Miller, L. S. (1994). Community college resource development: Foundations and fundraising. In G. A. Baker, III (Ed.). *A handbook on the community college in America: Its history, mission, and management* (pp. 360–374). Westport, CT: Greenwood.

Mullin, C. M., & Honeyman, D. S. (2007). The funding of community colleges: A typology of state funding formulas. *Community College Review,*35(2), 113–127.

Phillippe, K. A., & Sullivan L. G. (2005). *National profile of community colleges: Trends and statistics* (4th ed.). Washington, DC: American Association of Community Colleges.

Planty, M., Hussar, W., Snyder, T., Kena, G., KewalRamani, A., Kemp, J., Bianco, K., Dinkes, R. (2009). *The Condition of Education 2009* (NCES 2009–081). National Center for Education Statistics, Institute of Education Sciences, U.S. Department of Education. Washington, DC.

Tollefson, T. A. (2009). Community college governance, funding, and accountability: A century of issues and trends. *Community College Journal of Research and Practice, 33*(3), 386–402.

U.S. Census Bureau (2007). *Table PINC-04. Educational Attainment: People 18 Years Old and Over, by Total Money Earnings in 2007, Work Experience in 2007, Age, Race, Hispanic Origin, and Sex.* Washington, DC: U.S. Census Bureau.

U.S. Census Bureau (2009). *State government finances: 2007.* Washington, DC: U.S. Census Bureau.

U.S. Government Accountability Office (2008). *Workforce development: Community colleges and one-stop centers collaborate to meet 21st century workforce needs.* Washington, DC: U.S. Government Accountability Office.

Wattenbarger, J. L. (1994). Resource development in the community college: The evolution of resource policy development for community colleges as related to support from local, state, and federal governments. In G. A. Baker, J. Dudziak, & P. Tyler (Eds.). *A handbook on the community college in America: Its history, mission, and management* (pp. 333–339). Westport, CT: Greenwood Press.

Zumeta, W. & Frankle, D. (2007). *California community colleges: Making them stronger and more affordable.* San Jose, CA: National Center for Public Policy and Higher Education. Retrieved September 2, 2009, from: http://www.highereducation.org/reports/calcc/calcc.pdf

CHAPTER TEN

COMMUNITY COLLEGE GOVERNANCE

This chapter will focus on governance in the community college. Information presented will be framed in accordance with a Conceptual Model of Community College Governance which depicts governance in these institutions. The focus of this chapter is twofold: (1) to provide an overview of the general governance processes at the state, local, and campus levels; and (2) to present four influences (e.g., national, statewide, and local needs, ideological differences, internal influences, external influences), which serve to "truly" guide governance in these institutions.

When reading this chapter, consider the following questions:

- How is community college governance defined? What aspects does it entail?
- What is the structure of community college governance? What entities and documents form governance at the state, local, and campus levels?
- What are the four influences which impact community college governance? How are these influences related? What role do they play in influencing policy, practices, and governance structures in community colleges?

Governance in the community college is a complex web of forces. Numerous stakeholders at the state (e.g., governor, legislators, and state superintendent), local (e.g., trustees, alumni, community members), and campus (faculty, staff, students) levels vie to have a voice, influence, and impact the management process and structure. While the involvement of these stakeholders provides for increased accountability of community colleges and balances individual/group interests, it can: (a) complicate or enhance the vision and direction of institutions (Davis, 2001); (b) lead to overly bureaucratic decision-making processes or the assurance of a democratic process; and (c) facilitate the existence of an excessively regulatory governance system. Amey, Jessup-Anger, & Jessup-Anger

(2008) note that community college leaders must understand: (1) policy issues and challenges facing community colleges at all levels (e.g., federal, local); (2) workforce development needs, institutional finance, and the educational needs of students; and (3) the role of community colleges in the educational system, at all levels (elementary to doctoral education). Leaders who understand and maneuver successfully through the intricacies of the governance structure will benefit in several interrelated areas:

- *Positioning.* Leaders who understand power dynamics, policymaking, and influence within their own institutions as well as within state, district, and/or local governing boards will be better poised to position their institutions (e.g., staff, faculty, resources) to: (a) reap the benefits of political favor; (b) advocate for more resources; (c) promote effective policy; and (d) facilitate the vision and mission of institution.
- *Legal Boundaries.* With a well-grounded knowledge of governance in the community colleges, leaders will know their personal and institutional legal boundaries. Leaders should be able to answer questions such as: Where does authority for this decision reside? What decisions can they make? What are the legal ramifications of the decisions? What decision-making powers are unclear? These are all aspects of the legal boundaries of governance. A leader who knows the answers to these questions can more effectively, ethically, and lawfully operate their institutions.
- *Public Good.* By understanding the nature of community college governance, leaders are able to be more effective in advocating for change, which can positively affect the students, faculty, staff, and local communities that they serve. Their leadership for the public good is enhanced by a better understanding of policy, decision-making authority, and law.

Throughout this chapter, the term *governance* is defined as the bodies (e.g., trustees, legislature, faculty senate), documents (e.g., state constitution, state codes, system-wide and campus policies), and internal (e.g., board dynamics) and external influences (e.g., blue ribbon panels, state planning commissions, business industry) that affect decision making in the community college. These bodies, documents, and influences will be the central focus of this chapter, which will be framed in accordance with the *Conceptual Model of Community College Governance* (see Figure 1). It has a twofold purpose that will: (1) provide a general description of the governance process at the state, local, and campus levels

Governance in the Community College

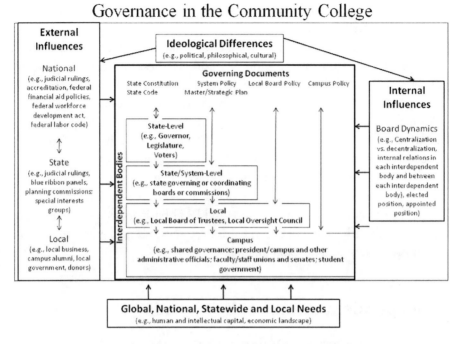

Figure 1 Conceptual Model of Community College Governance

and examine the documents that guide decision making at these levels; and (2) provide an overview of the factors affecting, influencing, and driving governance in the community college, including: (a) national, statewide, and local needs; (b) ideological differences; (c) internal influences; and (d) external influences.

The conceptual model of community college governance provides an overview of three specific areas which guide governance in the community college. First, it examines the governing entities involved in decision making on four levels: (a) the state level, which includes elected statewide leaders (e.g., governor, lieutenant governor, legislature); (b) the state/system level, which focuses on state-level governing boards and coordinating commissions; (c) the local level, in which decision making is guided by local boards of trustees; and (d) the campus-level, including all stakeholders in shared-governance processes (e.g., campus administration, faculty, staff, students). Second, the model identifies documents (e.g., state constitution, state code, master plan, state system policy, local board policy, campus-level policy) which guide decision making in the community college. Each of these documents is associated (in general) with the four governing entities previously mentioned. For example, state constitution and state code guide, articulate, and drive the functions of state-level entities; master plans and system policy direct the operations of state/system-level governing boards and commissions; and so on.

Finally, the model depicts four distinct internal and external factors which influence governance in the community college, these include: (a) national, state, and local human and intellectual capital needs as well as their economic landscape(s); (b) ideological differences including (but not limited to) political, philosophical, and cultural viewpoints, perspectives, and realities; (c) internal influences, which include issues such as board dynamics (centralization vs. decentralization), interdependent relations, as well as position types (e.g., elected vs. appointed board); and (d) external influences on a national, state, and local level; these external influences include some of the following: judicial rulings, blue ribbon panels/commission, and local businesses (see Figure 1). In sum, these four influences are the true driving forces behind community college governance, policy, and decision making.

Independent Bodies and Governing Documents

Beginning with Joliet Junior College in 1901, community college governance mirrored that of the public high schools. Early community colleges were housed in high schools and governed by secondary-level administrators (Cain, 1999), and their leadership was overseen by local school boards (Potter & Phelan, 2008). Initially, the educational leaders who operated these high school/colleges were granted large amounts of freedom and authority (Alfred, 2008). By the 1920s and 1930s, the community college, as known today, began to take form. The founding of the American Association of Community Colleges (formerly the American Association of Junior Colleges) in 1920 (AACC, 2009), and the advances in accreditation standards by regional associations (Eells, 1931) catapulted community colleges as recognized players in postsecondary education. In trying to shed their image as an extension of high schools, community college oversight transitioned from secondary school boards to local community college boards as well as statewide governing boards (Richardson & de los Santos, 2001).

During the 1920s and 1930s, community colleges gradually shifted their governance structure to mirror that of the universities (Cain, 1999). As these institutions have matured, their governance structures have become more complex and dynamic. As noted by Alfred (2008), "community colleges have evolved from small organizations administered by leaders with almost unlimited authority to complex multifaceted organizations staffed principally by specialist and part-time personnel in departments and administrative units detached from the center for the organization" (Alfred, 2008, p. 80). Today, community college governance differs vastly from state to state. In some states, community colleges operate under powerful statewide boards; in others, power is vested in local community college governing boards. Generally, money dictates where the power resides. Funding proportions from local government and state government are reflective of control bestowed at each level (Tollefson, 2009). Due to the wide range of governance patterns seen in the community college, Cain (1999) notes "the pattern is that there is not a true pattern" (p. 97). What remains fairly consistent across states is the type of documents under which community colleges operate, though their influence varies from state to state. These documents serve to direct the governing functions of the community college. These documents include: (1) the state constitution; (2) state statutes/code; (3) state master plans/ statewide strategic plans; (4) state/system-level policy; (5) local board policy; and (6) campus-level policy. Though federal policy can play a role in community college governance, its role is limited. Almost invariably, the order of importance of the aforementioned documents is as presented above. However, regardless of their order of authority, all must be abided by at the campus level. Thus, there is a gauntlet of laws, codes, regulations, and policy that shape the operations of community colleges.

State Level

State-level governance often includes many individuals (e.g., governor, lieutenant governor, house speaker, state senate) who directly and indirectly influence and manage community colleges at the statewide level. The composition and authority of state-level governance can vary greatly from state to state. As chief state officers, governors, by virtue of their positions, are key players in the makeup of statewide governing boards. They usually appoint a substantial portion and sometimes all of the members of the chief state governing boards. Their appointments are typically subject to the approval of the state senate or legislature (ECS, 2007). In some states, especially those where more than one governing board shares power, governors serve as voting members of at least one state governing board. For example, in the state of Alabama, the governor appoints 10 of the 12 members of the Alabama Commission for Higher Education (ACHE, 2009) and is the president of the State Board of Education (ALSDE, 2009).

   While governors usually have primary appointment authority, board power is balanced in some states with appointments from the lieutenant governor and house speakers, though their appointments are usually fewer in number than those of the governor (ECS, 2007). Legislators are also key players in statewide governance. They set the legal guidelines from which all public institutions of higher education operate; this includes community colleges. The guidelines established by state legislatures often bear significant influence on community college operations. Voters are also statewide power players in the community college. Their role in shaping community college policy is twofold: (1) they elect the governor and other members of the legislature, who conceptualize, write, and pass state statutes (Davis, 2001); and (2) through statewide ballot initiatives, they can enact voter-approved mandates which affect the governing of community colleges. Take for example, voter-approved initiatives in California's and Michigan's Proposition 209 and Proposal 2. These initiatives effectively ended affirmative action programming and services in those states. To this day, they have a direct and influential role in shaping community college policy, governance, and the usage of state funds (Richardson & de los Santos, 2001).

Much of the powers maintained at the state level for elected officials (e.g., governor, lieutenant governor) and the people (the electorate) reside in constitutional and state-level authority. Either state constitutions and/or statutory code delineates the number of appointments that can be made, who makes the appointments, and how often they are made. Often, community colleges are guided by state master plans or strategic plans (e.g., California Higher Education Master Plan, State Plan for Alabama Higher Education, and Access to Higher Education in Alaska). These are usually created by state-level governing boards, but in many cases are approved by the state legislature. Thus, at the state level three types of documents can exist that guide the operations and govern the community college: (a) the state constitution; (b) state code; and (c) master plans/statewide strategic plans.

State/System-Level Governing Boards

State/system-level governing boards are the most common. These boards serve to facilitate "statewide education planning, program approval, and monitoring, and budget and policy recommendations to governors and legislature" (Schuetz, 2008, p. 92). Beyond those common responsibilities, state/system-level governing boards differ vastly from state to state. As a result, scholars have attempted to create typologies which best present categories of boards based on similar functions; this includes some of the following: (a) Lovell & Trouth's (2004) *state community college structures and degree of centralization* typology; (b) Richardson & de los Santos's (2001) *conceptual model of state structures for community colleges;* (c) McGuinness's (2003) *models of postsecondary education coordination and governance in the states;* and (d) Tollefson's (1999) *five models of state-level coordination/governance of community colleges.* Of these typologies, we are presenting Tollefson's taxonomy, as it is the most clear and concise model.

Tollefson's (1999) taxonomy classifies state-level coordination and governance into five groups: (1) State Board of Education; (2) State Higher Education Board or Commission; (3) Statewide Community College Coordinating Board; (4) State Community College Governing Board; and (5) State Board of Regents. A description of these coordination/governance boards follows:

- *State Board of Education.* Tollefson (1999) identifies several states (e.g., Alabama, Idaho, Iowa, Kansas, Michigan, Oregon, and Pennsylvania), which operate under the model of a state board of education (p. 26). In these states, power is usually decentralized with primary decision-making authority deferred to local boards of trustees. Lovell and Trouth (2004) note that state boards of education do not focus solely on issues facing the community college; rather, they provide general oversight to K-12 and postsecondary institutions.
- *State Higher Education Board or Commission.* There are a number of states (e.g., Arkansas, Maryland, Massachusetts, Missouri, Montana, Nebraska, New Jersey, New Mexico, New York, Ohio, Pennsylvania, and Texas) that operate under the control of state higher education boards or commissions (Tollefson, 1999). In these states, the boards/commissions oversee the development of new programs and degree offerings as well as "budget submission/recommendation authority" (p. 26). Under the model, community colleges are also governed by local boards of trustees. Local board powers (e.g., contract approval, faculty hiring authorization, approval of annual rank promotion, approval of administrative salaries) differ from state to state.
- *Statewide Community College Coordinating Board.* The most common system of governance seen in states (e.g., California, Colorado, Florida, Michigan, Mississippi, New Hampshire, North Carolina, Oregon, South Carolina, Washington, Wisconsin, and Wyoming) is a statewide community college coordinating board. These boards "typically exercise moderate control primarily over budgets and programs" (Tollefson, 1999, p. 26). Statewide coordinating boards can work in tandem with

local boards of trustees. An example of this is in California, where 72 community college districts have local oversight from elected board members.

- *State Community College Governing Board.* Some states (e.g., Colorado, Delaware, Kentucky, Maine, and Minnesota) operate under the centralized control of state community college governing boards. Usually, these boards hold substantial powers, including the ability to "hire and fire presidents, faculty and staff; hold title to land, buildings and equipment; and establish all policies for the state system" (Tollefson, 1999, p. 26). These boards also can have power over a wide array of other areas, such as: (a) long-range planning; (b) financial issues, management, and administration; (c) tuition and fees; and (d) matters of academic programming and degrees.

- *State Board of Regents.* There are a number of states (e.g., Alaska, Georgia, Hawaii, Louisiana, Montana, Nevada, North Dakota, Rhode Island, Tennessee, Vermont, and West Virginia) that are governed by a state board of regents. Similar to state community college governing boards, state boards of regents have substantial and centralized power, and authority over community colleges. However, the state board of regents directs community colleges as well as other postsecondary institutions.

State/system-level governing boards promulgate two types of policy which affect community colleges. As already noted, governing boards often are involved with the development of state master plans and statewide strategic plans. State/system-level boards are integral to revising these documents. In many states this process can lead to substantial changes to statewide postsecondary education planning on a semi-regular basis. In all, a vast majority of states have at least one state planning document, including Alabama, Alaska, Arizona, Arkansas, California, Connecticut, Florida, Georgia, Hawaii, Idaho, Illinois, Indiana, Iowa, Kansas, Kentucky, Louisiana, Maine, Maryland, Massachusetts, Minnesota, Mississippi, Missouri, Montana, Nebraska, Nevada, New Jersey, New York, North Carolina, North Dakota, Ohio, Oklahoma, Oregon, Pennsylvania, Rhode Island, South Carolina, South Dakota, Tennessee, Texas, Utah, Vermont, Virginia, Washington, West Virginia, and Wyoming (SHEEO, 2009). In addition to state plans, state/system-level governing boards also articulate policies directly to the districts and colleges they represent. This policy must be adhered to at the local governing board and campus levels.

Local Boards of Trustees

The vast majority of states have some form of local governance, usually in the form of local boards of trustees. This is especially the case in large community college systems (e.g., California) where local boards of trustees represent specific districts or locales (Miller & Miles, 2008). Many local governing boards possess hiring/firing authority at the campus level. For example, Garfield (2008) notes that they hold hiring authority of district chancellors, campus presidents, and other high-ranking executive leaders. In general, local boards establish policies to be implemented by campus leaders. Primary responsibilities of these governing boards include: (a) serving as a safeguard to the campus(es) in which they represent; by doing so, local board leaders allow the campus to focus on serving local community needs; (b) articulating the missions of the institutions they serve; (c) serving as a mechanism for community college accountability; and (d) providing and advocating for sufficient institutional resources (Davis, 2001).

There are two primary types of local governing board: elected boards and appointed boards. In general, comprehensive community colleges have elected boards; whereas, noncomprehensive systems have appointed boards. Vaughan (2006) articulates primary differences between the two. On elected boards, "would-be trustees campaign for board membership, much as they would if they were running for any political office" (p. 24). This includes seeking endorsements, raising money, courting constituent groups, and getting out the vote (GOTV) measures. Once elected, these board members serve a specified term, and must run for reelection in order to continue their membership on the board. As a result, elected board members hold office subject to the will of the local community, at least in theory. Some community colleges are governed by appointed boards, as opposed to elected boards. Similar to statewide boards, appointment authority for local governing boards usually rests under the power of chief state officials, namely the governor. However, appointment authority can also rest in "other political leaders, or by a combination of the two" (p. 24). Since appointed board members do not run for office, their primary manner in which they are held accountable is through their appointer. The dynamics that result from appointed and elected boards will be addressed later as part of the internal influences section.

As noted, local governing boards establish policy that governs the campus(es) in which they represent. Davis (2001) affirms the need for these policies to focus on the institutional mission of community colleges rather than day-to-day operations. Davis notes that when boards micromanage their institutions, they undermine the authority of executive-level institutional leaders and fail to focus on macro-level issues and policies that are the areas in which their input is most needed. Either way, local board policy dictates campus-level governance.

Campus-Level Governance

Most community colleges operate through a system of shared governance at the campus level. Shared governance refers to a process of governing by which multiple stakeholders (e.g., administrators, faculty, staff, and students) are involved as collaborators in the decision-making process. This occurs through formal input channels (e.g., committees, task forces, planning councils) as well as through official representative bodies (e.g., faculty senate, faculty union, student government), which participate in campus governance. That being said, shared governance is often window dressing. As noted by Cain (1999):

> What can be said about the governance of the colleges is that they generally follow hierarchical models and are ruled in a top-down manner, with information flowing— usually on paper—from a group of managers to the other groups on campus: faculty, classified staff, and students (p. 98).

Despite the top-down approach to governance in many community colleges, faculty involvement in governance has increased since the 1980s (Davis, 2001). Although shared governance began in the 1960s when colleges opened up the decision-making process to a greater number of constituents, shared governance has been defined as a means to involving various stakeholders in the governance process and pinpointing primary decision-making authority to specific individuals and entities. Formal input channels and representative bodies voice their concerns on issues, and advocate for cooperative resolutions to issues (Cain, 1999). Each person or entity (e.g., president, faculty senate) in the decision-making process has a distinct role:

- *President.* Presidents receive directives from governing boards at the state and local level. They are responsible for implementing these directives at their respective campuses. Due to their role in facilitating the desires of governing boards, presidents spend a substantial portion of their time: (a) establishing and maintaining relationships with governing board members (Miller & Miles, 2008); and (b) working to bridge the desires, interests, and direction of internal and external governing entities to provide clear direction for their institutions (Davis, 2001). Internally, presidents are the chief officers governing their institutions.

They dictate internal policy, shape the institutional mission, guide planning, and have authority over administrators and staff members.

- *Faculty Senate.* Faculty input ranges in nature and form. Some institutions have informal mechanisms to participate in governance (e.g., councils), whereas others have sophisticated faculty senates that elect their representatives (Miller & Miles, 2008). Faculty senates are made up of faculty who represent various disciplines and colleges/schools within the institution. They serve as the formal authority by which faculty input is maintained. Faculty senates usually hold reasonable power in institutional decision-making processes, with greater levels of authority in academic and instructional matters (Garfield, 2008). Mostly, faculty senates represent full-time faculty members with minimal involvement (if any) from part-timers (Miller & Miles, 2008).
- *Faculty Union.* Faculty unions are another common form of faculty governance and representation. They serve as formal authorities for institution (employer) to faculty (employee) issues, affairs, and representation. Unions serve as strong representatives of faculty; "many decisions that are made solely by management and the board in a nonunion environment must first be negotiated with the exclusive representative in a union environment" (Garfield, 2008, p. 26). At times, this can lead to a slower decision-making process; however, faculty have a powerful and respected voice in campus governance.
- *Student Government.* Student government is comprised of students elected by their peers to represent their interests and needs to the college. Similar to the faculty senate, student government officials usually represent various disciplines and colleges/schools within the institution (Miller & Miles, 2008). Their role is to advocate for issues of concern to students (Davis, 2001). This is often accomplished through committee participation and direct communication with senior-level officials. In actuality, student governments have very little power in campus decision making, due to: (a) yearly changes in student delegates; (b) lack of institutional memory; and (c) tertiary power beneath administrative and faculty interests (Miller & Miles, 2008).

The president (along with his/her cabinet), faculty, staff, and students contribute to campus-level policies which guide operations at the campus level. These policies must align with policy generated at previous levels (e.g., state constitution, state code, state/system-level policy, local governing board policy). Combined, all levels of policy contribute to a complex matrix of governance. Of course, the policy, governance, interests, and power of all independent governing entities and documents are shaped by needs, special interests, and influences of the various stakeholders.

Influences on Community College Governance

As illustrated in the *conceptual model of community college governance*, there are four primary types of influences that impact governing in the community college: (1) national, statewide, and local needs; (2) ideological differences; (3) internal influences; and (4) external influences. Taken as a whole, these four influences are the driving forces behind community college governance, policy, and decision making. They are the context where "true" governance takes place. The information previously presented regarding the governing entities and documents that guide community college governance is a simplistic and elementary view of community college governance. In reality, interests, power, and resources dictate the real governing of these institutions.

National, Statewide, and Local Needs

A primary mission of the community college is to "serve local community needs." This value has become paramount in the psyche of both community colleges and society, an unspoken mutual interest of interdependence. Davis (2001) affirms this value in stating that "the nation, the state, and the community want the college to serve the public interest" (Para. 6). Often, serving the public interest means providing for the human and intellectual capital needs of local and state economies through workforce development programming. Through terminal degree offerings (e.g., certificates, associate's degrees), the community college prepares students to fill current and emerging voids in the state/local workforce. For example, the shortage of nurses throughout the nation has been widely discussed in academic, business, and healthcare circles. The community college has responded to this shortage by providing Licensed Vocational Nursing (LVN) and Registered Nursing (RN) programming. In fulfilling the workforce needs of local and state communities, community colleges provide curricular offerings that would not be seen at four-year institutions (e.g., Sacramento City College's railroad program). Serving local needs also entails being responsive to the fiscal landscape facing society as a whole. Currently, this is a major facet of community college operations as retirees, the unemployed, veterans, and other students flood the community college to get retrained during poor economic times.

Meeting its mission of serving local communities, and society as a whole, has a direct impact of governance in the community college. Friedel (2008), in her article titled *The effect of the community college workforce development mission on governance*, explicates the direct role that the community college plays in responding to local, regional, and state workforce development needs. She outlines two cases, one in Kentucky and the other in Iowa in which local, regional, and state needs directly dictated substantial changes in community college governance. For example, the need to transition to a more highly trained citizenry was identified as a major factor in making Kentucky more appealing to current and potential industrial firms. Subsequently, a powerful coalition of business and education entities was formed (referred to as JobQuEST) to advocate for large-scale educational reforms that would maximize minimal state resources in an effort to more strategically position the state to develop the human capital needed for the workforce. The University of Kentucky Community College System was viewed as being responsive to workforce development needs. As a result, the legislature passed the Postsecondary Improvement Act. This act merged this system with the Kentucky Technical College System resulting in the establishment of the Kentucky Community and Technical College System (KCTCS). As noted by Friedel, "the primary vehicle for accomplishing the legislation's goal of offering access to two-year liberal arts and technical degrees, remedial instruction, workforce training, and continuing education would be through the merger...a new governance structure was established" (p. 50). This serves as a prime example (among many) that showcases the mergence of human and intellectual capital with economic needs and how governance was used as a mechanism to drive a new configuration to better meet state and local workforce development needs.

Ideological Differences

Ideological differences significantly impact community college governance. This occurs on three primary levels: (a) through political differences; (b) through core philosophical differences; and (c) through cultural differences. In terms of political differences, Davis (2001) notes that in a number of states, community college board members are appointed by the governor. Thus, every statewide political election can lead to a foundational shift in board makeup and ideology. Further, even in states where board members are elected, the fickleness of the electorate, voter turnout, and political tide can lead to substantial changes in board makeup. Thus, political differences can result in sweeping change in community college governance on board membership at the state and/or local level. Political shifts in governance have both benefits and drawbacks. The benefits include: (a) maintaining a balance of ideology; (b) changing policies, practices, and structures that are viewed as ineffective; and (c) new ideas that can contribute to positive organization change. The drawbacks include: (a) inconsistency of operations, vision, and mission that allow for longitudinal monitoring of accountability; (b) the loss of experience and institutional memory among board members; and (c) institutionalized networks that take time to establish being undermined, as networks serve to facilitate the development and implementation of an issue.

Davis notes that philosophical differences also impact community college governance. State/system-wide governing boards, local governing boards, and campus presidents can face direct conflict in institutional direction, vision, and mission as a result of their beliefs, "loyalty conflicts with the value of truthfulness, fairness conflicts with mercy, and concern for the individual conflicts with concern for the community" (Davis, 2001, Para. 11). When opposing viewpoints are not addressed in a manner that is respectful of differences and collaborative, conflict can consume the operations of community colleges and inhibit their success. Community college leaders (e.g., state/local trustees, campus officials) should see philosophical differences more as strengths for holistically addressing issues and concerns facing their institutions than as challenges to their integrity, direction, and outcomes. Often, philosophical differences serve to stall collaborative decision making. This can stall, divide, and alienate institutional affiliates, thereby, hindering or stopping altogether organizational changes needed for the community college to actualize its mission.

Finally, differing cultural viewpoints can also inhibit community college governance. Cultural misunderstandings and ethnocentrism can lead to discord at the state, local, and campus levels. Leaders must strive to better understand the issues, concerns, interests, and needs of varying cultural groups and how cultural perceptions can shape worldviews. Leaders who succeed in this regard will have enhanced relationships, support, and resources that can contribute to the success of the institutions they serve. For example, culturally proficient leaders are able to work effectively with a wide range of institutional constituents through their ability to understand, accept, and affirm varied cultural values, views, customs, and realities. This affords them the necessary knowledge to infuse within the decision-making process the thoughts, perceptions, and needs of communities that they serve.

Internal Influences

There are a number of internal influences that affect governance in the community college, which are classified under the umbrella of board dynamics. There are three general types of board dynamics: (a) power as impacted by centralization versus decentralization; (b) relations between and among interdependent bodies; and (c) term of office (e.g., elected, appointed, length of term). These three types of board dynamics impact community college governance as follows:

Centralization/Decentralization. As noted earlier, funding levels dictate where primary authority resides between state (e.g., elected officials, state/system-level governing boards) and local-level governance (e.g., local governing boards, campus-level governance). Generally, funding proportions from local government and state government are reflective of their authority in the governance process (Tollefson, 2009). In centralized governance structures, state officials and state/system governing boards have substantial control of community colleges. In some cases, boards even have authority to the point of approving faculty hiring/firing at the local campus level. In decentralized governance structures, power and authority is placed at the local level. When this occurs in states with local trustees, they may feel that their power in larger matters is reduced. As a result, they may turn to micromanaging presidents. Thus, centralization/decentralization has a direct impact on governing powers. Sometimes, states have a balance of centralization and decentralization. This can result in conflict, as authority lines are unclear. In "good times, ambiguity causes few problems. However, in lean years local boards often blame the state authority and state officials blame the local trustees" (Davis, 2001, Para 17).

Relations Between/Among Interdependent Bodies. Issues of centralization and decentralization can lead to the development of strong state-wide community college systems (in centralized structures) and strong local systems (in decentralized structures). However, this does not withhold players on state and local levels from vying for power. Centralized structures can lead educational leaders at the local level to feel disenfranchised. It also can lead to animosity from local officials toward state officials as orders from above can conflict with the best interests of local communities and their colleges. In contrast, decentralized structures can make those serving on state governing boards feel that their voice is not impacting changes they desire. When boards disagree about the vision and mission of colleges, discord between boards can ensue. However, disagreements about a college's direction can also occur within boards. Internal relationships, power, views, jockeying for control, especially when political, philosophical, and cultural values differ, can lead to ineffective state, local, and campus governance. In sum, centralization and decentralization structures have their strengths and shortcomings. When each is implemented within an institution in an effective manner and in accordance with the contextual factors of each local area (e.g., communication with key constituents, needs of local community, local culture and philosophy), they have the potential and ability to serve as a strong governance structure. Ultimately, this serves to clarify and improve relations between independent governing boards.

Term of Office. As noted, some community college boards are elected while others are appointed. There are benefits and drawbacks of both. Elected boards are beneficial in that they are accountable to the will of the electorate. Thus, if an elected board member makes a decision that is contrary to public opinion, they lose credibility, become marginalized, and can be removed from office. Also, elected boards usually represent specific districts or locales. This provides an equal voice at the table for constituents based upon geographic region. Elected boards have drawbacks: (1) usually only a small percentage of voters elect them, and these voters are usually not representative of the demographic makeup of the community it serves. As such, accountability to the electorate is only held when voters vote; (2) since they run for office, they are forced to fundraise and seek endorsements; this can place them in a position where they are (in essence) "owned" by special-interests groups (e.g., unions and associations) (Davis, 2001); (3) elected boards members must also run for reelection; this can hinder their focus on governing, and place their efforts on staying in office, rather than maintaining and/or improving their office (Vaughan, 2006). This issue can be compounded when terms of office are short (it can also be a benefit when boards are ineffective); and (4) their actions in office can, and often are, motivated by political interests. When these interests align with the college's interests, students benefit; however, when they do not, it is to the detriment of students (Miller & Miles, 2008).

Appointed board benefits include: (a) a more central focus on college issues (at least in theory), since board members do not run for office; (b) since they are not elected offices, they do not have to campaign for office (e.g., raise funds, seek endorsements). As a result, they may owe fewer political favors; and (c) ideally, the appointer (usually the governor) appoints individuals with expertise conducive to meet the needs of the college(s) they represent; and not, for the purpose of self-promotion/interests. However, appointed boards have drawbacks as well: (a) some "believe that appointed board members will be loyal to the appointing official, not to the community college" (Vaughan, 2006, p. 24); (b) they are not accountable to the electorate for their decisions. In all, benefits and drawbacks of elected and appointed board structures are evident; and (c) oftentimes, appointees are ardent donors or supporters to the political leader by whom they are appointed. This can be detrimental to community colleges when board members with little knowledge of education and issues facing community colleges are appointed.

External Influences

External influences are entities (e.g., accreditation associations, courts, federal government, blue ribbon commission, planning commissions), individuals (e.g., donors, campus alumni), and documents (e.g., federal code/acts) that influence community college governance. There are a number of external influences on each level. We will examine influences at the national, state, and local levels that we believe have the most impact on governance in the community college.

At the national level, three primary types of external influences are seen. The first is the Supreme Court of the United States. This judicial branch of government enacts national policy mandates, which influence the operations of the community college. One example of this is noted by Cohen (2001) who states that in the 1970s, the court "ruled that Southeastern Community College (North Carolina) was within its rights in denying the admission of a severely deaf student to its nursing program because the student's disability would preclude her taking part in the clinical aspect of the nursing program" (p. 18). Supreme Court influence on the community college is infrequent; however, when it occurs, it can create sweeping changes in policy, practices, and structures. This can lead to long-standing institutional change, overruling local and state governing bodies.

The second primary national external influence for community colleges are accreditation associations. While these associations represent regional locales (e.g., the Higher Learning Commission of the North Central Association of Colleges and Schools represents several states including Arkansas, New Mexico, Wyoming), they are recognized at the federal level by the U.S. Department of Education. Accreditation associations play an influential role in ensuring the successful operations of colleges. A prime example of the role accreditation associations can play in institutional governance is seen in the case of the late Compton Community College (now a branch of El Camino Community College). Due to egregious financial instability, fiscal mismanagement, and unethical operations, the California State Community College Chancellor's office removed the leadership and local governing board authority in an effort to prevent the college from losing its accreditation. Despite these actions, the Accreditation Commission for Community and Junior Colleges (ACCJC) of the Western Association of Schools and Colleges (WASC) revoked Compton College's accreditation (El Camino Community College, 2008). This serves as a primary example of the ramifications imposed on local and campus governing officials when their actions do not represent the will of the people. It also illustrates the strong external influence accreditation associations have on community college governance, even to the point of determining a college's existence. Accreditation associations serve as a strong authority on institutional governance, as accreditation is tied to: (a) funding colleges receives at the federal, state, and local level; (b) the reputation and prestige of institutions; (c) the transferability and worth of degrees awarded; and (d) the quality of teaching and learning at colleges. Thus, colleges exist at the will of these associations.

The third major national external influence is the federal government. Financial aid policies, federal labor code, and the Federal Workforce Development Act are just a few examples (among many) that illustrate the federal government's role as a strong external influence on community college governance. Often, these funds come with guidelines, policies, and regulations that dictate how they are to be used. When institutions do not meet these rules, the federal government will revoke funding. A current example of the role funding plays in institutional governance is the new plan announced by the Obama administration to increase community college graduation rates by five million more students by the year 2020 (Biden, 2009). In order to support this effort, the Obama administration has indicated that nine billion dollars in federal grants will be provided to community colleges. However, these monies come with strings attached. They include stringent benchmarks for degree completion, preparation of graduates for the workforce, and career placement (Field, 2009). Inevitably, these benchmarks will influence community college governance as local governing boards align policies, practices, and structures to better position institutions to receive federal funds.

At the state level, there are four primary forms of external influences that affect community college governance: (a) State Supreme courts; (b) blue ribbon panels; (c) planning commissions; and (d) special interest groups. Similar to the U.S. Supreme Court, state supreme courts issue rulings as well as clarify/interpret law (e.g., prior rulings, state initiatives). When rulings take place that deal with labor codes, education, and voting (among a host of other issues), community college governance responds. Blue ribbon panels also play a role in institutional governance. Blue ribbon panels are comprised of stakeholders (e.g., citizens, students, faculty, and administrators) who are concerned about a specific topic (e.g., production of students of color in the sciences, faculty intellectual rights). Through a series of meetings, often accompanied with research, panels render reports that are designed to influence community college leaders (e.g., statewide, state/system-wide, local, campus) to enact policies, procedures, and practices that impact the issue in which they are concerned. Often, the implementation of their recommendations is based upon the publicity of the panel, the prestige of its membership, and the organizations/entity that sponsored it. In essence, blue ribbon panels consist of coalition building among established and influential leaders. The end results are changes to policy which can directly improve an issue under consideration.

Planning Commissions are local, regional, or statewide groups comprised primarily of educational leaders as well as other affiliates (e.g., business representatives) who engage in long-term planning for specific locales. Usually, these commissions produce reports that are given to governing boards and state authorities (e.g., legislature) to be considered for ratification. Sometimes, they operate as mechanisms for dialogue on planning without official ratification. Many state-level master plans and strategic planning documents are created by planning commissions with representatives from various levels of postsecondary education. Thus, planning commissions can exert strong influence on state and local governance.

Finally, special interest groups also play a large role in institutional governance. Special interest groups can range in size, power, and interest. The most powerful special interest groups are unions and associations. These groups can have direct control over governing boards, especially those that are elected. In state government, special interest groups are so powerful that they are often referred to as "the third house," the branch of government where true decisions are made. Community college governing boards at all levels can be susceptible to the money, political favor, and endorsements, which come from these groups. At one end, these groups can erode decision making and place groups without their financial backing (namely students) at a disadvantage in the governing process. At the other end, they can lead to stronger advocacy, better board members, and a respected voice in governing processes.

Local-level groups, entities, and persons can also have a direct influence on community college governance. In general, four primary external groups influence governance on this level: (a) the local business community; (b) campus alumni; (c) local government; and (d) donors. When these groups come together, they can become powerful external influences on governance.

A primary aspect of the mission of community college is to "serve local community needs," thus local business can often influence institutional governance. As future employers for community college graduates, local industry heavily influences governance through: (a) donating resources (e.g., computers, software, and equipment) and services to community colleges; and (b) providing internships for students. Their influence can be presented through special interest groups (e.g., chambers, associations), and through individual contact (especially for large regional employers) with local governing board members and campus presidents. Campus alumni are another group that can exert external influence on community college governance, primarily through: (a) financial support; (b) existing social networks (i.e. on the campus and in the community; and (c) through positive publicity for the institution. Though community colleges do not have the strong alumni base that four-year institutions enjoy, community college alumni can influence community college governance. This is particularly common when they are individuals of great political or economic stature (e.g., community leaders, publicly elected officials; successful business owners; the wealthy). Local government leaders can directly influence community college governance whether they are alumni or not. Through social networks, political affiliations, and access to resources, they can encourage (and incentivize) community college boards and presidents to make decisions on issues that are important to them. In this light, they can operate in a similar fashion as special interest groups.

Of the local entities mentioned, donors (especially large donors) likely have the most influence on community college governance. For example, large donors to community colleges can greatly improve the quality and the success of these institutions, especially in difficult financial times. When additional funding streams are crucial to the fiscal viability of institutions or to community college leaders' reputations, contributors can greatly influence decision making. Large donors who have the potential of donating on multiple occasions are especially crucial to community colleges; however, institutional leaders must not erode the governing process by guaranteeing the enactment of new policies and practices in order to attain gifts. This is often easier said than done, especially when institutions face reductions in state and local government funding coupled with increasing student enrollments. This focus on donations and fundraising is very much welcomed by institutions, especially by presidents who are increasingly pressured to self-sustain their institutions.

Case Study

In this chapter, we have presented the complexities involved in community college governance. We have shown that governing these institutions is anything but a straightforward, simplistic, and linear process. Thus, leaders must shed their idealistic and elementary view of governing these institutions. Rather, they must recognize that leading community colleges will require strong analytical, political, intuitive, and human relations skills; in doing so, it will facilitate their success in a complex, multifaceted, dynamic, and complicated governing process. In consideration of this convoluted process of governance, leaders may find it easier to work in isolation. While this may work in the short-term, not following a shared-governance process by neglecting the interests of governing entities, documents, and influences will be catastrophic to the well-being of the institution. Disenfranchising stakeholders will ultimately result in votes of no confidence for presidents and simple removal or reassignment for other leaders. In essence, "if you don't become a governance player, then you get played by the governance." In analyzing and resolving the case study presented below, leaders should be attentive to the material covered in this chapter with special attention given to the nexus of interests, influences, power, and resources in shaping governance.

Chancellor, Ned Doffoney
North Orange County Community College District
Anaheim, California

An Athletic Scandal?

Background

Central Valley College (CVC) is a large urban community college with a diverse population of more than 20,000 students. The college is in its ninth decade of operation, offering more than 100 academic and technical programs. The college also offers a full range of intercollegiate athletic programs including football. Because of its history of success and focus on local students and programs, the college football receives significant local media attention. The community is the largest community in the central valley of California. Predominately Latino and poor to middle class, the community has a strong tradition of support for athletic programs. The demographic makeup of the college, similar to the community, is 38 percent Latino, 32 percent White, 8 percent African American, 18 percent Asian, and 1 percent Native American. The gender makeup of the college is 58 percent female and 42 percent male. The 2006 football team at CVC is predicted to be among the best teams ever. The coaching staff, accustomed to winning, has recruited outstanding local talent and supplemented that local talent by inviting more than 20 out-of-area athletes to compete for a roster spot on the local college team. Athletes flock to this program due to the football team's reputation of sending a great number of athletes to Division 1 football programs. Subsequently, some even make it to the National Football League (NFL). It is the summer of 2006 just four weeks before football practice officially begins. Players are gathering, yet coaches are not allowed to "coach" prior to enrollment. Potential players gather for personal, unsupervised conditioning sessions.

Statement of the Problem

You are the college president in your fourth year of assignment. You receive a telephone call on Sunday afternoon from the college public information officer (PIO) informing you that in four hours there will be a television news conference by the local chief of police accusing 10 CVC football players of raping an 11-year-old girl. The College PIO asked that you be prepared to give a response to the media regarding the college's position on these accusations. By 5 pm there are more than 200 media request from every major media outlet in the west. In addition, state policymakers, the state chancellor's office, and local governing board members are asking for an immediate response from you. Information vital to the circumstances are as follows:

- In an alleged crime that the local police chief calls "disturbing," as many as 10 African American men, most of whom are community college football players, are accused of raping an 11-year-old Latina;

- The girl, a runaway from a group home, claims she was raped multiple times by the men on Saturday night at a local apartment complex;
- Police investigation indicated that housing arrangements for several of the occupants that reside in the apartment unit where this sexual assault is said to have occurred were made by the head football coach at CVC;
- Neighbors who live around the apartment told reporters the men always seemed polite and have been seen tossing footballs around the complex's common areas;
- The suspects who have been taken into custody were arrested on suspicion of child molestation with a victim under 14 and oral copulation with a victim under 18. Under California law any sexual conduct with a person under 14 is a felony. For about the last six years, many Division I coaches have referred promising recruits to the CVC program in the hopes of improving grades while facing top-notch competition;
- The infusion of Division I-caliber talent has transformed CVC into a consistent top-10 program. In the past, the school's roster has been filled with African American players from Florida, Georgia, and Alabama.
- The chairman of the board is in Argentina, legal counsel is on vacation in Arizona, and the athletic director is in the hospital undergoing an operation. The head football coach and the accused men are immediately available. While CVC is a pigskin paradise for Division I coaches, it is a purgatory for the players.

In addressing this issue, consider the following: (1) What implications does this case have for state, local, and campus governance? (2) What are the reasons in involving or not involving multiple stakeholders in addressing this situation? (3) What are the influences (e.g., internal, external, philosophical) that you should consider in addressing this case? and (4) What governing documents (e.g., state law, local governing board policy) must you be attentive to in this case?

References

AACC (2008). *About us.* Washington, DC: American Association of Community Colleges. Retrieved September 2, 2009, from: http://www.aacc.nche.edu/About/Pages/default.aspx

AACC (2009). *Who we are.* Washington, DC: American Association of Community Colleges. Retrieved November 16, 2009, from: http://www.aacc.nche.edu/About/Who/Pages/default.aspx

ACHE (2009). *Mission statement.* Montgomery, AL: Alabama Commission for Higher Education. Retrieved June 30, 2009, from: http://www.ache.alabama.gov/AboutUs/Mission.htm

ALSDE (2009). *About us.* Montgomery, AL: Alabama State Department of Education. Retrieved June 30, 2009, from: http://www.alsde.edu/html/boe.asp

Alfred, R. L. (2008). Governance in strategic context. *New Directions for Community Colleges,* 141, 79–89.

Amey, M. J., Jessup-Anger, E., & Jessup-Anger, J. (2008). Community college governance: What matters and why? *New Directions in Community Colleges,* 141, 5–14.

Biden, J. (2009, July 21). Community colleges are crucial. *The Sun News.* Retrieved August 3, 2009, from: http://www.thesunnews.com/158/story/990694.html

Cain, M. S. (1999). *The community college in the twenty-first century: A systems approach.* Lanham, MD: University Press of America.

Cohen, A. M. (2001). Governmental policies affecting community colleges: A historical perspective. In B. K. Townsend & S. B. Twombly (eds.). *Community colleges: Policy in the future context* (pp. 3–22). Westport, CT: Ablex Publishing.

Davis, G. (2001). *Issues in Community college governance.* Washington, DC: American Association of Community Colleges. Retrieved September 2, 2009, from: http://www.aacc.nche.edu/Resources/aaccprograms/pastprojects/Pages/issuesccgovernance.aspx

ECS (2007). *State-level coordinating and/or governing agency.* Denver, CO: Educational Commission of the States. Retrieved June 30, 2009, from: http://mb2.ecs.org/reports/Report.aspx?id=223

Eells, W. B. (1931). *The junior college.* Boston, MA: Houghton Mifflin.

El Camino Community College (2008). *Campus history.* Compton, CA: Compton Community Educational Center. Retrieved September 2, 2009, from: http://www.compton.edu/campusinformation/CampusHistory.aspx

Field, K. (2009, July 29). For community colleges, federal aid would come with strings attached. *The Chronicle of Higher Education.* Retrieved August 3, 2009, from: http://chronicle.com/article/For-Community-Colleges-Aid/47493/?utm_source=at&utm_medium=en

Friedel, J. N. (2008). The effect of the community college workforce development mission on governance. *New Directions for Community Colleges,* 141, 45–55.

Garfield, T. K. (2008). Governance in a union environment. *New Directions for Community Colleges,* 141, 25–33.

Lovell, C. D., & Trouth, C. (2004). Statewide community college governance structures: Factors that influence and issues that test effectiveness. In J. C. Smart (ed.). *Higher education: Handbook of theory and research, vol. XIX* (pp. 133–174). Cambridge, MA: Springer.

McGuinness, A. C. (2003). *ECS State notes: Models of postsecondary education coordination and governance in the states.* Denver, CO: Education Commission of the State.

Miller, M. T., & Miles, J. M. (2008). Internal governance in the community college: Models and quilts. *New Directions for Community Colleges,* 141, 35–44.

Potter, G. E., & Phelan, D. J. (2008). Governance over the years: A trustee's perspective. *New Directions for Community Colleges,* 141, 15–24.

Richardson, R., and de los Santos, G. (2001). Statewide governance structures and two-year colleges. In B. K. Townsend, and S. B. Twombly (eds.). *Community Colleges: Policy in the Future Context* (pp. 39–56). Westport, CT: Ablex Publishing.

Schuetz, P. (2008). Key resources on community college governance. *New Directions in Community Colleges*, 141, 91–98.

SHEEO (2009). State planning documents. Denver, CO: State Higher Education Executive Officers. Retrieved September 2, 2009, from: http://www.sheeo.org/links/links_results.asp?regionID=53&issueID=17

Tollefson, T. A. (1999). Mission, governance, funding, and accountability trends in state systems of community colleges. In T. A. Tollefson, R. L. Garrett, W. G. Ingram & Associates (eds.). *Fifty state systems of community colleges: Mission, governance, funding and accountability* (pp. 23–32). Johnson City, TN: Overmountain Press.

Tollefson, T. A. (2009). Community college governance, funding, and accountability: A century of issues and trends. *Community College Journal of Research and Practice*, 33(3), 386–402.

Vaughan, G. B. (2006). *The community college story* (3rd ed.). Washington, DC: Community College Press.

CHAPTER ELEVEN

LEADERSHIP DEVELOPMENT
IN THE COMMUNITY COLLEGE

This chapter focuses on the role of leadership development in preparing community college leaders. Therefore, we will: (a) examine challenges and opportunities facing community college leaders; (b) address the skills needed to successfully confront these challenges; (c) identify various leadership development programs designed for community college leaders; and (d) discuss the need for assessing the success of these programs.

When reading this chapter, consider the following questions:

- What are the leadership development needs within your own institution? What are the implications of these needs for the future of your institution?
- What skills do you believe community college leaders need? Do you believe doctoral programs and leadership institutes are meeting these needs?
- What role do leadership development programs (e.g., doctoral programs, leadership institutes) play in preparing aspiring and current community college leaders?

In the coming years, the community college will experience unprecedented turnover in its leadership, especially among its senior ranks (Shults, 2001; Weisman & Vaughan, 2001; 2006). Weisman & Vaughan (2006) note that 84 percent of community college chief executive officers (CEOs) plan to retire by 2016. Primarily, the "impending" leadership void is being created by educators who entered the community college in the 1960s and 1970s and have served in these institutions for decades (Phillippe & Sullivan, 2005; Shults, 2001). On the verge of retirement, the presidential ranks are becoming progressively older. In 1996, the average age of a community college president was 54; in 2001, it had risen to 56. By 2006, the average age of a president had increased to 58 (Weisman & Vaughan, 2006). While the average age of a community college president is 58, Duree (2007) notes that 44 percent of presidents are between the ages of 60 and 69, supporting the assertion that administrator turnover is forthcoming.

The aging trend among community college leaders is also evident in the ranks of chief academic officers (CAOs) (e.g., vice presidents of academic affairs, vice chancellors for academic affairs) (see Amey, VanDerlinden, & Brown, 2001; Evelyn, 2000; Shults, 2001). For example in 1985, the average age of a CAO in the community college was 49.1 years (Moore, Matorana, & Twombly, 1985). However, by 2008, the average age had risen to 54 years, further suggesting that retirements are looming among these administrators (Mizak, 2008). The retirement of a large portion of senior faculty members also poses severe challenges to leadership channels. Typically, senior faculty members fill the leadership pipeline. As noted by Nevarez and Keyes (2007), "historically, the path to higher education administration has been via tenure-track faculty member, to chair, dean, vice president, to president" (p. 82). This is affirmed by Duree (2007) who states that 84.4 percent of presidents have taught full-time or part-time in the community college prior to assuming the presidency. Furthermore, 47 percent assumed the presidency directly from positions in academic affairs.

Challenges to Leading in the Community College

As retirements loom among executive-level administrators, there is a critical need to develop the next generation of leaders who are prepared to assume the dynamic, complex, and challenging roles that their positions demand. Thus, the importance of providing leadership preparation; focus on preparing leaders with the skills, knowledge, and experiences needed to become effective leaders is essential for the vitality and advancement of the institutions they serve. The need to prepare a new kind of executive leader is of the utmost importance, as the roles and duties of higher education leaders have changed greatly from previous generations. Leaders today need to realize the fundamental organizational changes required to better meet the needs of constituents and the necessity for growth and transformation of individuals and institutions (Hoff, 1999; Ramaley, 2000).

In contrast to other sectors (e.g., business), higher education has few internal mechanisms to train new and aspiring administrators for successive levels of leadership. Consequently, the lack of leadership succession planning in community colleges, especially among senior administrative ranks, places those promoted to new leadership posts at a disadvantage, as skills and knowledge needed for success in these positions are learned on-the-job. To counter the lack of preparation, an approach that focuses on building the leadership capacity of prospective leaders should be institutionalized within the everyday practices of the college.

Leadership development can serve to prepare leaders with the multifaceted skills necessary to meet these needs. It can serve as a tool to replenish the leadership pipeline, prepare leaders so that they are effective at transforming institutions to meet the needs of students and constituents, and diversify the administrative ranks with leaders attuned to the needs of a global marketplace. Leadership development should encompass academic and professional development opportunities such as doctoral programs, conferences, and leadership institutes, which provide guidance, mentorship, knowledge, experiences, networks, and activities that prepare leaders to effectively serve the wide-ranging missions, demands, and diverse needs of the community college.

Primary Challenges Facing Community College Leaders

There are a number of challenges facing today's community colleges and, consequently, its leaders. These issues are dynamic and complex due to the evolving mission, changing demographic landscape, and societal pressures on the community colleges. The following merely serves as a snapshot of the challenges encountered by these institutions:

- *Complexity of the Position.* The community college has multiple roles (e.g., career technical education, remediation, transfer, meeting community needs), and these roles are continually evolving due to internal (e.g., faculty pay, student retention) and external demands (e.g., funding, accountability). Thus, leading these increasingly dynamic institutions requires that leaders are able to multitask, possess effective leadership skills, and handle multiple pressures that the position brings.
- *Funding.* The chronic lack of funding experienced by community colleges poses significant challenges to the community colleges mission of open access. Funding shortages result in lack of funding for student services, high numbers of adjunct faculty, and minimal institutional resources among other factors. While other institutions of higher education can confront these challenges with capital campaigns, community colleges are at a disadvantage as they lack the kind of support that four-year universities experience. For example, Townsend & Twombly (2001) contend that "the community college has sometimes been viewed as a

poor cousin of elite liberal arts colleges and research universities" (p. vii). These views have implications directly tied to alumni support, state/ federal funding allocations, fundraising, and bond initiatives.

- *Academic Success.* Community colleges offer access to the most under-served students with the greatest needs, as their "open door" policy is consistent with their mission focused on access. However, these institutions have been criticized for low degree attainment and transfer rates. Even when controlling for students who state that they desire to graduate or transfer, the success rate is low. For example, the three-year graduation rate for first-time freshman in the community college is less than 27 percent for all racial/ethnic groups (U.S. Department of Education, 2006).

- *Assessment.* As a whole, community colleges struggle in assessing local community impact and student success. Often, this is attributed to the multiple purposes and foci of these institutions. The assessment of the community college is challenged by its varied missions and its decentralized governance structure, which provides it with a great deal of autonomy. Improved assessment is needed in the community college to: (a) improve academic outcomes of students; (b) inform current and future practices; (c) justify future funding, resources, and support from state governments; and (d) satisfy guidelines for accreditation agencies.

- *Diversity.* The disproportionate representation of diverse leaders among the administrative ranks is not reflective of the population these institutions serve. This has implications in the following ways: (a) preparing students for a diverse global marketplace; (b) promoting civic engagement and social justice; (c) creating quality role models; (d) providing cultural brokers/translators/transformers; and (e) encouraging effective critical pedagogy, planning, and programming that accounts for diversity. These points are further expounded upon in Chapter 6, *Faculty in the Community College.*

Leadership "Crisis" or Leadership Opportunity

Some scholars have gone to great lengths to herald the approaching transition of community college leaders, describing it as a "crisis" (Katsinas, 2002; Korb, 2006; Shults, 2001). This claim is made in relation to the lack of leaders being prepared to assume the leadership ranks in community colleges. It is vague what is meant by this "crisis" other than the typical administrative turnover experienced in all sectors of society due to the retirement of the baby boomer generation. However, there is another way to construe this phenomenon; it should be seen as an opportunity to improve the effectiveness of community college leadership.

As noted in Chapter 4 on the *Achievement Gap and the Role of Community Colleges*, the retention, graduation, and transfer rates of students, particularly students of color, in the community college is abysmal. Clearly, new ideas, perspectives, and educational approaches are needed to increase student academic success. In this light, these retirements are not a crisis; rather, it is an opportunity to improve the diversification of leaders and educational outcomes. That being said, the primary challenge posed by these retirements is the potential loss of institutional memory within these organizations (Shults, 2001; Phillippe & Sullivan, 2005). As the "old guard" is replaced with new leadership, the historical context needed to understand the importance of policies, processes, and programs may be lost. However, Phillippe & Sullivan (2005) assert that these changes provide opportunities, as "the potential for new energy and insight balances some of the losses" (p. 76).

Some of these new insights may come from a more diverse leadership. Weisman & Vaughan (2006) provide data indicating that 88 percent of community college presidents are White, while only 8 percent are Black, 4 percent Hispanic, and 1 percent Asian American/Pacific Islander. Furthermore, they state that only 29 percent of these presidents are female, while 71 percent are male. These statistics indicate a clear problem of representation between the percentage of racial/ethnic and gender diversity in society and among community college students and that of the workforce in administrative ranks. It is important for the administrators to reflect on the diverse makeup of the students they represent in order to serve as mentors/role models and work toward creating an inclusive campus environment. The lack of diversity within the administrative ranks in many community colleges raises an important question: Do its principles of access, equity, and diversity extend only to its student body? If so, a mixed message is being sent to its constituency. One that says—we welcome diversity among students but not among the leadership ranks. Furthermore, the paucity of leader diversity in the community college presents a nearly untapped resource to fill the broken leadership pipeline. If diversified, these leaders may bring to the leadership ranks new cultural lenses, a commitment to diversity, the ability to relate to diverse constituencies, and insights on challenges facing students that may enable the community college to better address the needs of a continuously changing student population. That being said, not all minorities are proponents for diversity-related initiatives and ideals.

Skills Needed by Community College Leaders

A variety of leadership development programs/initiatives have been useful in developing community college leaders. In doing so, they have focused on developing the knowledge, skills, and disposition needed for success (e.g., budgeting, ethics, governance, human relations, cultural proficiency, facilitating institutional change, conflict resolution). However, there remains a need to rethink the way community college leaders have been trained. Traditional leadership development programs have been criticized for replicating leadership approaches, structures, and ideologies that are not attuned to the current realities faced by community colleges. For example, most doctoral programs, which develop community college leaders, train students for the positions in the professoriate or as researchers; however, in discussions with current administrators seeking their doctorates, they state that there is a need to develop practical skills that are aligned with the everyday challenges faced by community college leaders.

Research by Nevarez and Keyes (2007) indicates than only 29 percent of executive-level community college administrators in California believe that their academic programs provided them with the training and skills necessary for successful leadership. Furthermore, 70.4 percent stated that there was a need to integrate leadership training and skills into current academic programs. Other scholars also affirm the disconnect that exists between leadership preparation and the skills needed to be successful in the field (see Brown, Martinez, & Daniel, 2002; McPhail, Robinson, & Scott, 2008). To illustrate this disconnect, Table 1 presents findings derived from three studies on this topic (Brown, Martinez, & Daniel, 2002; Nevarez & Keyes, 2007; Wallin, 2002). On the left side of Table 1, a set of skills was identified by a variety of community college leaders as being essential skills for effective community college leadership.[1] These skills contrast with the current areas of leadership development occurring in doctoral programs, which are featured on the right side of Table 1 (Brown, Martinez, & Daniel, 2002).

In examining the themes across Table 1, it is apparent that the primary skills needed for community college leaders, as identified by the leaders themselves, encompasses two areas: human relations and budgeting/finance. In contrast, the preparation received in doctoral programs focuses on developing research skills and the technical knowledge needed for success in the professoriate. While these skills are important for aspiring faculty members, the gateway for many

---

[1] Skill sets are ranked, ties are indicated by (*) asterisks.

Table 1 Leadership Skills Needed & Skills Emphasized in Doctoral Programs

Leadership skills needed			Doctoral program emphasis
Wallin (2002)	Nevarez & Keyes (2007)	Brown et al., 2002	Brown et al., 2002
1. Budget management	1. Strategic planning and management	1. Effective writing skills	1. Statistical research methodology
2. Developing positive relationship with local political leaders	2. Interpersonal communication skills	2. Conflict resolution, mediation, and negotiating skills	2. Faculty and staff development
3. Developing positive relationships with state political leaders	3. Budgeting and fund development	3. Understanding and application of "change"	3. Interpretation of surveys and research
	4. Laws and legal issues	4. * Understanding of community college mission	4. Understanding of organization theory and culture
	5. Technology training	5. * Institutional effectiveness: assessment and analysis	5. Effective writing skills
		6. Understanding of collaborative decision making	6. Teaching and learning styles and methodologies
		7. Understanding of interpersonal communication	7. Understanding of the community college mission
		8. * Developing and communicating a vision	8. Understanding and application of "change"
		9. * Effective public speaking skills	9. Curriculum development
		10. Effective listening and feedback skills	10. Statistical software application

Skill sets are ranked, ties are indicated by (*) asterisks.

community college presidents, they do not adequately prepare aspiring leaders with the skill sets needed for success in administrative posts. This presents an opportunity to ensure that leadership programs, including doctoral programs, are attuned to the realities of the profession. It also illustrates the critical need for professional development for leaders beyond doctoral programs.

Skills Provided by Doctoral Programs

There are current efforts to address these contradictions, the focus of which has been on the unclear role of the EdD and PhD (Schulman et al., 2006). The lack of distinction between the EdD and PhD serves as an additional element contributing to the incongruencies between what leaders state they need, and what they are getting. Levine (2005) stated that educational leadership programs were not preparing academic leaders for the demands of the profession. Some efforts are underway to address Levine's concern. As an example, the Carnegie Foundation launched a new initiative entitled, the *Carnegie Project on the Education Doctorate*; its purpose is to critically analyze and redefine the state of doctoral education. The foundation seeks to implement a widespread overhaul of the EdD and PhD curriculum to meet distinct needs of both researchers and practitioners. For practitioners, the goal is to create curriculum that focuses less on preparing students for the professoriate and more on providing a venue where greater efforts are made to link theory to practice (Carnegie Foundation, 2009).

Skills Provided by Leadership Development Programs

In examining unpublished data from 66 community college executives (e.g., presidents, chancellors, vice chancellors) who participated in the study published by Nevarez & Keyes (2007), it is clear that leadership development programs are meeting some of the needs identified by these educational leaders. According to the community college leaders who participated in the survey, the top five skills/ abilities that they have gained from leadership training include:

- Increased time management skills
- More understanding of the challenges associated with educational leadership
- Increased strategic-planning skills
- Increased decision-making skills

- Increased communication skills
- Increased confidence level

Based upon this data, it seems that leadership development programs are meeting the human relationship needs of leaders, an important void identified in doctoral education training. Unfortunately, the budgeting/finance skills received the lowest score in this study. Thus, it is imperative that leadership development programs improve this area of training in order to address the top two concerns identified by community college leaders.

Types of Leadership Development

Leadership development programs have flourished due to concerns regarding the sufficiency of the pipeline to replenish the ensuing leadership vacancies. Leadership development programs can serve a variety of needs, as they can: (a) provide the disposition and vision needed to effectively lead community colleges; (b) set a venue where the technical aspects of the profession are learned, rehearsed, and practiced; (c) provide a setting where formed relationships lead to networks of professional support; (d) prepare leaders with a genre of skills needed to lead the highly fluid community college; and (e) attune leaders to emerging statewide and national trends and demands.

There are two main types of leadership development programs; (1) doctoral programs; and (2) leadership institutes. In general, these programs share comparable characteristics in that "they focus on building support networks and provide instruction in basic areas...But they also vary on many counts, especially length, structure, experience level addressed, and extent of firsthand contact with top administrators" (Leon & Nevarez, 2007, p. 364).

There are similarities across leadership development programs, while the specificities of each leadership program type are unique. The authors used the following criteria to provide a broad preview of programs across the country, which exemplify the two types of leadership development programs. These criteria included:

- The identification of programs reflective of various regions across the nation;
- The selection of a variety of institutes that cater to the needs of specialized populations (e.g., women leaders, leaders of color, senior-level leaders);

- The inclusion of established institutes with a focus on topics including technical skills, human relations, fundraising, and human resources;
- The identification of programs varying in length and scope; and
- The selection of institutes that are sponsored by a variety of entities (e.g., associations, foundations, universities, consortiums), which address the varying range of quality between the institutes.

Doctoral Programs

Doctoral programs (EdD and PhD) link theory, research, and practice relevant to training community college leaders. These programs are driven by the theoretical and conceptual underpinnings of leadership theory. Although the focus of these programs is to prepare community college leaders, each program has distinctive features (e.g., transformational leadership, social justice, policy) as illustrated in Table 2. An emerging trademark of these programs is the cohort-based model, in which students are grouped with other aspiring leaders throughout the duration of their program. The intention behind this structure is to increase cohesiveness, support, and networking among cohort members, which subsequently can serve as a mechanism to increase the academic success of its students.

A doctoral degree is widely viewed as a baseline requirement for executive-level leadership in the community college. Weisman & Vaughan (2006) note that 88.4 percent of community college presidents possessed doctoral degrees. Thus, there is a significant value in attaining a doctoral degree for aspiring and current community college leaders. As the demand for executive leaders to possess a doctoral degree continues to increase, the number of degrees conferred in the area of community college leadership has been stagnant.

The programs presented above provide a glimpse into what higher education programs focus on in preparing community college leaders. A comprehensive list of these programs is available on the Council for the Study of Community College and American Association of Community Colleges websites. These programs serve as an authority on preparing executive-level administrators, though they have been criticized for not adequately preparing leaders to effectively serve their institutions (Brown, Martinez, & Daniel, 2002; Land, 2003; Raines & Alberg, 2003). This is due to a lack of balance between theory and practice as well as a central academic focus on community colleges.

A cursory review of existing programs on community college leadership quickly reveals a paucity of programs specifically focused on community college

Table 2 Doctoral Programs

Name	Program overview	Distinctive features
California State University Education Doctorate (EdD)	"The CSU's EdD programs are designed to equip leaders with the necessary knowledge and skills to achieve reforms to improve student achievement." These programs have a dual focus of preparing P-12 and community college leaders. There are currently ten programs, which are regionally represented across the state of California. There are plans to increase this number.	Five primary features: 1) Reform: Program focuses on educating leaders to achieve reform and improvement in public education. 2) Involvement of professional partners: Local K-12 and community college educators form partnerships to address regional needs. 3) Cohort-learning model: learning occurs through active problem solving with peers. 4) Scheduling options: EdD classes are held in the evenings and on weekends to allow participation of full-time working professionals. 5) Rigorous focus on applied research: Rigorous focus on applied research to improve student learning.
Community College Leadership Program (CCL Program) at Colorado State University	The Community College Leadership Program (CCL Program) is designed to meet the needs of persons interested in leadership positions at community colleges and other higher education institutions. The CCL Program offers current leaders the opportunity to improve their practice. The CCL Program offers aspiring leaders the opportunity to develop the cognitive, emotional, and interpersonal skills required for success in such appointments.	Four primary objectives: 1) To provide a comprehensive and progressive doctoral curriculum that develops the skills needed to successfully lead community colleges; 2) To develop students' research skills and abilities to enable them to expand the knowledge base concerning community colleges, effective teaching, and student learning; 3) To instill or reinforce a commitment to the critical engagement of diversity; and 4) To assist students in exploring ways to strengthen commitments to open access, the comprehensive mission, and instructional quality.

(Continued)

Table 2 (Continued)

Name	Program overview	Distinctive features
The Community College Leadership Program (CCLP) at Oregon State University	The Community College Leadership Program (CCLP) prepares teachers and administrators for leadership roles in technical and community colleges and similar organizations. The CCLP focus is on the application of quality research to the problems and opportunities in community colleges.	Five program features: 1) CCLP students enroll as members of a cohort with the goal of participating in an active learning community. 2) Classes are scheduled for an intensive weekend once a month at an off-campus conference center in Oregon. 3) Instructional methods include group and individual projects, scholarly discussion, and a professional internship. 4) A portfolio, oral exam, and the defense of original research reported in a dissertation are needed to complete the program. 5) A major professor guides each student through the program.
Community College Leadership Program (CCLP) at the University of Texas, Austin	This CCLP is the oldest community college doctoral program. The CCLP has focused on the preparation of key leaders for American and Canadian community colleges. A second objective has been to establish a service-oriented "field base" with community colleges from across North America for student recruitment and graduate placement, and to serve further as a laboratory for CCLP research and development efforts. A third objective has been the establishment of a research agenda that significantly impacts the quality of teaching, learning, and student services in open-door institutions.	The program consists of: 1) A cohesive program of study in a specialty area and related fields specifically tailored to the needs and career goals of individual students, 2) Sequences of appropriate field placements including such experiences as supervisory internships and administrative practicum, 3) Coursework in research and evaluation methodologies. 4) Upon completion of the program, each graduate will (a) have a broad understanding of the impact of social and cultural factors on education, (b) have the ability to communicate effectively in written and oral form in a variety of settings, (c) have advanced special expertise—body of knowledge and skills—which prepares the individual to assume a position of educational leadership, and (d) will be able to plan, develop, conduct, interpret, and apply research for specific purposes

Higher Education Program (HEP) at George Mason University	The Higher Education Program at George Mason University prepares individuals for positions of leadership in teaching, research, and administration at community colleges, four-year colleges, and universities around the globe. At the master's and doctoral levels, the interdisciplinary curriculum focuses on leadership, the scholarship of teaching and learning, and assessment. The program also offers coursework to prepare students for positions in academic affairs and student affairs.	The program rests on the four core principles that prepare graduates to handle the changing needs of today's college students. 1. *Ethical leadership*. Effective leadership derives from ethical integrity and a respect for the diversity of others. 2. *Assessment*. Assessment allows for educational improvement by measuring whether an individual, program, or institution is achieving the desired goals. 3. *Information technology*. Information technology has been identified as a primary focus for Mason's excellence. It fits the needs and goals of the region and the nation, and our faculty and students creatively use and critically examine information technology for their academic goals. 4. *Diversity*. This program prepares leaders who will foster educational and work environments free from discrimination. Further, students and faculty will encourage diversity of thought in the classroom and in research.

Source: See http://www.soe.cahs.colostate.edu/Graduate/PhD/CCL/; http://www.dacce.gmu.edu/; http://edadmin.edb.utexas.edu/cclp/; http://www.calstate.edu/edd/index.shtml.

Note: Programs presented in alphabetical order, when possible direct quotes from program Web sites are provided.

leadership. What is found is that programs have a generalized higher education focus. Additionally, there is a proliferation of online and/or for-profit programs for community college leadership (e.g., Argosy University, Walden University). It is clear that alternative formats of instruction provided by these institutions create greater access to doctoral education focused on community colleges than has been traditionally provided by public institutions. Like their public university counterparts, the issue of assessment to determine program effectiveness continues to gain greater visibility, especially in consideration of the accountability movement that permeates higher education.

Leadership Institutes

Leadership institutes are coherently planned efforts to develop a set of skills among leaders through the building of support networks and specialized instruction. In contrast to doctoral programs, leadership institutes emphasize the acquisition of practical skills. These institutes provide administrators with "concrete examples found in traditional professional development activities and institutes" (e.g., technical writing, mock interviews, case studies, interactive discussions, development of networks) (Amey, 2004, p. 8). An emphasis is placed on skill development, reflection, and applicability to addressing the realities faced by the home institution.

Institutes can vary based upon duration, structure, and experience level. In general, leadership institutes are sponsored by foundations, universities, consortiums and associations. Unfortunately, funding problems have a tendency to cripple the number and quality of these institutes, since funding typically comes from soft money. The need to formally institutionalize effective leadership institutes to protect them from the instability of the economic landscape is of importance. Table 3 illustrates some of the most prominent leadership institutes across the country coupled with a brief description of each program's focus and distinctive features. These institutes are typically attended by current and aspiring community college leaders, and serve to enhance their knowledge, skills, and leadership disposition.

Many leadership development institutes cater to specific populations (e.g., women, people of color) in order to address disparities in leader representation. As illustrated by the institutes above, there is a strong emphasis on improving the leadership pipeline for women in the community college as evidenced by programs such as the Asilomar Leadership Skills Seminar, The Leadership Tools for Women, and the National Institute for Leadership Development

Table 3 Leadership Institutes

Name	Program Overview	Distinctive Features
Admin 101 sponsored by the Association of California Community College Administrators (ACCCA)	ACCCA's Administration 101 is a five-day seminar focusing on the unique nuts and bolts of California community college administration. It provides an overview of the most crucial technical and legal aspects of administration as it applies to California's unique community college system. Case studies provided by current leaders help attendees apply the rules and regulations in real-world situations.	The ACCCA's Administration 101 seminar focuses on; 1. California Community College Governance 2. Instruction and student services 3. Institutional dynamics/strategic planning and administrative roles: The culture and politics of institutions 4. Budget 5. Human resources 6. Leadership and skills implementation 7. Leading through change; and 8. Balancing Your life.
Asilomar Leadership Skills Seminar sponsored by the Community College League of California	The Asilomar Leadership Skills Seminar began in 1984. The Seminar is an intensive four-day experience that focuses on the issues facing women who have made a commitment to community college administration, either in their current position or as a future goal.	This leadership seminar focuses on the following areas: 1. Emotional intelligence; 2. Budgeting and finance; 3. Cultural proficiency; 4. Leading change; 5. Leadership and ethics; 6. Finding balance; 7. Campus politics; 8. Career choices & paths; 9. Governance; and 10. Applications and interviews.
Community College Leadership Academy sponsored by the Hispanic Border Leadership Institute	The Community College Leadership Academy at Arizona State University is dedicated to assisting community college institutions to redefine their delivery of services to the escalating	Academy hallmarks include the following: 1. Two academies per calendar year; 2. Each academy to be 3–4 days long; 3. Intensive engagement (discussion, workgroups);

(Continued)

Table 3 *(Continued)*

Name	Program Overview	Distinctive Features
	population of students from diverse origins and backgrounds by meeting the need for prepared staff. The purpose of the Community College Leadership Academy is to provide leadership training to develop mid-level community college administrators (particularly persons of color and women) who want to serve this growing new majority population of students.	4. Pre- and post-reading and writing assignments via Internet; 5. Provide each participant with a notebook, contents with handouts, power point presentations, overhead transparencies, and so on; 6. Technology will be used extensively, for example, Website; 7. Features recognized practitioners and noted scholars; 8. Support to continue contact with fellow participants, presenters, and CCLA faculty and staff for networking, educational advancement, and employment opportunities; and 9. Site locations of seminars may rotate to states with large concentration of potential participants
Community College Executive Leadership Experience sponsored by the National Association of Student Personnel Administrators (NASPA)	The Community College Executive Leadership Experience (CCELE) is a selective, two-year executive program in which senior student affairs officers spend the first year working with a coach and the second serving as a coach to a new class of fellows. Commencing with an initial two-day program prior to the NASPA Annual Conference.	Fellows will participate in a number of activities including: 1. Conducting a self-assessment of leadership skills; 2. Developing a plan to reach professional development and leadership goals; 3. Engaging in strategic thinking and planning that have institution-wide implications; 4. Examining critical issues, leadership challenges, and policies affecting community colleges; 5. Perfecting the skills needed to become a campus spokesperson; and 6. Enhancing entrepreneurial thinking.
Executive Leadership Institute (ELI) sponsored by the League for Innovation	ELI provides the opportunity for potential community college presidents, or those in transition, to analyze their abilities, reflect on their interests, refine their skills, and engage in leadership discussions with an unparalleled faculty of community college leaders.	ELI features the following activities: 1. Presentations and discussions with distinguished community college leaders explore a wide range of topics; 2. Experienced CEOs and institute graduates present personal perspectives on the rewards and costs of being a president;

	3. Participants enhance their interview skills through presidential interview simulations under the guidance of national presidential search consultants; 4. Presidential search consultants critique the professional résumés and applications of institute participants; and 5. Participants join an essential network of ELI graduates.
Future Leaders Institute (FLI) sponsored by the American Association of Community Colleges (AACC)*	Future Leaders Institute (FLI) is an innovative five-day leadership seminar designed for mid-level community college administrators who are ready to move into a higher level of leadership. These individuals are currently in positions that are responsible for multiple employees, including faculty, administrators and/or staff. FLI focuses on the following areas: 1. Leading institutional change; 2. Assessing leadership style; 3. Building and motivating teams; 4. Dealing with conflict and challenging people; 5. Understanding legal issues; 6. Building community through diversity, access and inclusion; 7. Sustaining an ethical culture; 8. Understanding and using technology; and 9. Visioning with a global perspective.
Leadership Tools for Women Conference sponsored by the Institute for Community College Development	The Leadership Tools for Women is a conference designed specifically for women working in higher education who wish to heighten their understanding of the contemporary issues facing women as they move to assume leadership roles in their institutions. The Leadership Tools for Women program focuses on developing the following skills: 1. Communication, 2. Collaboration, 3. Professionalism, and 4. Ethics.
National Institute for Leadership Development (NILD)	NILD is touted as the premier program for developing women community college leaders. NILD provides leadership development opportunities through five-day conference workshops. The NILD brings together community college leaders to ignite new passions and possibilities in higher education. There are two primary foci of NILD. 1. Rejuvenate intellectually, emotionally, physically and spiritually. Reconnect with mentors and colleagues. 2. Become part of the national movement to supply more women to the community college leadership pipeline.

(Continued)

Table 3 (*Continued*)

Name	Program Overview	Distinctive Features
Presidents Academy Summer Institute (PASI) sponsored by the American Association of Community Colleges (AACC)	The AACC Presidents Academy Summer Institute, designed expressly for member presidents, is a powerful mix of seasoned and first-time CEOs who benefit from working with each other in educational sessions and in small groups.	The Institute provides an opportunity for in-depth examination of various topics in an open but protected environment, using veteran presenters and actual case studies. This institute features sessions on: 1. Roles of the president and the spouse and expectations for the engagement of the spouse in college and community events; and 2. Leading during challenging economic times.

Source: http://www.pc.maricopa.edu/nild/national_conference.html; http://www.league.org/eli/index.cfm; http://www.asu.edu/educ/hbli/CCLA/CCLA.html; http://www.ccleague.org/i4a/pages/index.cfm?pageid=3300; http://www.accca.org/i4a/pages/index.cfm?pageid=3291; http://www.aacc.nche.edu/newsevents/Events/fli/Pages/default.aspx; http://www.aacc.nche.edu/newsevents/Events/pasi/Pages/default.aspx; http://www.naspa.org/programs/ccele/default.cfm; http://www.iccd.cornell.edu/iccd/leadershipPrograms/leadershipTools/ICCDLeadershipToolsforWomen2009.html

Note: *AACC also sponsors FLI advanced for senior-level administrators. Programs presented in alphabetical order; when possible direct quotes from program websites are provided.

(NILD). Additionally, many institutes focus on specific levels of leadership (e.g., entry-level, mid-level, senior-level) in order to address specialized skills and knowledge needed to effectively function at various levels of leadership. For example, entry-level leaders need to possess technical skills; whereas, senior-level executives require a greater emphasis on having strong conceptual skills (e.g., strategic planning, visionary leadership, facilitation of organizational change). Independent of one's leadership level, human relation skills are a crucial skill to have at all levels.

Due to the increased recognition of the importance of leadership development, many community colleges have begun Grow Your Own Leadership (GYOL) programs. GYOL programs are typically sponsored, developed, and operated by individual institutions, though some programs are regional (e.g., the Coastline Leadership Academy sponsored by Coastline Community College, the Community College Leadership Institute sponsored by Pitt Community College). There are many benefits to GYOL programs; they include: (a) the ability to develop a curriculum that proactively addresses local leadership issues; (b) filling a leadership skill development void; (c) serving as catalysts to developing and maintaining the leadership pipeline; and (d) providing a platform where intensive mentoring of aspiring leaders occurs. These programs are particularly useful for aspiring leaders who are not interested in leaving the institution in order to rise through the ranks of college administration or enrolling in a doctoral program.

While benefits abound for these locally tailored institutes, GYOL programs are not without some drawbacks. Many programs can suffer from chronic funding shortages, which can cripple the quality and consistency of the programs. Additionally, administrative support of these programs can waiver as changes among the senior leadership ranks occur. GYOL programs also lack the prestige and strong national networks that are attained at national leadership institutes.

Furthermore, while certain GYOL programs are progressive in preparing individuals who are open to organizational change and possess the skills necessary to confront the challenges faced by community colleges, some programs will invariably replicate leadership approaches and practices that may not be attuned to the realities facing community college institutions.

Preferably, institutions will opt to support up-and-coming leaders by allowing them to maximize on benefits from both national leadership institutes and GYOL programs. Lester (2008) contends that GYOL programs can serve to diversify the leadership ranks within the community college. However, in order to meet this objective, experts suggest that program organizers "be intentional about how they attract, how they facilitate access, and how they construct the programming" (p. 827).

Assessment

The need for ongoing assessment of the effectiveness of leadership development programs is of critical importance. Especially in this era of accountability where programs are being scrutinized to determine whether proposed outcomes have been achieved and subsequently determine if further support is warranted. Additionally, it is imperative to assess these leadership development programs to ensure that professional standards are met and that programmatic offerings are not fragmented and/or misaligned. Assessment efforts will identify key components of leadership development that are successful and areas that need to be created, expanded, revamped, or eliminated.

It is important to assess "the worth of these programs to their stakeholders, including sponsors, participants, employers, and other beneficiaries" (Weissner & Sullivan, 2007, p. 93). Assessment of programs are needed in four areas: (a) participants' reaction to the program, including subjects addressed, quality of presenters and logistics; (b) the nature and extent of the learning that occurred during the program; (c) the extent to which attitudes and actions changed as a result of the program; and (d) the outcomes and benefits of the program.

Preferably, program assessments will use quantitative and qualitative analyses to examine the immediate and long-term impact of the programs. This approach will allow for a comprehensive overview of the impact of the program and determine whether: (a) the program met its intended purpose/outcome; (b) programmatic adjustments are needed to improve its effectiveness; and (c) sponsors should continue their funding support. Effective components of leadership development programs should include the following:

- It is structurally sound where the purpose and objectives are clearly defined.
- The curriculum of the leadership program is attuned to the profession's skill requirements.
- There is a focus on transformational leadership and organizational changes are emphasized.
- It involves multiple entities to support the overall structure of the

program.
- It ensures that senior administrators serve as mentors and that these interactions are ongoing.
- There are networking opportunities and a plan to sustain these relationships through hands-on learning.
- It links theory to practice through problem-based learning.
- Programs are sustained, supported, and evaluated.

Case Study

The importance for leadership development has been established in this chapter. In the following case study, consider major points discussed in this chapter (e.g., leadership demographics, challenges facing community college leaders, skills needed by community college leaders, leadership development programs). When identifying resolution(s) to the case study presented, be attentive to the role of professional development in enhancing the leadership of aspiring and current community college leaders.

President Karen Nicodemus
Cochise College
Sierra Vista, Arizona

A House Divided

Background

High Desert Community College (HDCC), a comprehensive community college offering certificate and associate's degree programs, serves a large geographical area (approximately 6,000 square miles) and is located on an international border with Mexico. The college was first established in the early 1960s with a single residential campus (now referred to as the East Campus) located on approximately 540 acres; the campus was located equal distance between two thriving communities within the district's service area. In the late 1970s, a second campus (West) was established approximately 40 miles from the original campus, on approximately 36 acres, in a growing area of the service area. In addition, the district has continued to grow by establishing three outreach centers as well as a robust online campus. Today, the college serves approximately 14,000 students with most of its recent growth realized through a special partnership serving active military students, its online campus, and outreach centers. Both the East and West campuses have seen fairly stable or declining enrollments over the past decade.

The East and West campuses serve distinctly different student and community populations. The East Campus, which continues to be the district's only residential campus, serves a largely Hispanic community population. The majority of the students are commuters, belonging to minority groups, with many first-generation students of traditional age; as a result of this large population, the district enjoys status as a Hispanic-Serving Institution (HSI) and has received several major HSI grants. The East Campus is also perceived as being the support campus (academic and maintenance) for one of the three outreach centers. The West Campus is located in a community that is heavily influenced by the presence of a major Army post and a large influx of retirees. The West Campus serves an older student population and one that includes a number of active military personnel, dependents, and military retirees. The West Campus provides support (academic and maintenance), as needed, to the two remaining outreach centers. The Center located on the military post falls under the direction of the West Campus dean of instruction and represents approximately 50 percent of the district's overall full-time student equivalency (FTSE.) FTSE is the basis of state funding; therefore, overall the West Campus now represents a significant source of state funding.

Both campuses are served by approximately the same number of full-time faculty, but the West Campus also has a significant proportion of the district's part-time faculty. The West Campus has a large evening, as well as daytime, enrollment; the East Campus is primarily a daytime campus. Personnel familiar with faculty and staff at both campuses often compare and contrast faculty and staff attitudes and relationships with students between the two campuses. Specifically, faculty at the East campus are often described as nurturing, family-oriented, relationship-based, similar to the values reflective of the local culture. In contrast, faculty at the West campus are often described as more detached, less familiar with students and their personal lives, and more businesslike in their relationships with students. Those critical of the East campus refer to faculty as "coddling students" while those critical of the West campus refer to faculty as "detached and demanding." In reality, students at each site are highly complimentary of the role faculty play, the knowledge the faculty bring as instructors, and the dedication they demonstrate to their jobs and the college.

Over the past 40 years, the district's service area has changed dramatically. The major employer of the East Campus' two major feeder communities left the area in the early 1980s. As a result, both communities located at equal distance from the original campus have changed dramatically in demographics and per-capita income. At the same time, expansion of the Army post has resulted in major population growth in areas closer to the East Campus. This shift in population (over 50 percent of the district's service area population is now located in the East Campus' area) has further complicated lingering issues between the East and West campuses.

Notwithstanding efforts to bridge the two campuses and turnover in faculty and staff over the past four decades, there remains a sense of "us versus them" between the two campuses on a number of levels. After these many years, a feeling of competition or resentment appears to be embedded and accepted within the culture of the district. The East Campus believes its own well-being has been compromised by redirecting district resources to the building of the West Campus. As noted by one faculty member, at the time the West Campus was established, faculty, furniture, and other resources were moved to the campus with no consideration for the existing, original campus. This resentment over resources is echoed within the community that was once thriving, but is now overshadowed on many levels, by the larger community now located to its west. The West Campus and the primary community it serves feel it has been underserved, given the growth in population and proportion of students served by the campus and its outreach center located on the post. There is some resentment that residential living is not available on the West Campus or any of the district's athletic programs.

In addition, the district's senior administration consisting of the president, vice president for instruction (VPI), vice president for student services (VPSS), vice president for administration (VPA), and vice president for information technology (VPIT) are housed on different campuses. The president and VPI typically spend 80 percent of their time at either the

West Campus or in off-campus meetings. The remaining vice presidents spend 80 percent of their time at the East Campus. The senior administration has district responsibilities; other administrators include campus instructional deans, a dean with district oversight of student services and dean of extended campus, which includes online campus and 2 of the 3 outreach centers.

In 2000, the district placed before the voters of its service area a secondary property tax question in support of a comprehensive master facilities plan to address significant facilities needs across the districts. The voters rejected the issue, with the major opposition coming from the more populous West Campus area while the East Campus area overwhelmingly supported the plan. Although the district has been able to downsize the plan using other available resources and is in the process of addressing facility issues at both the East and West Campus, some see the failure of the bond election as another tangible example of the lack of support across the district for both campuses.

Statement of the Problem

You have experience as a senior administrator at another community college within the state and have some limited knowledge of the district's service area and history. You are excited to be starting your career as a president at HDCC, having been recently hired to replace the district's retiring president. During the search process, you were able to quickly pick up that the East and West campuses see themselves as rivals for resources even though you have found no evidence that one campus is favored in the budgeting process. In visiting with different campus-based faculty, within the same disciplines, it also appears that academic policies/expectations may not be consistently applied across the district. Some faculty members have also expressed concerns with the growth of the online campus at the expense of enrollments in face-to-face classes.

After accepting the position, you have the opportunity to visit more in-depth with the retiring president. The president has advised you that there also exists among some district governing board members very strong feelings about the status of the East Campus. The concern is with the infrastructure costs of maintaining an overbuilt campus for the current student enrollment. As a result, the governing board members elected from the East Campus area are very sensitive to any perceived threat to the campus, while the majority of the board members reside in the West Campus service area.

The district is facing a comprehensive accreditation visit in five years; the last accrediting team noted the challenge of bringing a district perspective to the campuses/centers while also celebrating and allowing for the diversity within the district. Some of the team's issues included the district administrative/management structure and its effect on consistent academic and support services, including assessment of student learning.

You believe that the problems, which divide the campuses, are related to its leadership (e.g., governing board members, campus administrators, faculty, and staff). Thus your role as a leader is to ensure that both campuses work in unison to meet the needs of its students. How would you approach this issue?

References

Amey, M. J. (2004). Learning leadership in today's community colleges. *Community College Journal*, 74(4), 6–9.

Amey, M. J., VanDerlinden, K. E., & Brown, D. F. (2002). Perspectives on community college leadership: Twenty years in the making. *Community College Journal of Research and Practice*, 26, 573–589.

Brown, L., Martinez, M., & Daniel, D. (2002). Community college leadership preparation: Needs, perceptions, and recommendations. *Community College Review*, 30(1), 45–73.

Carnegie Foundation (2009). *Carnegie Project on the Education Doctorate.* Stanford, CA: Carnegie Foundation.

Duree, C. A. (2007). *The challenges of the community college presidency in the new millennium: Pathways, preparation, competencies, and leadership programs needed to survive.* Unpublished doctoral dissertation, Iowa State University.

Evelyn, J. (2001). Community colleges face a crisis of leadership. *Chronicle of Higher Education* (April), 47(30), A36–A37.

Hoff, K. S. (1999, October). Leaders and managers: Essential skills required within higher education. *Higher Education*, 38, 311–331.

Katsinas, S. G. (2002). Looking back and looking forward: A century of community colleges in America. *Community College Journal of Research and Practice*, 26, 555–557.

Korb, J. L. (2006). Community college leadership at a crossroads: Where crisis intersects opportunity. *Dissertation Abstracts International*, 66(8), 2814.

Land, P. C. (2003). From the other side of the academy to academic leadership roles: Crossing the great divide. *New Directions for Higher Education*, 124, 13–20.

Leon, D., & Nevarez, C. (2007). Models of leadership institutes for increasing the number of top Latino administrators in higher education. *Journal of Hispanics in Higher Education*, 6, 356–378.

Lester, J. (2008). Future trends and possibilities for creating more gender equitable community colleges. *Community College Journal of Research and Practice*, 32(10), 822–837.

Levine, A. (2005). *Educating school leaders.* New York: Education Schools Project.

McPhail, C. J., Robinson, M., & Scott, H. (2008). The cohort leadership development model: Student perspectives. *Community College Journal of Research and Practice*, 32(4), 362–374.

Mizak, P. (2008). *An examination of community college Chief Academic Officers and oncoming presidential vacancies.* Unpublished doctoral dissertation, the State University of New York, Buffalo.

Moore, K., Martorana, S. V., & Twombly, S. (1985). *Today's academic leaders: A national study of administrators in two-year colleges.* University Park, PA: Center for the Study of Higher Education.

Nevarez, C., & Keyes, K. (2007). Higher education leadership training: Learning to lead. *The John Ben Shepperd Journal of Practical Leadership*, 2, 81–95.

Phillippe, K. A., & Sullivan L. G. (2005). *National profile of community colleges: Trends and statistics (4th Ed.).* Washington, DC: American Association of Community Colleges.

Raines, S. C., & Alberg, M. S. (2003). The role of professional development in preparing academic leaders. *New Directions for Higher Education,* (Winter) 124, 33–39.

Ramaley, J. A. (2000). Change as a scholarly act: Higher education research transfer practice. *New Directions for Higher Education*, (Summer), 110, 75–88.

Shulman, L. S., Golde, C. M., Bueschel, A. C., & Garabedian, K. J. (2006). Reclaiming education's doctorates: A critique and a proposal. *Educational Researcher*, 25–32.

Shults, C. (2001). *The critical impact of impending retirements on community college leadership.* Washington, DC: American Association of Community Colleges.

Townsend, B. K., & Twombly, S. B. (Eds.) (2001). *Community colleges: Policy in the future context.* Westport, CT: Ablex Publishing.

U.S. Department of Education (2006). National Center for Education Statistics, Integrated Postsecondary Education Data System (IPEDS), Spring, Graduation Rates component.

Wallin, D. L. (2002). Professional development for presidents: A study of community and technical college presidents in three states. *Community College Review*, 30(2), 27–41.

Weisman, I. M., & Vaughan, G. B. (2001). *The community college presidency 2001. Research Brief No. 3.* Washington, DC: American Association of Community Colleges.

Weisman, I. M., & Vaughan, G. B. (2006). *The community college presidency 2006.* Washington, DC: American Association of Community Colleges.

Wiessner, C., & Sullivan, L. (2007, October). Constructing knowledge in leadership training programs. *Community College Review*, 35(2), 88–112.

CHAPTER TWELVE

EMERGING TRENDS IN THE COMMUNITY COLLEGE

This chapter will summarize the mission of the community college in light of emerging trends facing these institutions. Particular attention is paid to: (a) challenges to "open access"; (b) bachelor's degrees; (c) the presidential initiative on community colleges; (d) increasing numbers of part-time faculty; (e) new and returning students; and (f) minority student initiatives.

When reading this chapter as well as others, consider the following questions:

- In light of current trends, what are challenges to "open access" in the community college?
- What are the primary arguments for and against the offering of baccalaureate degrees at the community college? What are the implications of both?
- What impact will the proposed presidential initiative have on community colleges? How, if at all, will it affect student success?
- What role do part-time faculty members play in the community college? What considerations must be taken into account in consideration of the increasing numbers of community college part-time faculty?
- What is the community colleges' commitment to "lifelong learning"? How is the current financial climate and overall institutional structure affecting this mission component?
- What are minority student initiatives? What role do they play in supporting community colleges in creating student success?

In this book, we have discussed a wide range of topics (e.g., historical legacy of the community college, governance, finance), challenges (e.g., community college achievement gap, current financial climate), theories (e.g., theories of Erickson, Marcia, Chickering, Helm, and Bennett), and research (e.g., Spady, Bean & Metzner, Tinto, Hagedorn). Our goal has been to provide aspiring and current community college leaders with a framework for: (a) providing foundational knowledge needed to understand community college operations; (b) contextualizing current realities, problems, and opportunities facing community colleges; (c) examining, critiquing, analyzing, and operationalizing the functions and operations of the community college; and (d) challenging leaders to construct, deconstruct, and restrict new policies, programs, services, and practices which improve the overall success of community college students. As a result, we have presented readers with the breadth and depth of knowledge needed to facilitate success in these institutions. It is incumbent upon leaders to use the information presented to enforce effective practices and enact changes to improve these institutions for the betterment of their students as well as society.

Unlike previous chapters, where we have provided a context for viewing the past and current landscape of the community college, this chapter will focus on these contexts as well as the future. At this juncture of the book, we believe that leaders should have gained the foundational knowledge necessary to engage in an in-depth analysis of previously presented content areas. More importantly, the content presented can allow leaders to use this book to guide and control the future trajectory of their institutions. In doing so, they can be proactive in planning for these trajectories. This will enable the leaders to align their institutions for academic success. Purposively, we have centered this book on the mission of the community college. We have done so to illustrate its evolving role in the historical, contemporary, and future of the community colleges. In this chapter, we will summarize the mission of the community college in order to contextualize our thoughts, reflections, and insights for their future. We do this as all emerging trends in the community college, in one way or another, impact its mission.

The mission of the community college is six fold; it includes: (a) open access to education; (b) comprehensive educational programming; (c) serving the community; (d) teaching and learning; (e) lifelong learning; and (f) students' achieving academic/career goals. These interrelated values are the core ways in which the community college progresses towards its vision of encouraging "broader postsecondary education for the people" (Deegan & Tillery, 1985, p. 5).

Open Access

Providing the opportunity for all who desire to engage in postsecondary education to do so is referred to as open access. Open access is a concept deeply rooted in the progressivist movement (mid-1800s onward) and emerged as a value of the civil rights movement. As a result, the expansive growth of the community college in the 1960s is in large part a result of its open-access mission. In the community college of today, diversity among students and to a lesser degree among its faculty, staff, and administrators is a direct result of open access. As the community college looks to the future, especially in this current fiscal climate, its ability to remain dedicated to open access will be challenged. Open access is largely responsible for the notable student diversity seen in the community colleges; however, maintaining high percentages of students of color in these institutions may be difficult if the "open-access" aspect of the community college mission is eliminated. The emergence of enrollment caps should be of primary importance to all community college leaders. As McPhail (2009) notes:

> "In tough times, it is highly likely that the open door mission of community colleges will come under attack (again) by those who have historically restricted opportunities for individuals from diverse backgrounds. If this is allowed to happen and tolerated, some community colleges may see a reversal in decades of progress" (Para. 6).

This challenge is already underway. In New Mexico, Rhode Island, Tennessee, Maryland, and North Carolina among other states, enrollments are surging while state resources are dwindling (Bushong, 2009; Hoover & Wilson, 2009). However, this is merely the tip of the iceberg. In California's behemoth community college system (comprised of 110 institutions), colleges have raised their fees by 30 percent in the 2009–10 school years. Even more alarming, the number of courses offered has been reduced, effectively cutting enrollments, which may prevent nearly 250,000 students from enrolling in the California community college system (Nealon, 2009). The implications of California's decision to postpone "open access," may signal the end of an era. At the very least, this decision has, and will continue to spark discussion and critique around the nation about the community colleges mission of "open-access."

Comprehensive Educational Programming

Comprehensive educational programming refers to the wide range of academic programs offered by the community colleges. Though preparation for a four-year university has remained an integral function of the institution since the early 1900s, remedial education, vocational-technical, and continuing education functions quickly emerged to the forefront and are core aspects of today's community colleges. Largely this is a direct result of the dedication of the community colleges to meet the needs of their local communities. Today, academic programming in the community colleges is expansive, ranging from career technical education to leisure/hobby courses. This broad ranging programming has allowed community colleges to address the ever increasing needs of a wide range of students and their interests. As a result, this is consistent with "meeting the needs of local communities," another primary aspect of the community college mission. While the wide range of programming offered by the community college is noteworthy, it does have its drawbacks. For example, our experience has shown that students come into the community college with varying remediation needs. Some of the students are within a semester or two of entering college-level coursework; others are years away from this level of coursework. As a result, meeting the needs of students through comprehensive programming can be difficult, especially when needs of the students are wildly disparate. Although it is honorable that these institutions engage in educating students with a broad spectrum of skills, the ability of the community college to do so effectively and efficiently remains a challenge.

Though not necessarily a new phenomenon, an increasing trend in the community college is the offering of baccalaureate degrees. The American Association of Community Colleges (2009) reports that 31 public and 52 independent two-year colleges offer bachelor degrees. Typically, bachelor's degrees are offered in various fields in which public state universities are: (a) not producing enough graduates in order to meet regional demands (e.g., nursing, education); (b) not providing equitable access for all students due to distance or cost issues (Shultz, 2009); and (c) not offering academic programming that is historically avoided and neglected by four-year colleges and universities. These efforts have been criticized by some scholars and practitioners for: (a) leading the community college away from their mission; (b) offering second-rate bachelor's-degrees; (c) complicating issues of capacity; (d) being inappropriate for community colleges to undertake due to their faculties' lack of bachelor's-degree level-expertise; and (e) adding new responsibilities that detract from areas in need of attention (e.g., low graduation and transfer rates). Proponents of the community college bachelor's degree argue that they are creating a seamless avenue for community college students to have "open access" to bachelor's degrees (see Mills, 2003); thereby better enabling these institutions to: (a) meet their mission of "open access," "serving local community needs," and "student success" (i.e., aiding students in achieving their academic/career goals); (b) increase graduates who are contributing to the local tax base through higher earnings; (c) meet human capital and intellectual needs of the local, state, and regional workforce; (d) allow students to attain a bachelor's-level education in a more personable environment; and (e) attain baccalaureate degrees at a lower cost. Either way, it is a trend that does not show signs of slowing.

Serving the Community

Serving the needs of local communities has been a core value of community colleges since their inception. The rationale that was used to justify the establishment of many community colleges was their role in providing higher education programming, which addresses the workforce development and higher learning needs of local communities (e.g., human, social, cultural, intellectual capital) (Cohen & Brawer, 2003). By doing so, individuals benefit themselves and their communities as follows:

1. *Socially.* Social benefits include: (a) increased local, state, and federal tax base through lower annual earnings; (b) increased diversity in the workforce; and (c) independence from social services that lead to draining tax revenue and reductions of programs in a variety of social service areas.
2. *Politically.* Political and civic benefits include: (a) increased likelihood of civic engagement (e.g., voting, community service, engagement); and (b) representation in influential political positions (e.g., federal, state, local boards, commissions, committees, and posts).
3. *Economically.* Economic benefits include: (a) increased earning potential and subsequently philanthropic donations; (b) increased likeliness of job satisfaction, attainment, and security. As a result, students make more money to better support themselves, their families, and communities.
4. *Psychosocially.* Psychosocial benefits include: (a) increased adaptability to workforce needs; (b) increased likelihood of solidified social and professional networks; and (c) increased likelihood of being diversity minded, as a result of increased interactions with individuals from other cultures.
5. *Cognitively.* Cognitive benefits include: (a) increased likelihood of becoming a critical consumer; (b) increased job skills (e.g., writing, reading, communication); and (c) increased adaptability to learning (e.g., professional, social settings).

While the benefits of a college education are numerous, community colleges have struggled to graduate enough students to meet the demand of many regions' workforce needs. Thus far, the Obama administration has been very supportive of the community college. Jill Biden, Vice President Joe Biden's wife, is an english professor at Northern Virginia Community College and has served as proponent of administrative support for community colleges. In July of 2009, the Obama administration announced a new plan to support community colleges around the country in graduating five million more students by the year 2020 (Biden 2009). While this is an extremely tall order, the Obama administration is set to provide nine billion dollars in federal grants to these institutions in order to aid them in reaching this goal. However, this funding will likely come with stringent benchmarks for degree completion, preparation of graduates for the workforce, and career placement, since many public leaders (e.g., government, education) are critical of the community colleges' success in graduating students. In essence, the critique being levied against community colleges is that they are not meeting their mission in serving the needs of their local communities, a charge that is now reverberating on a national level. This is an extremely important trend for educational leaders to be attentive to, as it may lead to a foundational shift in the manner community colleges are funded, viewed by the general population, and held accountable to this component of their mission. Currently, the vast majority of "state and local aid to community colleges is based on the number of students enrolled"; however, new funding guidelines for federal grants could shift, funding graduate production rather than enrollment (Field, 2009).

Teaching and Learning

Teaching and learning refers to the process that students receive instruction and learning from the teaching given. Clearly this is a cardinal principle of the community college, as it is evident in all of its functions (e.g., transfer, terminal degrees, remedial education, vocational-technical education, continuing education). The emphasis on teaching and learning in the community college is juxtaposed with that of the research universities where teaching and learning are not the primary foci. For example, 70.8 percent of community college faculty state that their primary interest is teaching and learning; in contrast, only 17.9 of public four-year university faculty hold teaching as their primary interest (Almanac, 2008–09b).

General education has been a central element of the community college since its conception in the mid-1800s and its inception in 1901. Early community college leaders such as William Rainey Harper desired that these institutions would assume the first two years of college instruction (e.g., general education); while the university would focus on research. While the teaching and learning mission of the community college remains active, it is clear that the method of achieving this mission has changed over time. As noted in Chapter 6 on faculty, the percentage of full-time tenured/tenure-track faculty is dwindling while the percentage of part-time nontenured-track faculty is increasing. This should raise several important considerations for community college leaders, such as:

- *Faculty Satisfaction.* Jacoby (2005) notes that most part-time faculty begin their tenure in the community college with the desire to become full-time faculty members. Unable to reach their goal of becoming full-time faculty members, part-time faculty "eventually become frustrated and discouraged," a trend that rises as they increase in age and tenure (p. 138). Thus, community college leaders should work to create policies, structures, and practices that integrate and engage part-time faculty into the overall life of the community college. In doing so, leaders should strive to increase the satisfaction of these faculty members by communicating to them that they are valued members of the institution.
- *Institutional Leadership.* Part-time faculty play a limited role in institutional governance (e.g., committees, taskforces, planning). The increase of part-time faculty, places a greater burden upon full-time faculty to serve in these capacities. As a result, leaders should be creative in incorporating part-time faculty as contributing members in institutional governance. This will entail a departure from the current makeup of faculty governance structures. The benefit of increasing their participation is lower levels of work for full-time faculty and increased input on institutional decision making.
- *Instructional Dean.* The influx of part-time faculty in the community college increases the role of the instructional dean. This occurs in several ways; it necessitates the dean's efforts in: (a) engaging part-time faculty into the college environment; (b) reconceptualizing policies and structures that allow part-time faculty to participate in the inner workings of the community college; and (c) ensuring that the quality of instruction, curriculum, and learning is maintained through standardized academic and programmatic expectations.

- *Institutional Success.* Some research suggests that part-time faculty is not as successful in graduating students as full-time faculty. For example, Jacoby (2006) found that community college graduation rates decreased as the percentage of part-time faculty in the institution increased. While the effect of part-time faculty on institutional success remains to be seen (as it is highly contextual in nature), it is incumbent upon leaders to implement faculty training, professional development, and support mechanisms to ensure their overall success in educating students. Also, community college leaders need to consider an array of assessment measures to ensure the competency among all faculty, including part-timers.

Lifelong Learning

Lifelong learning remains a core dedication of community colleges. Since its early years, it has provided opportunities for individuals to engage in leisure activities (e.g., machinery, cooking), take classes that improve their job skills (e.g., business finance, writing), complete their general education, and seek a total retool for the job market. Of these, the latter has increased as the job market and economy have decreased. Enrollments are soaring across the nation, courses are filled, and waiting lists are atypically long. For example, at Fresno City College in California, there were a total of 14,000 names on waiting lists for classes for the Fall of 2009 (Fontana, 2009). In Hillsborough Community College in Florida (also in 2009), lines for financial aid caused many students to wait for five hours or more in order to receive service (Kavanaugh, 2009). We can safely predict that issues of institutional capacity will continue to gain momentum in community colleges across the country due to tuition increases, limited enrollments, and increasing academic standards at four-year universities.

It is almost ironic that only a few years ago, Donald Read (2004) among others was encouraging community colleges to see the retirements as a new market for the community college to tap as a method of achieving institutional growth. Now, seniors, along with traditional college-aged freshman, adult students, the unemployed, and those who are seeking additional education to maintain employment are crushing the infrastructure of these institutions. Unfortunately, enrollment increases have been coupled with reduced state funds to community colleges, this has forced the leaders of these institutions to do more (e.g., programs, services), for more (e.g., students, community members), with less (e.g., state and local funds) (Zeidenberg, 2008). This is occurring while the need for lifelong learning is greater than ever, especially for those who have lost their jobs in the economic turndown. As community college leaders look to the future, they will be forced to make tough decisions if enrollments and services are on the rise and funding is not. Cuts will likely come, as will fee increases. This can easily translate into access denied. The question that leaders must consider at all times is twofold: (1) they must ask themselves how these trends will affect the students that they serve; and (2) how the current lack of access at public institutions (two-year and four-year) translates into students' increasing attraction to private not-for-profit and for-profit institutions, which are readily accepting applications.

Student Success

A cardinal component of the community colleges mission is to aid students in achieving their academic and career goals (i.e., student success). This mission, though embedded throughout the history of the community college, emerged in the 1960s and 1970s, when Cohen & Brawer (2003) noted that open access meant *the right to fail*. Today, persistence rates for students of color, particularly male students, reveal low rates of success. According to the U.S. Department of Education (2006), across all racial/ethnic groups, the lowest graduation rates are seen among Black, Hispanic, and Native American students at 16.5, 18.7, and 21.8 percent, respectively. Further, graduation rates for minority males are lower. For instance, graduation rates for male students from these groups are as follows: Blacks males, 16.2 percent; Hispanic males, 17.3 percent; and Native American males, 19.2 percent. In contrast, White and Asian American males graduate at 25.2 percent and 23.4 percent, respectively. While even the White and Asian American male graduation rates are extremely low, increased attention to the dismal graduation rates of Black, Hispanic, and Native American males has increased.

The consequences of continuously neglecting issues facing minority students in the community colleges, has, and will continue to have dire consequences at the local, state, and national levels. As a result, the emergence of Minority Male Initiatives (e.g., Maricopa Minority Male Initiative, A²MEND), and Minority Student Initiatives (e.g., Achieving the Dream) have forced community colleges to address poor success rates among their students. These initiatives take a comprehensive approach including dialogue, research, and action to address disparities in success of the students. While the long-term effect of these initiatives remains to be seen; at the very least, they are: (a) creating a space for difficult conversations about race, racism, and racialization; (b) forging part-nerships between and among internal and external entities; (c) implementing practices that are designed to improve the success rates of students of color and low-income students; and (d) providing a support structure of success for stu-dents that cater to their affective and cognitive development. By doing so, they are holding community colleges accountable for issues of student success.

Case Study

This chapter provided a general summary of the mission of the community colleges in light of current and emerging trends facing these institutions (e.g., minority student initiatives, part-time faculty, bachelor's degrees, and Obama administrations initiatives). Our goal has been to convey to lead-ers that all trends, in one way or another, relate directly to the mission of these institutions. These trends challenge community college leaders to serve as mavericks in realizing and advancing the mission of the commu-nity college. Below, we present a case study that requires leaders to utilize their understanding of the historical, current, and future trajectory of these institutions in responding to a leadership dilemma. In addressing the case study scenario, pay particular attention to the role of emerging trends (presented in this chapter) in resolving the case.

President Cathryn Addy
Tunxis Community College
Farmington, Connecticut

Converging Issues as an Opportunity for Change

Background

Doe Community College, located in an eastern city of 100,000, was founded in 1952. It has an enrollment of 6,780 FTE (full-time equivalent) and a headcount enrollment of slightly over 8,000 in credit classes. Noncredit enrollment is around 3,000 annually. There are 100 full-time faculty who teach a 12 credit load on average, 280 adjunct faculty, and approximately 60 other professionals and administrators. There is one campus of approximately 300,000 square feet on 10 acres of land, and one satellite campus 50 miles away in a rural area that opened in a renovated high school 20 years ago. Doe CC is one of 14 publicly supported community colleges in the state but gets one-third of its funding locally, drawn proportionately from each of the 17 school districts in its service area. Another one-third comes from the state according to a long established allocation formula, and the remaining one-third comes from tuition, fees, and auxiliary income from grants, noncredit enrollments, and other enterprises such as the bookstore and a small restaurant on campus run by the culinary students.

Over the last three years, the local districts have become more and more vocal about no longer being able to afford to provide funding to Doe, and have been threatening to withdraw from the partnership. The college has just been given an 18-month window in which to develop an alternate plan for the funding its needs at the local level. The state has made it clear that it does not intend to make up the difference, and has also limited the amount that can be raised from a tuition increase.

Programmatically, Doe CC has always been strong in the applied technology and science areas, and its students have reflected that: 80 percent (60 percent male) are enrolled in Associate of Applied Science programs, while the remaining 20 percent (80 percent female) are in Associate of Arts program areas. Recently the college has struggled to maintain its enrollment levels as the economic status of the region has suffered due to manufacturing jobs disappearing and little new growth occurring in any other sector of the economy. However, they have noted an increase in demand for students coming out of their allied health programs but have not had the funding to support expansion of their "flagship" nursing or dental hygiene programs, where the demand has been the strongest. They have also noted that more and more students are attending on a part-time basis and many of their classes at traditional prime times are not fully subscribed, but that they often have waiting lists for many of the classes offered in the late afternoon and at night.

The main campus reflects the industrial character of the surrounding city in which the college is located. The buildings are showing their age and in need of updating as well as repairs. Some issues that the college will have to face include new roofs, new wiring to accommodate the expansion of technology in the classrooms and offices, expanded parking facilities due to the recent demise of the local mass transit system, and a new chemistry lab to replace the one that was recently burned out when a lab experiment went awry. There are also needs at the satellite campus up north. Although initial renovations were paid for by a grant when that campus first opened, Doe must now pick up the tab for some deferred maintenance issues as well as the upgrading of its computer labs and library. There are also equipment needs due to the reinstatement of a Practical Nursing program that had been dormant for about ten years.

Finally, in the last two years, 64 percent of faculty members have become eligible to retire, as have 50 percent of the professionals and administrators. In addition the president (who has been at Doe since 1985) has just announced his intention to retire. Thus, an institution that has long been stable and steady is about to enter a new era, and many at the college are worried about its ability to survive the "boat rocking."

Statement of the Problem

You are the academic vice president of the college and have been at Doe for only five years. The president has spoken with you about his intention to name you as the interim president to bridge the time between his leaving and a new, permanent president arriving. If you accept this responsibility, you will have to decide the following:

- What are the four or five major issues that Doe Community College faces?
- What steps must the college undertake to address these issues, and in what order?
- What should the leadership of the college do to solve the present problems?
- What should the leadership of the college do to plan the college's future? and
- What knowledge and skills must the interim president possess to facilitate institutional change?

References

Almanac (2008–09b). *Opinions and attitudes of full time faculty members;* Aspects of job described as satisfactory or very satisfactory. Washington, DC: Chronicle of Higher Education.

American Association of Community Colleges (2009). *2009 fact sheet.* Washington, DC: Author.

Biden, J. (2009). Community colleges are crucial. *The Sun News* (July 21). Retrieved August 3, 2009, from: http://www.thesunnews.com/158/story/990694.html

Bushong, S. (2009). Community college enrollments are up, but institutions struggle to pay for them. *The Chronicle of Higher Education* (January 23). Retrieved August 3, 2009, from: http://chronicle.com/article/Community-College-Enrollments/29574/

Cohen, A. M., & Brawer, F. B. (2003). *The American community college,* (4th Ed.). San Francisco, CA: Jossey-Bass.

Deegan, W. L., & Tillery, D. (1985). *Introduction.* In D. Tillery & W. L. Deegan (eds.). *Renewing the American community college: Priorities and strategies for effective leadership* (pp. 1–5). San Francisco, CA: Jossey-Bass.

Field, K. (2009). For community colleges, federal aid would come with strings attached. *The Chronicle of Higher Education* (July 29). Retrieved August 3, 2009, from: http://chronicle.com/article/For-Community-Colleges-Aid/47493/?utm_source=at&utm_medium=en

Fontana, C. (2009). Valley colleges face record demand, budget cuts: Enrollment soars despite cuts in funding. *The Fresno Bee* (July 31). Retrieved August 3, 2009, from: http://www.fresnobee.com/local/story/1570068.html

Hoover, E., & Wilson, R. (2009). How a community college makes room: Scrambling to create classrooms as enrollments soar. *The Chronicle of Higher Education* (August 2). Retrieved August 3, 2009, from: http://chronicle.com/article/How-a-Community-College-Makes/47532/

Jacoby, D. (2005). Part-time community college faculty and the desire for full-time tenure-track positions: Results of a single institution case study. *Community College Journal of Research and Practice,* 29(2), 137–152. Retrieved August 03, 2009, from http://www.informaworld.com/10.1080/10668920490891629

Jacoby, D. (2006). Effects of part-time faculty employment on community college graduation rates. *The Journal of Higher Education,* 77(6), 1081–1003.

Kavanaugh, K. (2009). College students brave long lines for financial aid. *ABC Action News* (July 20). Retrieved August 3, 2009, from: http://www.abcactionnews.com/news/local/story/College-students-brave-long-lines-for-financial/rFzmRoghpkmz3GcJFji4LA.cspx?rss=794

McPhail, C. J. (2009). Open access fosters diversity across campuses. *Community College Times* (April 1). Retrieved August 3, 2009, from: http://www.communitycollegetimes.com/article.cfm?TopicId=8&Article.Id=1589

Mills, K. (2003). *Community college baccalaureates: Some critics decry the trend as "mission creep."* San Jose, CA: National Center for Public Policy and Higher Education.

Nealon, S. (2009). Seats hard to come by in community college classes. *The Press Enterprise* (July 31). Retrieved August 3, 2009, from: http://www.pe.com/localnews/inland/stories/PE_News_Local_S_community01.2667d87.html

Read, D. R. (2004). Tapping the evolving seniors market. *The Community College Journal* (April/May), 74(5), 44–50.

Shultz, M. (2009). Community colleges fight to give 4-year degrees: Two-year schools want to offer four-year degrees to increase access for students. *The Detroit News* (June 15). Retrieved

August 3, 2009, from: http://www.detnews.com/article/20090615/SCHOOLS/906150313/ Community-colleges-fight-to-give-4-year-degrees

U.S. Department of Education. 2006. National Center for Education Statistics, Integrated Postsecondary Education Data System (IPEDS), Spring, Graduation Rates component.

Zeidenberg, M. (2008). Community colleges under stress. *Issues in Science and Technology* (Summer), 53–58.

M. Christopher Brown II, *General Editor*

The *Education Management: Contexts, Constituents, and Communities* (EM:c³) series includes the best scholarship on the varied dynamics of educational leadership, management, and administration across the educational continuum. In order to disseminate ideas and strategies useful for schools, colleges, and the education community, each book investigates critical topics missing from the extant literature and engages one or more theoretical perspectives. This series bridges the gaps between the traditional management research, practical approaches to academic administration, and the fluid nature of organizational realities.

Additionally, the EM:c³ series endeavors to provide meaningful guidance on continuing challenges to the effective and efficient management of educational contexts. Volumes in the series foreground important policy/praxis issues, developing professional trends, and the concerns of educational constituencies. The aim is to generate a corpus of scholarship that discusses the unique nature of education in the academic and social spaces of all school types (e.g., public, private, charter, parochial) and university types (e.g., public, private, historically black, tribal institutions, community colleges).

The EM:c³ series offers thoughtful research presentations from leading experts in the fields of educational administration, higher education, organizational behavior, public administration, and related academic concentrations. Contributions represent research on the United States as well as other countries by comparison, address issues related to leadership at all levels of the educational system, and are written in a style accessible to scholars, educational practitioners and policymakers throughout the world.

For further information about the series and submitting manuscripts, please contact:

Dr. M. Christopher Brown II | *em_bookseries@yahoo.com*

To order other books in this series, please contact our Customer Service Department at:

(800) 770-LANG (within the U.S.)
(212) 647-7706 (outside the U.S.)
(212) 647-7707 FAX

Or browse online by series at www.peterlang.com